EMERGING TECHNOLOGIES IN EDUCATION

MATTHEW N. O. SADIKU
OLANIYI D. OLALEYE

Copyright © 2024 Matthew N. O. Sadiku and Olaniyi D. Olaleye.

All rights reserved. No part of this book may be reproduced, stored, or transmitted by any means—whether auditory, graphic, mechanical, or electronic—without written permission of both publisher and author, except in the case of brief excerpts used in critical articles and reviews. Unauthorized reproduction of any part of this work is illegal and is punishable by law.

ISBN: 979-8-89031-972-2 (sc)
ISBN: 979-8-88640-033-5 (hc)
ISBN: 979-8-88640-034-2 (e)

Because of the dynamic nature of the Internet, any web addresses or links contained in this book may have changed since publication and may no longer be valid. The views expressed in this work are solely those of the author and do not necessarily reflect the views of the publisher, and the publisher hereby disclaims any responsibility for them.

One Galleria Blvd., Suite 1900, Metairie, LA 70001
(504) 702-6708

CONTENTS

Preface ix
About the Authors...xv

Chapter 1 Introduction 1
1.1 Introduction 1
1.2 What are Emerging Technologies?.. 3
1.3 Some Emerging Technologies.. 4
1.4 Digital Natives 10
1.5 Benefits 12
1.6 Challenges.. 14
1.7 Global Impact of Emerging Technologies on Education 15
1.8 Conclusion 18
References 20

Chapter 2 AI in Education..26
2.1 Introduction 26
2.2 Review of Artificial Intelligence 28
2.3 Possibilities of Ai in Education 33
2.4 AI in Different Levels of AI... 36
2.5 Applications of AI in Education 37
2.6 Global Adoption of AI in Education 42
2.7 Benefits 45
2.8 Challenges 47
2.9 Future of AI Education 50
2.10 Conclusion 51
References 53

Chapter 3 Robotics in Education..59
3.1 Introduction 59
3.2 What Are Robots? 60

3.3 Educational Robotics 62
3.4 Applications 63
3.5 Benefits 68
3.6 Challenges 69
3.7 Global Use of Robots in Education 70
3.8 Conclusion 73
References 74

Chapter 4 Cloud Computing in Education 79
4.1 Introduction 79
4.2 Concept of Cloud Computing 80
4.3 Applications of Cloud Computing in Education 84
4.4 Benefits 87
4.5 Challenges 90
4.6 Global Use of Cloud Computing in Education 91
4.7 Conclusion 93
References 93

Chapter 5 Soft Computing in Education 98
5.1 Introduction 98
5.2 Overview of Soft Computing 99
5.3 Applications 102
5.4 Benefits 106
5.5 Challenges 107
5.6 Soft Computing in Education Worldwide 108
5.7 Conclusion 111
References 112

Chapter 6 Big Data in Education 116
6.1 Introduction 116
6.2 Characteristics of Big Data 117
6.3 Applications 120
6.4 Benefits 121
6.5 Challenges 124
6.6 Global Use of Big Data in Education 125
6.7 Conclusion 128
References 129

Chapter 7 Education 4.0	132
7.1 Introduction	132
7.2 Traditional Education is Lacking	134
7.3 Three Generations of Education	134
7.4 Emergence of Industry 4.0	139
7.5 Emergence of Education 4.0	140
7.6 Benefits	143
7.7 Challenges	145
7.8 Global Adoption of Education 4.0	146
7.9 Conclusion	149
References	150

Chapter 8 Digital Education	155
8.1 Introduction	155
8.2 What is Digital Education?	156
8.3 Applications	159
8.4 Digital Textbooks	162
8.5 Global Digital Education	165
8.6 Benefits	167
8.7 Challenges	170
8.8 Conclusion	172
References	173

Chapter 9 Online Education	178
9.1 Introduction	178
9.2 Need for Online Education	180
9.3 Online Teaching	181
9.4 Online Learning	183
9.5 Online Laboratory	185
9.6 Massive Open Online Courses	187
9.7 Enabling Technology	189
9.8 Presence	190
9.9 Quality and Effectiveness	190
9.10 Benefits	192
9.11 Challenges	194
9.12 Global Online Education	196

9.13 Conclusion 201
References 202

Chapter 10 3D Printing in Education 208
10.1 Introduction 208
10.2 What is 3D Printing? 209
10.3 Applications 211
10.4 Benefits 218
10.5 Challenges 220
10.6 Global Use of 3D Printing 221
10.7 Conclusion 225
References 226

Chapter 11 Virtual Reality in Education 230
11.1 Introduction 230
11.2 Concept of Virtual Reality 231
11.3 Applications 234
11.4 Benefits 237
11.5 Challenges 238
11.6 Global Use of Virtual Reality 240
11.5 Conclusion 242
References 243

Chapter 12 Augmented Reality in Education 248
12.1 Introduction 248
12.2 Concept of Augmented Reality 250
12.3 Applications of AR in Education 253
12.4 Benefits 258
12.5 Challenges 260
12.6 Global Use of Augmented Reality in Education 261
12.7 Conclusion 264
References 264

Chapter 13 Gamification in Education 268
13.1 Introduction 268
13.2 What is Gamification? 269
13.3 Components of Gamification 271

13.4 Applications.. 273
13.5 Benefits 277
13.6 Challenges.. 278
13.7 Global Use of Gamification in Education................................. 280
13.8 Conclusion 282
References 283

Chapter 14 Social Media in Education 288
14.1 Introduction 288
14.2 Social Media Basics 289
14.3 Popular Social Media.. 290
14.4 Applications... 293
14.5 Benefits... 297
14.6 Challenges.. 298
14.7 Global Use of Social Media in Education 299
14.8 Conclusion 302
References 302

Chapter 15 Future of Education 307
15.1 Introduction 307
15.2 Future of Technology.. 309
15.3 Future of Learning...313
15.4 Future of Teaching..315
15.5 Future of Online Education 317
15.6 Challenges..318
15.7 Global Future of Education 319
15.8 Conclusion 323
References 323

PREFACE

Education is the process of transferring knowledge, values, methods, skills, and beliefs from one individual to another. It is widely recognized as a source of human capital and insurance against poverty. It is one of the most precious gifts we can offer our future generation. Educators have a monumental task before them and face many challenges. Skills sought after in the job market evolve faster than their curriculums. Educators need to determine which technology is the best for their curriculum.

Technology has a significant impact on education and society. It has always dictated how we teach and learn. It has always been at the forefront of education at all levels and times. Thanks to ever-advancing technology, educators now have access to handy tools that are more effective than anything they have ever had access to before.

The 21st century has seen a rapid rise in the use of technology in all aspects of life, and education is no exception. The education industry is constantly being disrupted by technology. Traditional education methods are disappearing and are becoming increasingly digitized. Today, school and university students prefer incorporating the power of emerging technologies into their classrooms.

Emerging technology is a general term used to describe new technology. Emerging technologies have revolutionized the learning and teaching process in the last decade. They are revolutionizing the world of education, including schools, colleges, and universities worldwide, by facilitating individualized instruction and expanding access to higher education. They are changing how students learn and how educators deliver knowledge.

Technologies are making learning and teaching easier than ever before. Such emerging technologies in education include artificial Intelligence, robotics, 3D printing, social media, gamification, the Internet of things, cloud computing, and big data.

This book examines these emerging technologies and their impact on education. It is organized into fifteen chapters that summarize emerging technologies and their applications in education.

Chapter 1: Introduction: This chapter provides an introduction to the entire book. It gives a systematic review of emerging technologies in education, what they are, and what they offer for education. Emerging technologies have revolutionized the learning and teaching process in the last decade. Newly emerging technologies, such as artificial Intelligence, 3D printing, social media, big data, cloud computing, and gamification, are being introduced into the classroom.

Chapter 2: Artificial Intelligence in Education: Traditional education systems are known to be inflexible but are now changing to adapt to the technological advancements of today's world. One key technology that is poised to transform education is artificial intelligence (AI). AI is an emerging technology that the educational sector can benefit from. AI in education refers to the application of AI technologies in educational settings to facilitate teaching, learning, or decision-making. This chapter provides various applications of AI in education.

Chapter 3: Robotics in Education: The chapter explores the uses of robots in the education industry. Robotics, an offshoot of artificial intelligence, is the new kid on the block to captivate the imagination of the young generation. It is a branch of engineering that involves the conception, design, manufacture, and operation of robots. The robot revolution is going to change us as humans. Robots used in the educational system are typically known as educational robots. Robotics in education is a growing field where robots teach students subjects.

Chapter 4: Cloud Computing in Education: This chapter provides an introduction to cloud computing for education. Cloud computing refers to a setup of computing resources that can be shared anywhere, irrespective of users' location. It is an emerging new computing paradigm for delivering computing services. It is changing the way information technology services are provided. A cloud platform makes accessing educational resources easier for students and teachers. It is easy for educators to monitor coursework and access students' progress without meeting face-to-face.

Chapter 5: Soft Computing in Education: This chapter is a primer on the applications of soft computing in education. Soft computing is a newly emerging computing method that combines various knowledge, technology, and methods to set up an intelligent or automated system to solve complex problems under uncertain and inaccurate circumstances. Soft computing technology in education allows a degree of flexibility and customization that was never possible. This provision is helpful for both students and educators alike.

Chapter 6: Big Data in Education: The chapter provides a brief introduction to how big data is used in education. Education systems produce a huge amount of data about students and schools. This data generation includes registration, attendance, grades, disciplinary records, socioeconomic background, and instruction times. The amount of data is so vast that processing it with conventional means is difficult. As the data in the education system becomes larger, the application of big data tools becomes necessary. Big data is a state-of-the-art technique to collect, allocate, accomplish, and discover massive datasets. Big data has made a significant impact on the education system.

Chapter 7: Education 4.0: This chapter provides a brief introduction to the continuum described from Education 1.0 through 2.0 towards 3.0/4.0. Education 4.0 requires a new way of thinking for teachers and students. It seeks to align with Industry 4.0 and prepare students for the next industrial revolution. Its most important goal for all educational institutions is to motivate students and improve their learning outcomes. It is tipped as the future of education and poised to change information consumption.

Chapter 8: Digital Education: The chapter introduces the readers to digital education, which is the process of using digital technology in teaching and learning. It is also known as online education, technology-enhanced learning, digital learning, or e-learning. Digital education uses digital tools and technologies during teaching and learning. It prepares students for becoming digital citizens by acquiring skills for navigating and existing in the digital world.

Chapter 9: Online Education: In this chapter, we discuss the strengths, weaknesses, and potential of online education. Online education, often called distance education or web-based education, is currently the latest, most popular form of distance education. It is a form of open and distance education widely used in higher education. It provides university equivalent courses for millions of students across the globe. It has been exploding in recent years as an option in colleges and universities both within the US and abroad.

Chapter 10: 3D Printing in Education: This chapter presents an overview of 3D printing in education. The 3D printer uses raw material combinations and builds an object one layer at a time. 3D printing (also known as additive manufacturing or rapid prototyping RP) brings disruptive innovation in several sectors, including education. The use of 3D printing as a support tool in education is increasing. 3D printing technologies facilitate improved learning, skills development, and increased student and teacher engagement with the subject matter. It has been a wonderful new way to teach and motivate students.

Chapter 11: Virtual Reality in Education: This chapter addresses the use of virtual reality in education. Human beings are visual creatures. Virtual reality is a human-designed system with the help of computers and electronic devices such as cameras and sensors to interact with 3-D environments. Virtual reality is an exciting way of turning ordinary classrooms into wonder, inquiry, and adventure places. It increases students' engagement and interest in learning. A key benefit of using virtual reality in education is that you learn through experience.

Chapter 12: Augmented Reality in Education: This chapter introduces the readers to the use of augmented reality in education. Augmented reality is one of the cloud technologies that bridge the gap between what you see and what you imagine. It superimposes sounds, videos, and graphics onto an existing environment. It allows the students to see 3D objects in the classroom. Using augmented reality to create interactive and engaging learning experiences makes students more likely to collaborate and share ideas.

Chapter 13: Gamification in Education: This chapter presents an overview of gamification in education and its applications. Games are widely popular and entertaining. The games industry is one of the most lucrative due to the billion-dollar digital game sales. Gamification is the use of game-based elements and game principles in non-game contexts. It has emerged as a promising area for imparting education. It transforms students from passive participants to active ones. It assumes that students learn best when they are also having fun. Its goal is to maximize teaching and engagement by capturing student interest and inspiring them to continue learning [4].

Chapter 14: Social Media in Education: This chapter introduces the use of social media networks and how they are applied in various education areas. Social media (also called Web 2.0) refers to Internet-based and mobile-based tools that allow individuals to share and consume content through varied modalities such as text, image, and video. Social media such as Facebook, Twitter, Myspace, Google+, LinkedIn, and Instagram are used daily by millions of people worldwide, especially young people. Social media can powerfully enhance the way students learn. Students in higher education rely on social media as one of the key resources for information and communication.

Chapter 15: Future of Education: This last chapter addresses how higher education institutions and K-12 schools can best prepare students for the future. It predicts the future of education by examining the future of technology, the future of learning, the future of teaching, and the future of online education. Today's education trends are shaping tomorrow's workforce, requiring youths to be competent in a broad range of transferable skills such as problem-solving, critical thinking, creativity, and communication. In the future, education will become more intelligent, safer and more secure, more relevant, and intertwined with future jobs.

This book is a must-read for anyone who wants to learn about trends in education.

We are grateful for the support of Dr. Annamalia Annamalai, the department head of the Department of Electrical and Computer Engineering, and Dr. Pamela Obiomon, the dean of the College of Engineering at Prairie View A&M University, Prairie View, Texas. Finally, we want to express our profound gratitude to our wives, Janet and Ranti, for their prayers and support.

—M. N. O. Sadiku and O. D. Olaleye

ABOUT THE AUTHORS

Matthew N. O. Sadiku: He received his B. Sc. degree in 1978 from Ahmadu Bello University, Zaria, Nigeria and his M.Sc. and Ph.D. degrees from Tennessee Technological University, Cookeville, TN in 1982 and 1984 respectively. In total, received seven college degrees. From 1984 to 1988, he was an assistant professor at Florida Atlantic University, Boca Raton, FL, where he did graduate work in computer science. From 1988 to 2000, he was at Temple University, Philadelphia, PA, where he became a full professor. From 2000 to 2002, he was with Lucent/Avaya, Holmdel, NJ as a system engineer and with Boeing Satellite Systems, Los Angeles, CA as a senior scientist. He is presently a Regents professor emeritus of electrical and computer engineering at Prairie View A&M University, Prairie View, TX.

He is the author of over 1,120 professional papers and over 120 books including "Elements of Electromagnetics" (Oxford University Press, 7th ed., 2018), "Fundamentals of Electric Circuits" (McGraw-Hill, 7th ed.,2020, with C. Alexander), "Computational Electromagnetics with MATLAB" (CRC Press, 4th ed., 2019), "Principles of Modern Communication Systems" (Cambridge University Press, 2017, with S. O. Agbo), and "Emerging Internet-based Technologies" (CRC Press, 2019). In addition to the engineering books, he has written Christian books including "Secrets of Successful Marriages," "How to Discover God's Will for Your Life," and commentaries on all the books of the New Testament Bible. Some of his books have been translated into ten languages including French, Korean, Chinese, Italian, Portuguese, Russian, and Spanish.

He was the recipient of the 2000 McGraw-Hill/Jacob Millman Award for outstanding contributions in the field of electrical engineering. He was also the recipient of Regents Professor award for 2012-2013 by the Texas A&M University System. He is a registered professional engineer and a life fellow of the Institute of Electrical and Electronics Engineers (IEEE) "for contributions to computational electromagnetics and engineering education." He was the IEEE Region 2 Student Activities Committee Chairman. He was an associate editor for IEEE Transactions on Education. He is also a member of Association for Computing Machinery (ACM) and American Society of Engineering Education (ASEE). His current research interests are in the areas of computational electromagnetic, computer science/networks, engineering education, and marriage counseling. His works can be found in his autobiography, "My Life and Work" (Trafford Publishing, 2017) or his website: www.matthew-sadiku.com. He currently resides with his wife Janet in West Palm Beach, Florida. He can be reached via email at sadiku@ieee.org

Olaniyi D. Olaleye: He received his B. Eng. degree in 1989 from University of Ilorin, Kwara State, Nigeria, and his M.Sc. degree from University of Lagos, Lagos State in 1997. He obtained Ph.D. degree in Urban Planning and Environmental Policy at the Texas Southern University, Houston, Texas, in 2021. From 1990 to 1992, he was a Project Engineer at Ibcon and Associates in Nigeria. He worked as Head of Engineering Operations at Horlan Company Limited from 1993 to 1997. He joined Mountliegh Nigeria Limited, an Oil and Gas services company and worked as Civil and Structural Project Manager from 1997 to 2002. He joined National Engineering and Technical Company (A subsidiary of Nigerian National Petroleum Corporation - NNPC) and worked as Lead Civil / Structural Engineer from 2002 to 2007. From 2007 to 2016, he joined RasGas Company Limited in Doha, Qatar, and worked as Advisor Offshore Structures Engineering. He has published several professional papers in international journals. He has also written books on diverse fields. He is a registered professional Civil Engineer with the Council for the Regulation of Engineering in Nigeria (COREN). He is also a registered professional Structural Engineer with the Engineering Council in United Kingdom (UK). He is a registered Project Management Professional (PMP.) with the

Project Management Institute (PMI) in Pennsylvania, United States. He is a member of American Concrete Institute (ACI), and American Institute of Steel Construction (AISC). His research interests are in the areas of civil and structural engineering, project engineering, project management, urban planning, water resources and environmental engineering, environmental management, climate adaptation, and infrastructural sustainability. He can be reached via email at olaniyi.olaleye@tsu.edu or olaleye.o@gmail.com.

CHAPTER 1

INTRODUCTION

"Education is our passport to the future, for tomorrow belongs to the people who prepare for it today."
—Malcolm X

1.1 INTRODUCTION

The main goal of education is to impart knowledge and understanding that will form the foundation for lifelong learning. Education and technology have always developed hand-in-hand. Technology has a significant impact on education and society. It has always dictated how we teach and learn. It has always been at the forefront of education at all levels and times. Different devices such as chalkboards, pencils, radios, television, overhead projector, photocopier, and handheld calculator significantly impacted the pre-computer years. In this digitalized global age, technology is everywhere in education. It is sweeping through classrooms as developers create more and more products designed to enhance education.

Traditionally, education has relied on face-to-face strategies. Although these face-to-face strategies have various obvious advantages and have been regarded as the gold standard in education, they require students to live near a school. In modern times, students demand and need alternatives to face-to-face instruction. Meeting the need may involve using current and emerging technologies such as computers, the Internet, mobile technologies, 3D printing, and virtual reality.

Emerging technology is a general term used to describe new technology. Emerging technologies have revolutionized the learning and teaching process in the last decade. Newly emerging technologies, such as artificial intelligence, 3D printing, social media, and gamification, are being introduced into the classroom. Education is already seeing some uses for these technologies. These technologies will force schools to eventually abandon their conventional modes of learning and teaching to align themselves with the times [1]. They are revolutionizing the world of education, including schools, colleges, and universities worldwide. They are revolutionizing classroom practice by facilitating individualized instruction and expanding access to higher education.

These new technologies are changing how students learn and how educators deliver knowledge. Technologies are making learning and teaching easier than ever before. Figure 1.1 shows a typical modern classroom with laptops and mobile devices [2].

This chapter provides a systematic review of emerging technologies in education, what they are, and what they offer for education. It begins by explaining what emerging technologies are. It presents some of the emerging technologies. It explains digital natives and the students using the technologies. It highlights the benefits and challenges of the technologies. It addresses the global impact of emerging technologies in education. The last section concludes with comments.

Figure 1.1 A typical modern classroom, dominated by laptops and mobile devices [2].

1.2 WHAT ARE EMERGING TECHNOLOGIES?

Technology is essentially the organized application of knowledge to solve practical problems. It is also a collection of systems designed to perform some function. It can-alleviate some of the challenges facing today's education system. It affects how live and act in the society, particularly in education. In recent years, these technologies have been given various names such as, Information and Communication Technologies (ICT), Technologies in Education, Digital Technologies, Technologies for Learning, Technologies for Empowerment, and Emerging Technologies (ETs). Emerging technologies are new technologies that are at an early stage in their development. They refer to resources, tools, concepts, and innovations that have a disruptive potential to generate changes [3].

Some of the characteristics of emerging technologies are [4,5]:

(1) they may or may not be new technologies;
(2) they change rapidly, so they are always in a state of coming into being;
(3) they go through cycles of hyped expectations;
(4) they are in a continuous state of being understood and researched;
(5) they have the potential to transform social practices.

Figure 1.2 illustrates emerging technologies in education [6]. Emerging technologies are used in nearly every field imaginable such as-education, engineering, medicine, mathematics, and the military.

Emerging technologies (ETs) in education are essential tools, concepts, and innovations used in educational settings to serve various education-related purposes. They are used in different areas of education, such as distance learning, online education, virtual laboratory, teacher training, language learning, distance education, e-learning, and adult education. They promise to revolutionize the way students and teachers work and interact [5]. These educational technologies try to make learning more efficient, engaging, relevant, and entertaining. They are especially helpful in allowing teachers and students to generate and share academic work.

They can have considerable positive impacts on student performance. Many educators' jobs have become easier and more enjoyable through these technologies.

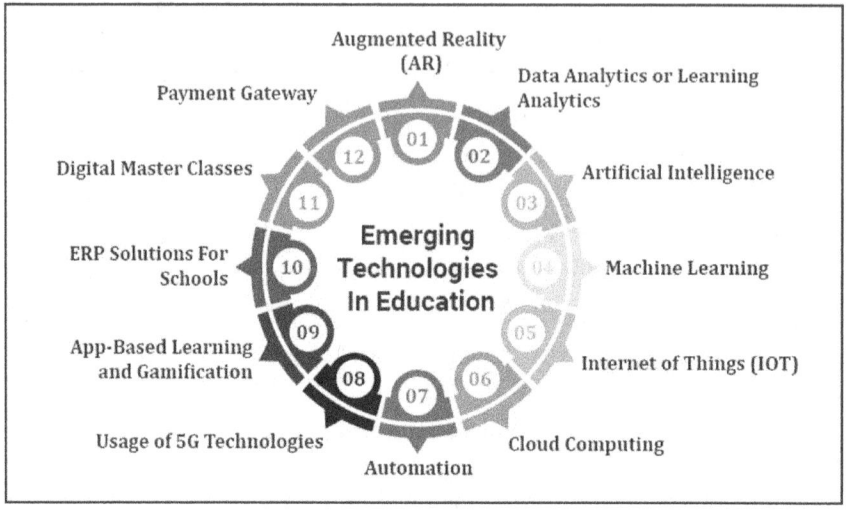

Figure 1.2 Emerging technologies in education [6].

1.3 SOME EMERGING TECHNOLOGIES

Emerging technologies (ETs) are tools utilized in diverse educational settings face-to-face, distance, and online) to serve various education-related purposes. Emerging technologies are paving the way for the future of education in ways we may have yet to see. We will cover some of these technologies [7].

- *Online Education:* Students enrolled in online schools do not attend a bricks and mortar school. Both core courses and electives, including lab courses, can be taken online. Online learning opportunities can increase educational productivity by accelerating the learning rate, reducing costs associated with instructional materials or program delivery, and better utilizing teacher time. Blended learning opportunities incorporate face-to-face and online learning opportunities to accommodate students' diverse learning styles. Online universities such as Athabasca recognize the value of online learning and are well-positioned to offer a blended education.

- *Artificial intelligence:* The umbrella term of "artificial intelligence" (AI) refers to a set of tools and capabilities like machine learning, expert systems, robotics, and natural language processing. AI is poised to play an important role in education as it expands to different parts of a school setting. AI harnesses big data, using machine learning to make predictions and decisions. Alexa is Amazon's AI voice assistant, much like Siri for Apple. Figure 1.3 shows the benefits of AI in education [8].

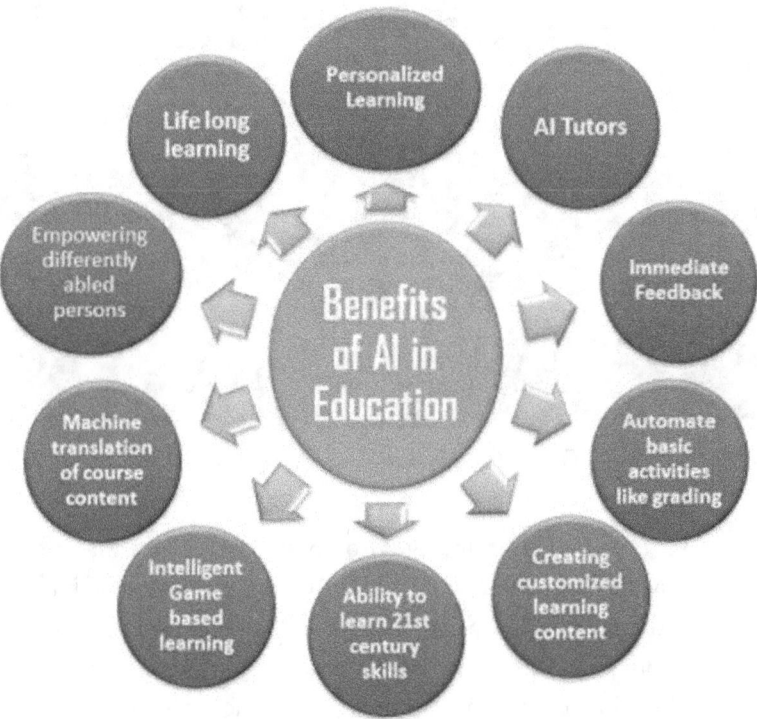

Figure 1.3 The benefits of AI in education [8].

- *Robotics:* This is one of the most exciting and rapidly growing fields in education today. Although the use of pedagogical robotics is still in its incipient stage, the literature on its advantages for classroom use is already abundant. Educational robotics helps to enhance strategic problem-solving, higher-order thinking, logical and analytical reasoning, computational thinking, teamwork, collaborative skills, and more. For example, educational service robots have appeared in the United States, Canada, Japan, South Korea, and Taiwan. A typical educational robot is shown in Figure 1.4 [9].

Figure 1.4 A typical educational robot [9].

- *3D Printing:* 3D printing (also known as additive manufacturing (AM) or rapid prototyping (RP)) was invented by Charles Hull in the early 1980s. Since then, it has been used in manufacturing, automotive, electronics, aviation, aerospace, consumer products, education, entertainment, medicine, space missions, the military, and chemical and jewelry industries [10]. The 3D printer allows students to perfect their designs before making an actual prototype. Moving learning from two dimensions (2D) to three dimensions (3D) allows students to consider all sides of a concept. Engineering students could directly benefit from 3D printing technology. A typical use of a 3D printer is shown in Figure 1.5 [11].

- *Internet of Things:* The Internet of things (IoT) is a giant network of connected things and people. The idea behind creating IoT was the amalgamation of the physical world into computer-based systems. Some of the examples of IoT include cell phones, washing machines, laptops, etc. IoT is an innovative technology that allows all smart devices to communicate with each other via the Internet. The education sector is deploying IoT devices to make education more collaborative, interactive, and accessible.. IoT devices are changing how we process and absorb information for the better. It has tremendous potential to create smarter and more connected schools and is already impacting the education sector by making learning simpler, faster, and safer. The IoT technology will make institutional management easier, tech-based, and more robust. It can also be used to manage attendance digitally, real-time location tracking of students, school bus tracking, detect human presence in some rooms, and more [12].

Figure 1.5 A typical use of 3D printer [11].

- *Big Data:* This refers to the data generated by learners while taking a training module or an eLearning course. The eLearning industry has been revolutionized by big data. With the help of big data analytics, it is easy for the experts to make captivating and customized modules. Big data allows eLearning experts to understand how users digest the information and which learning aspects appeal the most to them. Based on the learning patterns, eLearning experts can predict where learners may excel or struggle and improve their eLearning accordingly [13].

- *Cloud Computing:* This is essentially accessing computing services through the Internet. A cloud platform makes it easier for students and teachers to access educational resources. Virtual learning environments, such as web-based tools and applications, are one example of cloud computing. They save schools time, money, and resources. A key advantage of cloud computing is that it reduces the need for in-house investment in hardware and software. Students and educators can use web-based tools to collaborate online. Everyone in the education sector is experiencing the positive impact of cloud computing technology [14].

- *Social Networking:* Social networks, such as MySpace, Facebook, Twitter, Facebook, LinkedIn, Pinterest, and YouTube, are part of how students communicate. Many universities have adopted the online virtual world, Second Life, to provide students with an online platform to socialize with each other. A class can be fully connected to social media, including a Twitter stream, a Google Plus account, and a Facebook account. Many teachers use social media to communicate directly with their students and provide one-on-one attention to students' concerns.

- *Virtual Reality*: The application of virtual reality (VR) in education seems obvious. In education, VR hardware is being used to provide experiences that are hard or even impossible to bring to students today. VR learning experiences will shift the concept of an educational "classroom" to that of a "virtual global class." Virtual reality equipment will become cheap and of high enough quality to provide a comfortable immersive user experience. For example, students in healthcare (nurses, doctors, dentists, and pharmacists) and manufacturing can expect to see VR being increasingly used for training or learning technology. A typical use of virtual reality in schools is shown in Figure 1.6 [15].

Figure 1.6 Use of virtual reality in schools [15].

- *Game-based Learning*: Gameplay has proved to be a useful training and motivation tool. Students can have fun and learn while they play interactive games. They are already used to playing with YouTube, Facebook, and smartphones. Computer-based games play an important role in the education of students with disabilities. Online sites such as Vocabulary.com provide opportunities for gamification. Figure 1.7 shows educational game technology [16].

Figure 1.7 Educational game technology [16].

Other newly emerging technologies that may directly or indirectly affect education are distance education, simulations, Massive Open Online Courses (MOOC), augmented reality, 5G, biometrics, mobile technologies, e-textbooks, cybersecurity, wearable technology, and automation, and the list is practically endless. Emerging technologies in education all share a similar objective: to revolutionize or reshape the learning process for students. Educators can seek online and offline supports to use emerging technologies in meaningful ways. To understand the true impact of emerging technologies on education, we must consider those who will use the technologies.

1.4 DIGITAL NATIVES

The phenomenon of digital technologies transcends all cultural, racial, religious, and age boundaries. We live in an always-connected, digital age. Digitalization has accelerated exponentially, and educators' survival will depend on their ability to reshape their future. It has produced a distinctively new generation defined by digital media: the digital natives. Digital natives are those who were born into the digital age or after 1980.

Those born before that year—who have migrated online—are digital immigrants.

Teachers often assume the role of digital immigrants, while students often assume the role of digital natives. Digital natives are students growing up in a digital world, and educators must employ new approaches to make learning real and relevant to them. They are the kind of students who will use the emerging technologies for learning and teaching. Today's "digital natives" are a new generation of students who want all kinds of digital gadgets, such as personal computers, laptops, tablets, and personal digital assistants (PDAs) [17]. Examples of digital natives are shown in Figure 1.8 [18].

Figure 1.8 Examples of digital natives [18].

Digital natives use and understand various digital technologies such as the Internet, smartphones, and social media. They know more about these technologies than their parents. They exhibit Internet-related addictive behaviors. Erika Smith of the University of Alberta describes eight unsubstantiated claims in the different present discourses on digital natives [19]:

- They possess new ways of knowing and being.
- They are driving a digital revolution and thereby transforming society.
- They are innately or inherently tech-savvy.
- They are multitaskers, team-oriented, and collaborative.
- They are native speakers of the language of technology and have unique viewpoints and abilities.
- They embrace gaming, interaction, and simulation.
- They demand immediate gratification.
- They reflect and respond to the knowledge economy.

The majority of learners in classrooms today are digital natives. Our educational systems need to listen to the voices of the digital natives or face a future with disgruntled, disconnected learners.

In the digital age, the role of a teacher has fundamentally changed. Leaning heavily on tech in teaching is the only option modern educators have. Educators must keep in mind that digital natives experience life growing up much-differently than the previous generations. It is incumbent upon teachers to understand when and how to incorporate technology into the classroom. To facilitate learning by digital natives, educators should embed digital technologies in their teaching, learning, and assessment [20,21].

1.5 BENEFITS

There has been widespread excitement and hope about the transformative potential of emerging technologies in education. ETs transform both teaching and learning practices. Some benefits of implementing emerging technologies in education are presented as follows.

- *Improvement in Productivity:* Technology ushers in changes that help achieve significant productivity improvements. It supports both teaching and learning. It can expand course offerings, supports learning 24/7, builds 21st-century skills, increases student engagement, and accelerates learning. Online learning can potentially improve educational productivity, pay less tuition, and reduce the cost of instructional materials [22].

- *Improvement in Computer Proficiency:* Technology increases computer usage and improves computer proficiency. Computer-assisted learning programs have improved academic achievement, especially in mathematics.

- *Blended Learning:* Many educational institutions are adopting emerging technologies to bring high-quality educational outcomes to their students and to stay relevant in the changing world. The adoption has enabled them to provide a "blended learning" approach to delivering course content. Blended learning incorporates face-to-face and online learning opportunities to accommodate students' diverse learning styles.

- *Online learning:* Online learning through educational technology tools has been used as a paradigm shift in education to transmit knowledge and promote learners' engagement in learning environments. Educators must devise means to engage learners emotionally, behaviorally, and cognitively in a technology-supported learning environment.

- *Learning Aid:* Emerging technologies can have a far-reaching effect on teaching and learning. With their laptops, students can access distant experts and archives, communicate with peers, participate in social media, and be part of virtual communities. Technology better prepares students for their future careers.

- *Equity:* One important aspect of technology in education is its ability to level the field of opportunity for students of all ages, colors, and backgrounds. All students deserve to have the best education. Emerging technologies can shrink long-standing equity and accessibility gaps and adapt learning experiences to meet the needs of all students. They help remove barriers, such as race, ethnicity, national origin, sex, and disability, that students face.

1.6 CHALLENGES

It is challenging to pinpoint the roles and functions of technologies in education. Claims about what technology can do are hard to verify. In 1931, Thomas Edison falsely predicted that books would soon be obsolete in school and that films would alter education as no other technology had before. The barriers or challenges faced by implementing emerging technologies in education include the following.

- *Cost:* The cost of implementing the technologies can be prohibitive for some schools and districts, as they require significant investment in hardware and software.

- *Change is Hard:* Education is a field that is resistant to change, but technology is leading the educational experience to change. Change is hard, budgets are tight, or leadership cannot agree on the best tools to purchase and use. Technological change is accelerating at an exponential rate. With the rapid evolution of technology, educational capabilities are growing and changing daily.

- *Digital Divide:* Technology can be either inclusive or exclusive. Knowledge and ideas flow in one direction, North-to-South. The digital divide between the technology-haves and technology-have-nots is growing wider and wider. The development of education technology has occurred in a persistent inequality, and the process of making it equitable is still evolving. Some parents in rural, remote, or low-income areas lack Wi-Fi access and struggle to provide lunch, let alone laptops, for their children.

- *Job Safety:* New technologies have always threatened to take jobs away from human workers. Although some jobs have been eliminated by technological advancements, many new jobs have been created.

- *Disruptive Technologies:* Emerging technologies are potentially disruptive. Their potential to transform educational practices is both welcomed by some and opposed by others. Technologies are important and useful but are merely just the means to an end. People must take ownership of what they learn, how, where, and when they learn. Lifelong learning requires people must unlearn and relearn as the world changes.

- *Cannot Deliver Promise:* A main critique of the implementation of emerging technologies is that they have fallen short of delivering on the promise of transforming existing teaching and learning practices. Despite the inundation of technology within the classroom, critics notice that the role of technology is yet to be determined, and there has been virtually no improvement in the students' learning outcomes in the Western world over the past decade.

- *Too Fast to Master*: Newly emerging technologies for education are arriving and changing exponentially, too fast for the teachers to keep up. Teachers will always be behind the curve in using these technologies. Yet our students, the digital natives, are comfortable with the technologies and clamoring for their use in their education.

1.7 GLOBAL IMPACT OF EMERGING TECHNOLOGIES ON EDUCATION

The newly emerging technologies allow people to collaborate across distance and time.

To remain relevant, academic institutions at all levels must respond to global, social, political, technological, and learning research trends. The globalization of education will only be successful if there is collaboration among nations.

The New Media Consortium (NMC) has been charting the landscape of emerging technologies in teaching, learning, and creative inquiry on a global scale. There is an ongoing collaboration between the NMC and the EDUCAUSE Learning Initiative (ELI), an EDUCAUSE program.

Massive online open courses (MOOCs) are online education technology that allows every person to learn what he or she wants to learn, in his or her own time, at his or her own speed. Educators across the globe are doing some amazing things with MOOCs. We now consider how some nations are employing emerging technologies.

- *United States:* Education is fundamentally local. A lot has been written about the failure of the American educational system, from pre-K through postsecondary education. Critics argue that the American higher education system has become nothing more than a "failure factory," with graduation rates even lower than those of high schools. Technology can help alleviate many of the challenges facing the American education system. The federal government is making a massive effort to make affordable high-speed Internet and online teaching resources available freely to even the most rural schools [23]. Pressure is mounting for institutions at all levels all over the United States to improve student outcomes, reduce rising tuition costs, and engage in educational reform. In response, institutions are embracing technologies that promise to help them do more with less. Some are even using technological tools to recruit and retain students.

- *United Kingdom*: The UK education system is a world leader in the adoption and use of technology in the classroom, with teachers, students, and parents actively involved in the way devices are utilized at school. Alongside parents' involvement, the research found that UK schools are much more willing to involve students in the planning of technology use in schools too [24]. The UK is showing itself to be a prominent leader in the adoption of education technology (EdTech), which refers to the practice of using technology to support teaching and the effective day-to-day management of education institutions. It includes hardware (such as tablets, laptops, or other digital devices) and digital resources, software, and services that help aid teaching, meet specific needs, and help the daily running of educational institutions.

- *Europe*: The European Commission is the European Union's politically independent executive arm. The Commission aims at modernizing education by funding research and promoting digital technologies used for learning. It funds many activities on research and innovation for digital learning under several programs, including Horizon Europe and Digital European Programme, the Seventh Framework Programme, and the Competitiveness and Innovation Framework Programme. The Commission has published Guidelines for teachers and educators in primary and secondary schools on how to address disinformation and promote digital literacy in their classrooms [25].

- *China:* China is the world's largest developing country and has the world's largest education system. It is leading in the application of new digital technologies in education. Its education industry has reached a critical stage where online education needs to be enhanced. There has been an increasing demand for at-home study in China, opening the door for the country's intelligent education hardware market. Intelligent education products like e-dictionary pens, robots, educational tablets, and smart lights are becoming increasingly popular with students in China and finding solutions for the vexing problems of students [26]. Information and communication technology (ICT) has had a revolutionary influence on the reform and development of Chinese education.

- *India:* The Indian education sector has recently undergone a significant transformation. The growth in popularity of mobile learning platforms among students has led to the expansion of the e-learning market in India. Virtual reality, artificial intelligence, mobile learning, smartboards, gamification, personalized learning, augmented reality, cloud computing, experiential learning, project-based learning, and collaborative learning are some of the latest trends driving a rapid transformation in the Indian education sector [27].

- *South Africa:* South African higher education is currently facing challenges posed by a diverse student population with varied levels of preparedness, multilingualism, and large classes. The educational system is under pressure to provide equity of access to education. Directors of teaching and learning and senior academics in all of South Africa were also targeted.

- *Burkina Faso:* In Sub-Saharan Africa, educators are introducing the idea of using technology as an educational and developmental tool. Education has faced several challenges in the African nation of Burkina Faso, where teachers are routinely confronted with material shortages, lack of equipment, and lack of opportunity for self-conducted learning. To overcome these challenges, educators are using Emerging Learning Technologies (ELTs) to help improve the quality of teaching and to increase student access to these learning opportunities. The education system is divided into the following subsectors: preschool education, primary education, secondary education, and a tertiary sub-sector [28].

- *Malaysia:* In 2021, the Minister of Higher Education Malaysia announced a new program: 'Education Tourism,' also commonly known as, EduTourism, at Expo 2020 Dubai. This program will soon be launched to promote Malaysia as a choice destination for both tourism and education. Malaysia's higher education institutions will continue their excellent performances. New partnerships must be established between academia, the industry, and all other potential collaborators [29]. A private Malaysian university also supported the student's willingness to continue using cloud e-learning applications in their studies.

1.8 CONCLUSION

Technology is impacting all aspects of life, including education. It has been changing the education system gradually and progressively. Technology is a tool and is only helpful when it is properly implemented. Otherwise, they can leave us disorganized, frustrated, disoriented, or confused. Technologies undergo natural cycles of infatuation, adoption, maturity, and impact. New technologies rise, gain popularity, and then disappear. Today's emerging technology may be tomorrow's fad.

Education is set to experience a huge impact from emerging technologies. There is unanimity that technology is unavoidable and vital to our daily life. Education technologies like the radio, TV, and computer have failed to replace teacher-aided learning. Education will experience a great transformation from emerging technologies, the learning tools for developing 21st-century knowledge and skills. Education technology will bring about social change and better use of resources. Understanding the impact of technologies on education will advance the learning process.

Today, many institutions worldwide offer courses on emerging technologies in education and prepare teachers on how to handle the technologies. Educators, learners, parents, and policymakers need reliable methodologies for evaluating the effectiveness of such emerging technologies. Such evaluation is necessary for their impacts to be effectively integrated into learning and teaching settings to bring the best benefit to learners and teachers [30]. For more information on emerging technologies in education, one should consult the books in [31-52]. One should also consult the following related journals devoted:

- *International Journal of Emerging Technologies in Learning*
- *International Journal of Emerging Technologies & Vocational Education*
- *British Journal of Educational Technology*
- *Educational Technology*
- *Educational Technology & Society*
- *Journal of Education*
- *International Journal of Education*
- *International Journal of Higher Education*
- *International Journal of Technology in Education and Science*
- *International Journal of Educational Technology in Higher Education*
- *International Journal of Educational Methodology*
- *World Journal of Education*
- *IEEE Transactions on Education*
- *Australasian Journal of Educational Technology*

REFERENCES

[1] M. N. O. Sadiku, U. C. Chukwu, A. Ajayi-Majebi, and S. M. Musa, "Emerging technologies in education," *Journal of Scientific and Engineering Research,* vol. 7, no. 8, 2020, pp. 35-44.

[2] Z. Bernard, "Here's how technology is shaping the future of education," December 2017, https://www.businessinsider.com/how-technology-is-shaping-the-future-of-education-2017-12

[3] E. A. S. Neira, J. Salinas, and B. B. Crosetti, "A systematic review of the literature published between 2006 and 2016," *International Journal of Emerging Technologies in Learning,* vol. 12, no. 5, May 2017, pp. 128-149.

[4] V. Bozalek, D. Ng'ambi, and D. Gachago, "Transforming teaching with emerging technologies: Implications for higher education institutions," https://core.ac.uk/download/pdf/83123732.pdf

[5] G. Veletsianos, "A definition of emerging technologies for education," in G. Veletsianos (ed.), *Emerging Technologies in Distance Education.* Athabasca University Press,, chapter 1, · 2010, pp. 3-22.

[6] "Emerging technologies in education," https://www.tatvasoft.com/outsourcing/2022/06/emerging-technologies-in-education.html

[7] M. Poh, "8 Technologies that will shape future classrooms," July 2017, https://www.hongkiat.com/blog/future-classroom-technologies/

[8] D. Wadhwa, "Using artificial intelligence technologies for personalized learning and responsive teaching: A survey," *International Journal of Advance Research in Science and Engineering,* vol. 6, no. 1, November 2017, pp. 207-217.

[9] S. Brezgov, "Robots in education: Is the educational revolution just around the corner?" January 2020, https://scholarlyoa.com/robots-in-education-is-the-educational-revolution-just-around-the-corner/

[10] M. N. O. Sadiku, S. M. Musa, and O. S. Musa, "3D printing in the chemical industry," *Invention Journal of Research Technology in Engineering and Management*, vol. 2, no. 2, February 2018, pp. 24-26.

[11] "The future of stem education: Emerging technologies and trends [2023 updated guide]," February 2023, https://www.constructionplacements.com/future-of-stem-education/

[12] A. Bharti, "6 Top emerging technology trends in higher education," June 2022, https://www.datatobiz.com/blog/top-emerging-technology-trends-in-higher-education/

[13] J. Axelsson, " 6 Emerging technology trends changing eLearning," https://elearningindustry.com/technology-trends-changing-elearning-6-emerging

[14] "Here are the reasons why we need cloud computing in schools in Nigeria," https://edufirst.ng/education-in-nigeria/the-importance-of-cloud-computing-in-education/

[15] K. Walsh, "Real uses of virtual reality in education: how schools are using VR," June 2017, https://www.emergingedtech.com/2017/06/real-uses-of-virtual-reality-in-education-how-schools-are-using-vr/

[16] E. Kunnen, "Emerging technologies to enhance teaching and enable active learning," August 2015, https://er.educause.edu/articles/2015/8/emerging-technologies-to-enhance-teaching-and-enable-active-learning

[17] "The evolution of technology in the classroom," https://online.purdue.edu/blog/education/evolution-technology-classroom

[18] "Digital native," *Wikipedia*, the free encyclopedia https://en.wikipedia.org/wiki/Digital_native

[19] P. De Bruyckere, P. A. Kirschner, and C. D. Hulshof, "Technology in education," https://www.aft.org/ae/spring2016/debruyckere-kirschner-and-hulshof

[20] M. N. O. Sadiku, J. King, J. O. Sadiku, and S. M. Musa, *Digital Natives and Their Customs*. Atlanta, GA: Author's Tranquility Press, chapter 3, 2023.

[21] M. N. O. Sadiku, U. C. Chukwu, A. Ajayi-Majebi, and S. M. Musa, "Educating Digital Natives," *Proceedings of Frontiers in Education: Computer Science & Computer E+STEM+Online*, Las Vegas, July 2022.

[22] "Use of technology in teaching and learning," https://www.ed.gov/oii-news/use-technology-teaching-and-learning#:~:text=Technology%20also%20has%20the%20power,own%20instruction%20and%20personalize%20learning.

[23] S. Ahalt, K. Fecho, and S. C. Ahalt, "Ten emerging technologies for higher education," https://renci.org/wp-content/uploads/2015/02/EmergingTechforHigherEd.pdf

[24] "UK education system 'leads world in embracing technology,'" March 2022, https://www.avinteractive.com/markets/education/uk-education-system-leads-world-embracing-technology-28-03-2022/

[25] "Digital learning and ICT in education," https://digital-strategy.ec.europa.eu/en/policies/digital-learning

[26] K. Aisyah, "China's education technology on the rise," August 2021, https://opengovasia.com/chinas-education-technology-on-the-rise/#:~:text=Intelligent%20education%20products%20like%20e,the%20vexing%20problems%20of%20students.

[27] "10 latest innovations and technologies in the Indian education sector," https://varthana.com/school/10-latest-innovations-and-technologies-in-the-indian-education-sector/#:~:text=Virtual%20reality%2C%20artificial%20intelligence%2C%20mobile,and%20innovations%20driving%20this%20change.

[28] R. R. Zongo, "Integration of emerging learning technologies in secondary schools: A Burkina Faso case study, *Doctoral Dissertation*, University of Minnesota, January 2017.

[29] "Emerging technologies in education," December 2021, https://www.gulftoday.ae/business/2021/12/18/emerging-technologies-in-education

[30] M. Cukurova and R. Luckin, "Measuring the Impact of Emerging Technologies in Education: A Pragmatic Approach," in J. Voogt et al. (eds), *Second Handbook of Information Technology in Primary and Secondary Education*. Cham, Switzerland: Springer 2018.

[31] L. Goosen and T. N. Mukasa-Lwanga, *Emerging Technologies Supported in ICT Education*. Springer, 2017.

[32] A. Hebbel-Seeger, T. Reiners, and D. Schäffer, *Synthetic Worlds: Emerging Technologies in Education and Economics*. Springer, 2013.

[33] K. Reggie, F. Robert, and T. Philip, *Enhancing Learning Through Technology: Research on Emerging Technologies and Pedagogies*. World Scientific Publishing, 2008.

[34] D. Hung and M. S. Khine, *Engaged Learning With Emerging Technologies*. Springer, 2006.

[35] X. Ge, D. Ifenthaler, and J. M. Spector, *Emerging Technologies for TEAM Education: Full STEAM Ahead*. Springer, 2016.

[36] G. Veletsianos, *Emergence and Innovation in Digital Learning*. AU Press, 2016.

[37] M. Pacansky-Brock, *Best Practices for Teaching with Emerging Technologies*. New York: Routledge, 2013.

[[38] V. Bozalek et al., *Activity Theory, Authentic Learning and Emerging Technologies: Towards a Transformative Higher Education Pedagogy*. Routledge, 2014

[39] S. Yu, M. Ally, and A. Tsinakos, *Emerging Technologies and Pedagogies in the Curriculum*. Springer, 2020.

[40] D. Hung, *Engaged Learning with Emerging Technologies*. Springer, 2006.

[41] Z. Ma and L. Yan, *Emerging Technologies and Applications in Data Processing and Management*. IGI Global, 2019.

[42] L. Rouhiainen, *The Future of Higher Education: How Emerging Technologies Will Change Education Forever*. CreateSpace Independent Publishing Platform, 2016.

[43] T. C. Huang et al. (eds.), *Emerging Technologies for Education: Second International Symposium, SETE 2017, Held in Conjunction with ICWL 2017, Cape Town, South Africa, September ... (Lecture Notes in Computer Science, 10676)*. Springer, 2017.

[44] M. Bowdon and R.G. Carpenter, *Higher Education, Emerging Technologies, and Community Partnerships: Concepts, Models and Practices*. IGI Global, 2011.

[45] E. Popescu et al. (eds.), *Emerging Technologies for Education: 4th International Symposium, SETE 2019, Held in Conjunction with ICWL 2019, Magdeburg, Germany, September 23–25, 2019, Revised Selected Papers*. Springer, 2020.

[46] J. Murray and W. Kidd, *Using Emerging Technologies to Develop Professional Learning*. Taylor & Francis, 2017.

[47] A. D. Cheok, B. I. Edwards, and N. A. Shukor (eds.), *Emerging Technologies for Next Generation Learning Spaces*. Springer, 2021.

[48] C. Mouza and N. Lavigne, *Emerging Technologies for the Classroom: A Learning Sciences Perspective*. New York: Springer, 2012.

[49] K. Becnel (ed.), *Emerging Technologies in Virtual Learning Environments*. IGI Global, 2019.

[50] J. A. Delello and R. R. McWhorter, *Disruptive and Emerging Technology Trends Across Education and the Workplace*. IGI Global, 2020.

[51] T. Hao et al. (eds.), *Emerging Technologies for Education*. Springer, 2018.

[52] G. Veletsianos, G. (ed.), *Emerging Technologies in Distance Education*. Edmonton, AB: AU Press, 2010.

CHAPTER 2

AI IN EDUCATION

*"I think AI is coming about and replacing routine jobs.
It is pushing us to do what we should be doing anyway:
the creation of more humanistic service jobs."*
—Kai-Fu Lee

2.1 INTRODUCTION

We live in a dynamic era that offers great opportunities and unprecedented challenges. Efforts have been made to evolve the educational system to the requirements and needs of students in the 21st century. According to Nelson Mandela, "Education is the most powerful weapon you can use to change the world." Education is a process where teachers give systematic instructions while students receive them. It is a major determining factor for an individual's success in life. Education seems to be fixed in terms of time, place, and prescribed activities. Learning takes place continuously, especially for younger people. Traditional education systems are known to be inflexible but are now changing to adapt to the technological advancements of today's world. One key technology that is poised to transform education is artificial intelligence (AI). AI is an emerging technology that the educational sector can benefit from. Implementing AI has several benefits for students and teachers alike [1].

AI is a general-purpose technology that can perform tasks that previously required human beings. It can be regarded as the simulation of human mental capacity by machines. It is a research domain with many sub-disciplines, domains of expertise, and developmental dynamics [2]. AI is rapidly transforming many industries, such as healthcare, transportation, business, retail, construction, food industry, manufacturing, and education. Apple's Siri voice assistant, Amazon's shopping recommendations, Uber ride sharing, and Google Translate are common examples of how AI has invaded our daily lives [3]. AI has impacted almost all sectors of human life and provided a lot of benefits to various fields, including education. The field of education is where artificial intelligence is poised to make big changes.

Artificial intelligence in education (AIED) has become a field of scientific research for more than 30 years. AIED refers to the application of AI technologies in educational settings to facilitate teaching, learning, or decision-making. It is one of the emerging fields in educational technology. AIED is mainly concerned with the development of "computers which perform cognitive tasks, usually associated with human minds" [4,5]. Figure 2.1 shows the roles of AIED.

This chapter provides various applications of AI in education. It begins by giving a brief review of AI and various possibilities of AI in education. It covers how AI can be applied in elementary school, high school, and higher institutions. It presents some applications of AI in education. It discusses the global adoption of AI in education. It highlights the benefits and challenges of AI in education. It considers the future of education as far as AI is concerned. The last section concludes with comments.

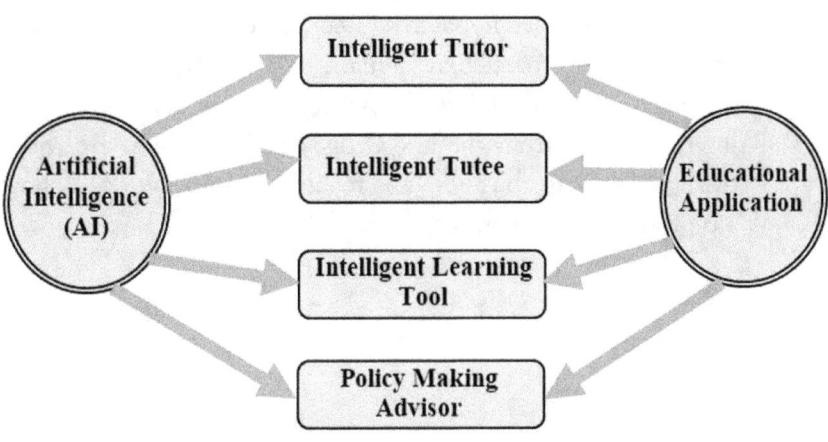

Figure 2.1 The roles of AIED.

2.2 REVIEW OF ARTIFICIAL INTELLIGENCE

The term "artificial intelligence" (AI) was first used at a Dartmouth College conference in 1952. Artificial intelligence refers to the ability of a computer system to perform human tasks (such as thinking and learning) that usually can only be accomplished using human intelligence. AI technology in education i allows a degree of flexibility and customization that was never before possible. It is revolutionizing schools and classrooms, making educator's jobs much easier. It is poised to revolutionize education.

AI is not a single technology but a range of computational models and algorithms. The concept of AI is an umbrella term that encompasses many different technologies. AI is not a single technology but a collection of techniques that enables computer systems to perform tasks that would otherwise require human intelligence. Artificial intelligence has the following main components [6-9]:

- *Expert systems:* AI is sometimes a stand-alone independent electronic entity that functions like a human expert. Expert system (ES) was the first successful implementation of artificial intelligence and may be regarded as a branch of AI mainly concerned with specialized knowledge-intensive domains like medicine. An expert system is computer software that simulates the judgment and behavior of a human expert. It is also known as an intelligent system or knowledge-based system. It encapsulates specialist knowledge of a particular domain of expertise and can make intelligent decisions. It has a knowledge base and a set of rules that infer new facts from the knowledge. Expert systems are widely used in healthcare, business, and manufacturing. Figure 2.2 shows a typical expert system.

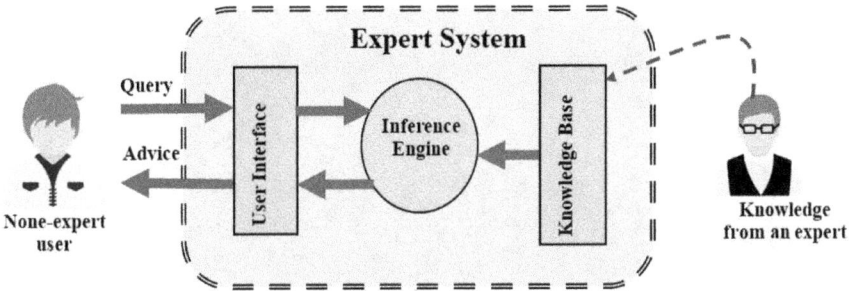

Figure 2.2 A typical expert system.

- *Fuzzy logic:* This makes it possible to create rules for how machines respond to inputs that account for a continuum of possible conditions rather than straightforward binary. The system needs absolute answers where each variable is either true or false (yes or no). However, these are not always available. Fuzzy logic allows variables to have a '" truth value" between 0 and 1. It uses approximate human reasoning in knowledge-based systems. It was introduced in the 1960s by Lotfi Zadeh of the University of California, Berkeley, known as the father of fuzzy set theory. Fuzzy logic is useful in manufacturing processes as it can handle situations that cannot be adequately handled by traditional true/false logic.

- *Neural networks:* These are specific types of machine learning systems that consist of artificial synapses designed to imitate the structure and function of brains. An artificial neural network (ANN) is an information-processing device that is inspired by how the brain processes information. They were originally developed to mimic the learning process of the human brain. The idea of ANNs was inspired by the structure of the human brain and by envy of what the brain can do. They are made up of artificial neurons, which take in multiple inputs and produce a single output. The network observes and learns as the synapses transmit data to one another, processing information as it passes through multiple layers. As shown in Figure 2.3, artificial neural networks are multi-layer fully-connected neural nets.

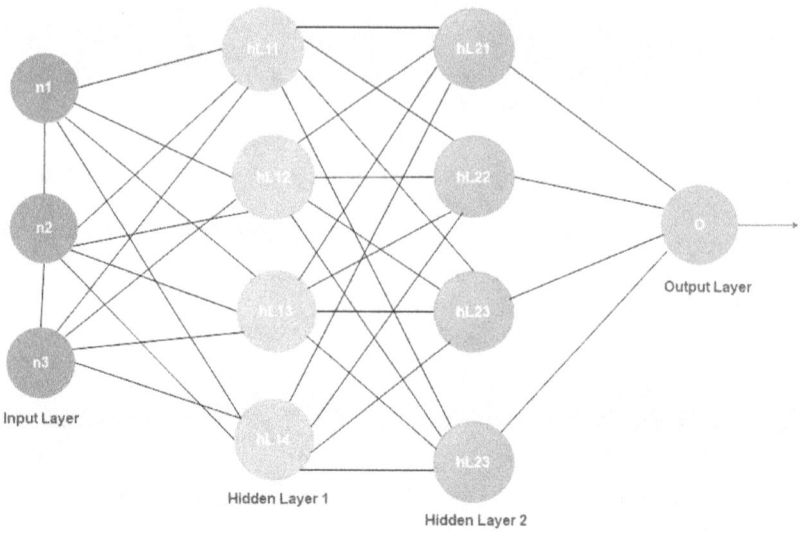

Figure 2.3 Artificial neural networks.

- *Machine Learning:* Machine learning (ML) is the study of computer algorithms that improve automatically through experience. It is the field that focuses on how computers learn from data. This field includes a broad range of algorithms and statistical models, making it possible for systems to find patterns, draw inferences, and learn to perform tasks without specific instructions. Machine learning is a process that involves the application of AI to automatically perform a specific task without explicitly programming it. There are two types of learning: supervised learning and unsupervised learning. Supervised learning focuses on classification and prediction. It involves building a statistical model for predicting or estimating an outcome based on one or more inputs. Unsupervised learning looks for internal structure in the data. Unsupervised learning algorithms are common in neural network models. Machine learning techniques have been currently applied in the analysis of data in various fields, including medicine, finance, business, education, advertising, cyber security, and energy applications. Figure 2.4 illustrates machine learning.

- *Deep learning*: The biggest breakthroughs for AI research have been in the field of machine learning, particularly in the field of deep learning. This component is a form of machine learning based on ANNs. Deep learning (DL) has enabled many practical applications of machine learning. DL architectures can process hierarchies of increasingly abstract features, making them especially useful for speech and image recognition and natural language processing. Deep learning networks can deal with complex non-linear problems. Recently, companies such as IBM, Microsoft, Google, Apple, and Baidu have invested in and developed deep learning. They have taken advantage of their massive data and large computational power to deploy deep learning on a large scale.

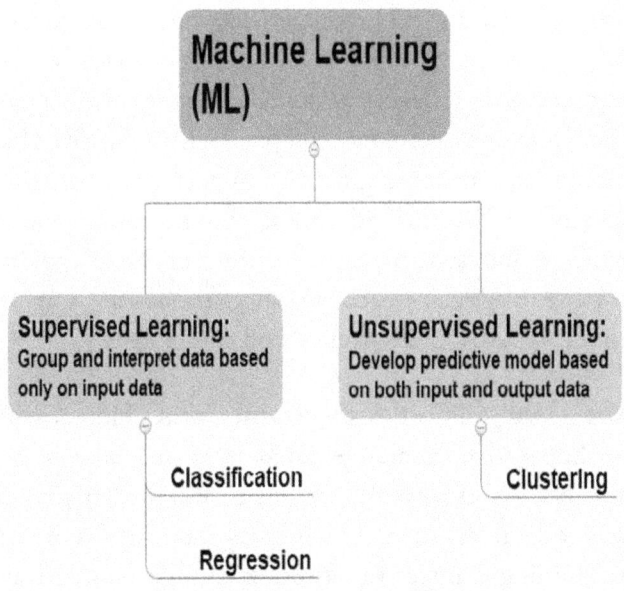

Figure 2.4 Machine learning.

- *Natural Language Processors*: For AI to be useful to humans, it needs to communicate with us in our language. Computer programs can translate or interpret language as it is spoken by ordinary people. Language is crucial worldwide in communication, entertainment, media, culture, drama, movies, and the economy. Natural language processing (NLP) refers to the field of study that focuses on the interactions between human language and computers. It involves the study of mathematical and computational modeling of various aspects of language. NLP is important because of the major role language, such as English, plays in human intelligence and the wealth of potential applications. NLP is commonly used for text mining, machine translation, and automated question-answering.

- *Robots:* AI is heavily used in robots, which are computer-based programmable machines that have physical manipulators and sensors. Sensors can monitor temperature, humidity, pressure, and time, record data, and make critical decisions in some cases. Robots have moved from science fiction to your local hospital. Jobs with repetitive and monotonous functions might even completely replace humans. A robot is an intelligent machine that can be programmed to take actions or make choices based on sensor input. It involves using electronics, computer science, artificial intelligence, mechatronics, and bioengineering. Robots are applied in many fields including, agriculture, education, manufacturing, entertainment, medicine, industry, space exploration, undersea exploration, sex, power grid, agriculture, construction, meat processing, household, mining, aerospace, electronics, and automotive.

- *Data Mining:* This deals with discovering hidden patterns and new knowledge from large databases. It may also be regarded as the process of discovering insightful and predictive models from massive data. It is an interdisciplinary subfield of computer science. Data mining exhibits a variety of algorithmic tools, such as statistics, regression models, neural networks, fuzzy sets, and evolutionary models. Data mining has been applied with considerable success in business, the retail industry, telecommunications, intrusion detection, biological data analysis, healthcare, geosciences, and computer security.

- *Computer Vision:* This is also known as machine vision. It is a scientific field that enables the machines to see. It emphasizes the development of techniques that allow a computer to recognize or otherwise understand the content of a picture. It performs tasks such as object detection, recognition, tracking, facial recognition, etc. Computer vision aims to develop visual interpretive skills equivalent to those of humans. Although humans often take visual skills for granted, visual interpretation requires intelligence. Computer vision entered all possible fields, such as pattern recognition, machine learning, computer graphics, 3D reconstructions, virtual reality, and augmented reality.

These computer-based tools or technologies have been used to achieve AI's goals. The AI tools are illustrated in Figure 2.5. Each AI tool has its advantages. Using a combination of these models, rather than a single model, is recommended. Artificial intelligence (AI) is rapidly transforming our world. It is incorporated into a variety of different types of technology. AI has the potential to impact nearly all aspects of our society, including automation, healthcare, business, education, engineering, law, manufacturing, transportation, and security. Some of these applications are illustrated in Figure 2.6.

2.3 POSSIBILITIES OF AI IN EDUCATION

Intelligent tutoring system (ITS), intelligent learning system (ILS) technologies, virtual reality (VR), and augmented reality (AR) education technology use artificial intelligence to create learning environments. Advances in these technologies fuel the applications of AI in education, including training, communications, administration, and resource management.

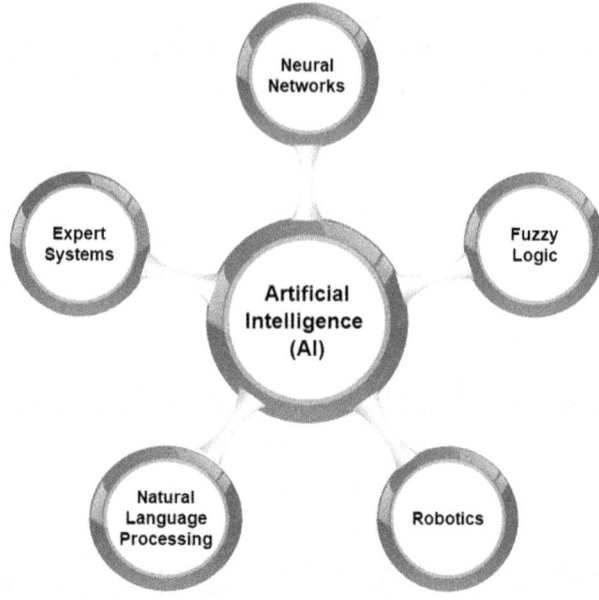

Figure 2.5 AI tools or components.

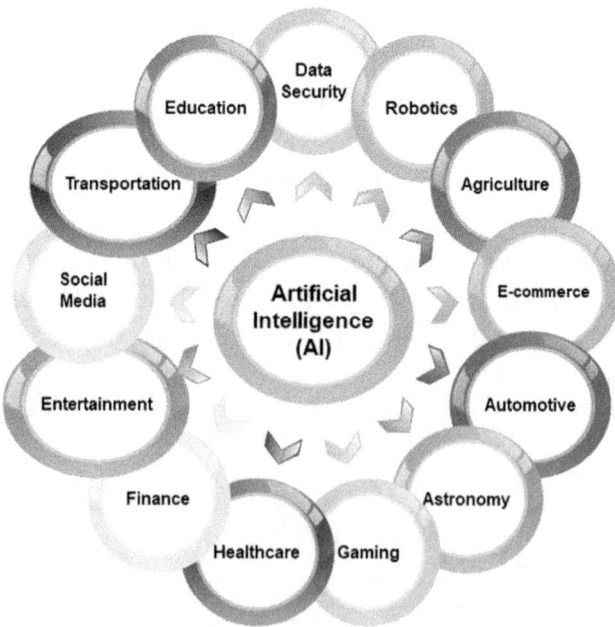

Figure 2.6 Applications of artificial intelligence.

Educators may soon find themselves teaching in a digital classroom with AI at its heart. The possibilities for artificial intelligence in education include the following [10]:

1. *Communication:* The pleasure of live communication is crucial for creating a favorable emotional atmosphere in a class. Students and teachers will be able to communicate instantly with one another and connect with other forms of AI around the world. Information from anywhere in the world is at students' fingertips.

2. *Personalization:* Unlike the traditional education system, AI-based systems promise to serve students of all capabilities and discover their full potential. Personalized learning opportunities can be offered to students. Students now have the advantage of personalized study plans, accessible from any user device or location. AI-based tools are helping them organize classes and customize the experience to match the student's background and ethnicity.

3. *Assessments:* Formulating assessment instruments using AI techniques can provide more conducive diagnostic outcomes than conventional tests. AI could help teachers assess students and streamline the grading process, with the added benefit of quickly taking the data and providing analysis for teachers, saving time for more classroom interactions. Assessing students' motivation, attention, and engagement could enhance their learning.

4. *Intelligent Tutoring Systems* (ITS): ITS has become popular since the early 2000s. It is essentially a computer system that aims to provide immediate and customized instruction or feedback to learners, usually without requiring intervention from a human teacher. ITS can be used to simulate one-to-one personal tutoring. While far from the norm, they are capable of functioning without a teacher having to be present and can effectively challenge and support the learner using different algorithms.

5. *Virtual Reality Learning:* Virtual reality (VR) is a simulated experience that enhances learning and engagement by allowing

users to view and interact with virtual items. It provides users an immersive experience via three-dimensional (3-D) visual and auditory simulations. It brings vivid experiences to the classroom for the purpose of increasing student engagement and enhancing learning. Combined with virtual and augmented reality, AI can bring a dynamic, immersive learning environment to the classroom. VR-assisted learning allows for educational support in authentic environments and extends the boundaries of the classroom. This application will be a stepping stone to real-world experiences with fully integrated AIs.

The future likely holds a lot of possibilities for AI and teachers who can take the opportunity to be informed of the possibilities and be open to discussions with students.

2.4 AI IN DIFFERENT LEVELS OF EDUCATION

AI applications in education are on the rise and are receiving a lot of attention at all levels of education. The promise of AI applications lies partly in their efficiency and efficacy. School children, and even kindergartners, who live in this generation are regarded as digital natives. Digital natives are children who were born after 1980. Early exposure to technology like the Internet, computers, and mobile devices fundamentally changes the way digital natives learn, behave, and operate [11]. As artificial intelligence is increasing in relevance, it is also finding its way into curricula for K-12.

- *Elementary School:* School children have grown up with technology at their fingertips in a world where education has changed, and the Internet is their primary source of entertainment and information. Chalkboards in the classroom are also a thing of the past. The availability of smart technology, such as interactive whiteboards, IT suites, and tablet-based learning, is becoming more commonplace in elementary schools. Nao is a humanoid robot that talks, moves and teaches children from ages seven and up everything from literacy to computer programming. This way, students are prepared to work alongside AI and develop the skills required to thrive in a digital workplace [12].

- *High School:* AI can be integrated into K-12 education. AI should be a critical element of any STEM curriculum. There is no rulebook for deploying AI in schools. Querium uses AI to deliver customizable STEM tutoring lessons to high school and college students. High school students with exposure to AI tools will be well prepared to make decisions involving AI technology, regardless of what industry they find themselves in. Therefore, it is of great importance to familiarize young people in school with the technical background and the underlying AI concepts [13].

- *Higher Education:* Higher education is entering into the unchartered territory of the possibilities opened by AI in teaching and learning. The AI technology will soon have a significant impact on higher education institutions. It is linked to the future of higher education. Some faculty members, teaching assistants, student counselors, and administrative staff may fear intelligent tutors, expert systems, and chatbots will take their jobs. Higher education institutions increasingly rely on algorithms for marketing to prospective students, enrollment, planning curricula, and allocating resources such as financial aid and facilities. Some AI applications provide student guidance and help students automatically schedule their course load. Colleges and universities can use AI for instruction by using educational software [14].

2.5 APPLICATIONS OF AI IN EDUCATION

Artificial intelligence has been applied in various industries and has become a part of our daily lives. Figure 2.7 shows a typical example of how AI changes the education industry [15]. There are several AI applications for education. Popular areas to incorporate AI technologies to facilitate students' learning include engineering education, higher education, mathematics education, language education, distance education, robotics education, computer science education, STEM education, medical education, musical education, and science education [16]. Companies using AI in education to enhance the classroom include Nuance, Knewton, Cognii, Querium, Century Tech, KidSense, Carnegie Learning, Kidaptive, Blippar, Thinkster Math, Volley, and Quizlet. These companies are merging the organic and the artificial by applying AI tools to innovate how people are educated [17]. Figure 2.8 compares traditional education with AI-driven education [18]. An application is the use of expert systems to assist with educational diagnosis and assessment. Other applications include the following.

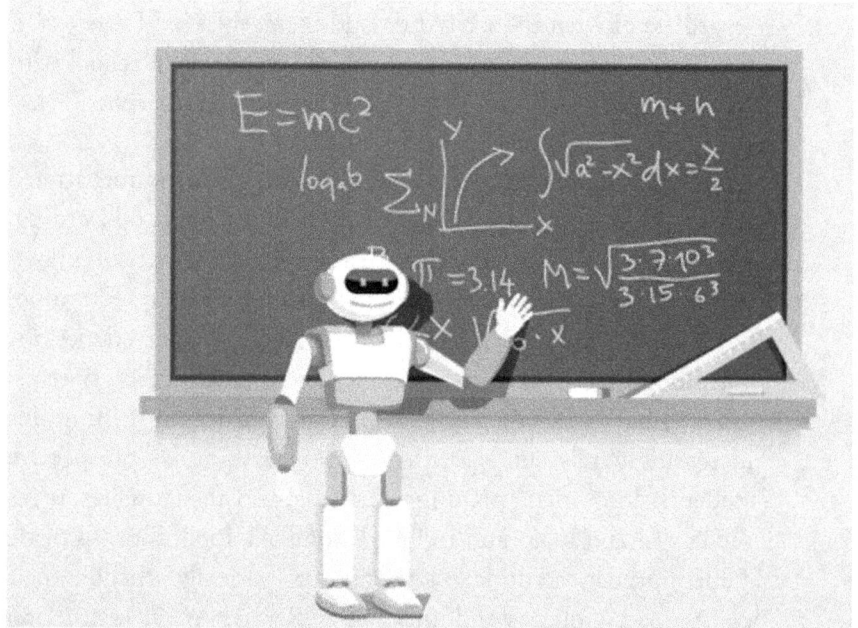

Figure 2.7 A typical example on how AI is changing the education industry [15].

- *In the Classroom:* While AI can never replace human teachers, it can play a great role in the classroom. AI can allow teachers to hand off all assignments to an AI for grading so the teachers can spend more time with students. Despite the cost and need for the Internet, AI is useful for tutoring. Since teachers cannot always be available for students, tutors are needed. Working with an AI tutor can help students with academic activities [19].

- *Personalized Education*: Traditional education is not flexible. AI will enable personalized or tailored education. AI can provide a level of differentiation that customizes learning specifically to an individual student. Artificial intelligence helps build a personalized study schedule for each learner, tailoring studies according to the student's specific needs. This approach opens up new ways of interacting with students with learning disabilities. Personalized education increases efficiency, improves accessibility, and scales processes [20].

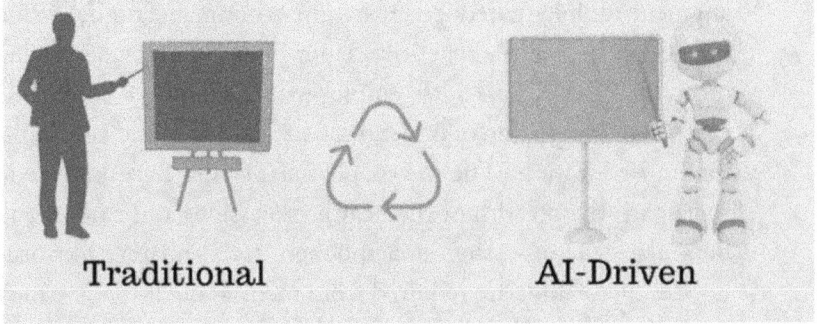

Figure 2.8 Comparing traditional education with AI-driven education [18].

- *Administration:* AI can simplify administrative tasks. It can automate the expedition of administrative duties for teachers and academic institutions. Technology can be used to automate grading tasks where multiple tests are involved.- This provision means that professors would spend more time with their students than spend long hours grading them.

- *Universal Access to Global Classrooms:* AI can help to eliminate boundaries, thereby facilitating the learning of any course from anywhere, anytime across the globe. AI tools can help make global classrooms available to all, including those who speak different languages. There will be a wider range of courses available online, and with the help of AI, students will be learning from wherever they are [21].

- *Medical Education*: Essentially, medicine serves common human needs and promotes patients' well-being. AI is critical for the future development of healthcare. The rate at which emerging health AI technologies are developing, being introduced into clinical practice, and being used by patients requires that healthcare professionals are well-equipped. Physicians must work with patients to make the implementation of AI technologies transparent and accountable [22]. AI can be used to check the effectiveness of the medical program and the satisfaction of the medical students. AI is being applied in healthcare for faster and more accurate diagnosis, to augment radiology, reduce errors due to human fatigue, reduce medical costs, replace repetitive, labor-intensive tasks, and reduce mortality rates [23]. Today, employers are making a compelling case for an integration of undergraduate, graduate, and continuing medical education. They need physicians who have knowledge that spans the breadth of the health professions and can leverage data platforms by using smartphones, social media, and other devices. New skills are required from medical doctors as we move to an age of artificial intelligence.

- *Marketing Education:* Artificial intelligence is transforming the marketing profession. It has several applications in marketing. These include sales forecasting, website experience personalization, speech recognition, content creation, chatbots, etc. For example, the chatbot is regarded as one of the most promising AI applications. Virtual assistant is used in online marketing. Learning to comprehend and use AI can be beneficial to students. Marketing students believe that they will work with AI tools during their careers [24].

- *Education 4.0:* This involves the integration of AI into the learner-centered education system. AI plays a key role in Education 4.0 since it is being empowered more and more by AI tools. Education 4.0 responds to the need of Industry 4.0, where man and machine work together to enable new possibilities. It puts the learner at the center of the ecosystem and enables him to go through experiential learning. Education 4.0 requires a new way of thinking for teacher and students. Being a good teacher requires acquiring a large set of different kinds of interdisciplinary skills. Today's student is a digital native comfortable with mobile and computing devices. New skills, new curricula, new teaching, new learning, new training, and flexibility in education are necessary. Education 4.0 is tipped as the future of education and is poised to change information consumption [25].

- *Chatbots:* Also known as talkbots or chatterbots, are artificial intelligence (AI) programs designed to simulate human conversation via text or speech. They may be regarded are mimic systems that imitate the conversations between two individuals. They employ different degrees of human-like appearance and behavior, such as facial expressions, compassion, humor, and tone of voice. Thus, chatbots are computer programs with a conversational user interface that emulates natural, conversational interpersonal exchange. Fueled by artificial intelligence (AI), chatbots are becoming a viable option for human-machine interaction Chatbots without education intentionality are used in administrative tasks such as student guidance and assistance. Those with education intentionality are used in fostering teaching and learning [26].

- *Teaching:* AI can potentially transform the traditional teaching and learning process through its advanced technology. AI works in teaching and provides facilities like instructing, tutoring, testing, grading, and feedback. Teachers serve as the link to preparing students to thrive in a world where AI is an integral part of their life and career. In the classroom, AI has become beneficial for the teacher. It goes on assisting a teacher rather than replacing them. Although AI provides many benefits for students and teachers, it cannot replace teachers. It makes the educator free from monotonous works work like assessing and grading students [27]. The AI software development system helps educators work on their weaknesses.

- *Learning:* Students learn in different ways. Some prefer reading written material, while others prefer problem-solving. Determining a student's learning style is crucial in making learning adaptive to the student's needs. AI methods are regarded as valuable tools because they can develop and replicate the decision-making process adopted by people. There are various AI techniques that have been used in adaptive educational systems. These include fuzzy logic, neural networks, and genetic algorithms [28]. Artificial intelligence combined with big data technology provides strong technical support for personalized learning, which is the basic ideology of modern education. Technology connects people from different geographical locations for global learning [29].

Other applications include personalized guidance, support, feedback, assessment tools, remediation, virtual assistants for students, mobile games, intelligent tutoring systems, educational robots, management education, smart education, engineering education, precision education, distance education, online education, foreign language education, sports education, physical education, audit education, and design education.

2.6 GLOBAL ADOPTION OF AI IN EDUCATION

The wave of interest in artificial intelligence is already impacting the world economy and has captured the attention of many analysts. AI has become a top priority on the agenda of different countries worldwide. Global adoption of AI technology in education transforms how we teach and learn. Several nations, such US, UK, China, and Japan, have listed AI as a major strategy to promote national competitiveness. AI applications can perform assessment and evaluation tasks at high accuracy and efficiency levels. Tech giants like Apple, Google, Microsoft, and Facebook compete in the AI industry, investing heavily in new applications and research. We will consider how some nations incorporate AI into their education systems.

- *United States:* The US Department of Education's Office of Educational Technology (OET) recognizes AI as a rapidly advancing set of technologies enabling new interaction between educators and students. Educators use AI-powered services in their everyday lives, such as voice assistants in their homes; tools that can correct grammar, complete sentences, and write essays. AI in education generally focuses on identifying what a student does and does not know through diagnostic testing and then developing personalized curricula based on each student's specific needs. AI-based education platforms in the US include Carnegie Learning, ALEKS, Jill Watson, Alexas, Siri Assistant, and Google Homes. Solutions for human-AI interaction and collaboration are already available to help people with disabilities. At the beginning of 2017, Einstein robots were born in the United States.

- *Europe:* For years, the European Commission has facilitated cooperation on AI across the EU to boost its competitiveness. The European Commission published Ethical Guidelines on using AI and data in teaching and learning for teachers. The Guidelines address how AI is used in schools to support teachers and students in their teaching and learning. Promoting excellence and trust in AI is a key priority of the Commission. Artificial Intelligence has great potential to transform education and training for students, teachers, and school staff [30].

- *China:* The Chinese have been working on creating smart education. In China, systems are already being used to monitor student participation and expressions via face recognition in classrooms. As we enter the AI era, the development of AI technology and the popularization of AI education has become the national strategy of China. The Chinese government has set 2030 as the deadline to integrate AI with the Chinese infrastructure. The government's ambitious plan would require huge amounts of research in AI, supported by professionals trained in the technology. China has started a grand experiment in AI education, which could reshape how the world learns [31]. Due to the magnitude of China's population, the impact of AI on employment in China will be more profound than in other nations. China is leading in advancing AI-centered education. For example, an elementary school introduced the cute robot "Xiao'pang" into the classroom and interacted with children in 2016.

- *Canada:* Artificial intelligence has made few inroads into Canadian education systems. AI is already being used for learning in Québec and the rest of Canada. Québec launched its Digital Action Plan for Education and Higher Education1 in May 2018. It states that,"The shift to digital is a unique opportunity for the development and growth of Québec and that digital technologies play a role in the educational success of our young people by offering them new ways to learn, communicate, share, create and collaborate. Some experts worry about the risks of AI for society if the forward march of intelligent machines is left unchecked [32].

- *United Kingdom:* A multitude of AI-driven applications are already in use in schools and universities. Many recent ITS use machine learning techniques, self-training algorithms, and neural networks to enable them to make appropriate decisions about what learning content to provide to the learner. Despite nearly three decades of work, AI's benefits and enormous potential remain mostly unrealized. Some within the scientific community worry that AI is Pandora's box with dangerous consequences [33]. Some institutions in the UK have established institutions, such as the Institute for Ethical AI in Education, to produce a framework for ethical governance for AI in education.

- *India*: By 2030, India will have the largest number of young people in the world, a population size that will be a boon only if these young people are skilled enough to join the workforce. Bringing AI to classrooms in India might just be the solution. Many Indian EdTech companies are developing AI-enabled intelligent instruction designs and digital platforms to provide learning, testing, and tutoring to students. AI is poised to redesign and reinvent the education sector in India. It will be an enabler in improving online education. The role of teachers in education systems is irreplaceable; AI will aid and improve a teacher's job. With the help of AI, students can get personalized curricula, tests, learning methods, and delivery [34]. The education sector in India will continue to open multiple avenues of AI intervention.

- *South Africa:* In some universities in South Africa, artificial intelligence is included in the undergraduate curriculum for engineering and computer science. The aim is to prepare for the fourth industrial revolution in South Africa. Students are required to complete projects in the final year of the undergraduate degree, which must include AI. To adequately prepare engineering and computer science graduates to face the challenges posed by the fourth industrial revolution in the workplace, it is imperative to provide students with the experience of solving real-world problems, including industry collaboration and experience [35].

2.7 BENEFITS

AI tools are gradually changing the landscape of education. They can help make global classrooms available to all. They help to promote immersive learning. AI-based tools have a high potential to support students, educators, and administrators throughout the student lifecycle. Today, AI applications in education (AIEd) are widely used by learners and educators. AI helps in enhancing educational quality. The benefits of AI for students, teachers, and schools include [36,37]:

- *Education at Any Time:* AI impacts how children can learn and from where. AI-based applications allow students to study whenever they are free time and receive feedback from teachers in a real-time mode.

- *Virtual Mentors:* AI-based platforms offer virtual mentors to track the students' progress. AI holds promise as a tool to monitor student performance.

- *Better Engagement*: Modern technologies like VR and gamification help involve students in the education process, making it more interactive and personalized.

- *Equality:* The use of AI is also being framed as a potential boom to equality. More students will have equal access and gain access to better-quality educational opportunities.

- *Opportunity to Find A Good Teacher:* Educational platforms have a lot of teachers, so the student has an opportunity to communicate with specialists from other countries.

- *Personalized learning*: AI-based solutions offering personalized learning are about to transform the school curriculum and the entire education sector.

- *Teacher's Aid*: AI can be a great ally to a teacher. AI can help an educator reduce the burden of administrative duties such as marking exams, grading students' assignments, planning, etc., and save a lot of time.

- *Teaching the Teacher*: Artificial intelligence makes comprehensive information available to teachers at any time of the day.

- *Connecting Everyone*: Education has no limits. AI can help to eliminate boundaries and make education accessible to everyone anywhere in the globe.

- *Global Learning*: AI tools can help make global classrooms available to all, fostering greater cooperation, communication, and collaboration among schools and nations. Remote proctoring can help simplify the exam invigilation process.

- *Cost Reduction:* AI can accelerate and reduce the cost of learning.

- *Improves Efficiency:* AI reduces the burden of daily repetitive tasks teachers and schools have to deal with. For example, students can useAI-powered tools to learn word pronunciation, meaning, and proper usage. From classroom interactions, coursework learning, and administrative processes, AI makes things better and more efficient.

- *Competitiveness:* Some educators regard AI as instrumental to their institution's competitiveness. AI has the power to become an equalizer in education and a key differentiator for institutions that embrace it.

- *Inclusivity:* Designers of AI applications and platforms must design with inclusivity in mind. They must address various capabilities and motivations of individuals. They must also avoid biases and assumptions with end users in mind during the design process. Designing for inclusion must identify who might be excluded.

- *Automation:* The area with the biggest automation potential is teacher's preparation and administrative responsibilities. Automation focuses on making mundane tasks easy for both students and teachers. For example, automated grading will allow teachers the time and freedom to do other things that are more important. AI can automate grading for nearly all forms of multiple-choice testing. Some of the benefits of artificial intelligence in education (AIED) are illustrated in Figure 2.9. In AI-powered education, academia still needs schools, classrooms, and teachers to motivate students and teach social skills.

2.8 CHALLENGES

Humans have some unique characteristics that AI cannot match. The human characteristics that machines or algorithms cannot replace include love and their abilities regarding perception, emotion, feeling, and cognition. Although the possibilities of AI are exciting, a number of challenges prevent the full realization of AI in various educational institutions. Those challenges include [38,39]:

- *Privacy:* Personal information is private. Many students do not want others to know their private information, such as their learning style and capability.

- *Limited Capability:* The capabilities of artificial intelligence in education are limited. AI tools cannot teach empathy, compassion, and other such emotions, which are an integral part of the overall development of personality. Love and emotion are among the human characteristics that cannot be replaced by machines.

- *Unanswered Questions:* There are a lot of unanswered questions about AI's role and how it will be managed in higher education.

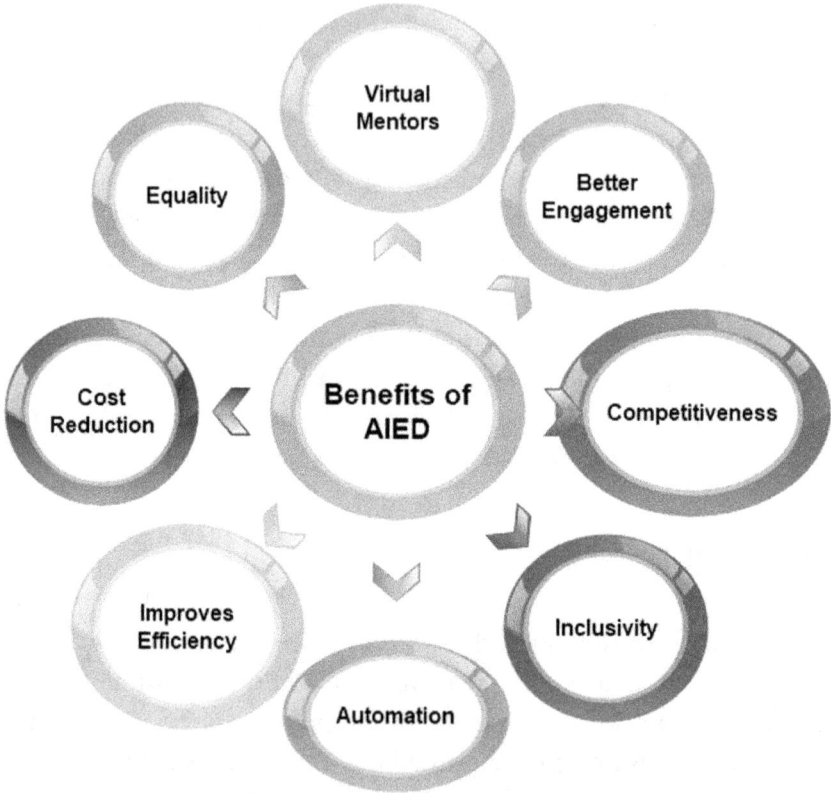

Figure 2.9 Benefit of artificial intelligence in education (AIED).

- *Trust:* Parents and school administrators may find it difficult to trust AI technologies used to influence or make decisions about student learning. AI can be abused or misused by humans, such as using personal information to identify citizen scores that breach trust and human rights.

- *Ethical Dilemma:* This is a situation in which the human being is confronted when he opposes, on the one hand, morality or conscience and, on the other, life. Another ethical dilemma faced by today's society is the "humanism" of the human being.

- *Cost:* The cost and time involved in developing and introducing AI-based methods may not be affordable by many public educational institutions. However, prices will come down as AI technology spreads.

- *No Personal Connection:* Machines lack social skills and personal connection.

- *Student's lack of Experience:* It is possible for students to have difficulties understanding AI and, in particular, ML due to their lack of experience. Sometimes, AI is not presented appropriately for the backgrounds of students, particularly high school students. Since complex math and programming are required to implement AI, educations must find an appropriate way to teach AI.

- *AI Literacy*: It is necessary to promote artificial intelligence literacy in society to enable the existing workforce to develop their artificial intelligence skills. AI literacy may be regarded as a person's overall level of acknowledge, method, application, and evaluation of AI. It will provide our graduates with the necessary knowledge and skills to solve problems as we move into the fourth industrial revolution. Figure 2.10 depicts some issues that AI literacy should address. There are more benefits when one compares the pros and cons of artificial intelligence in education.

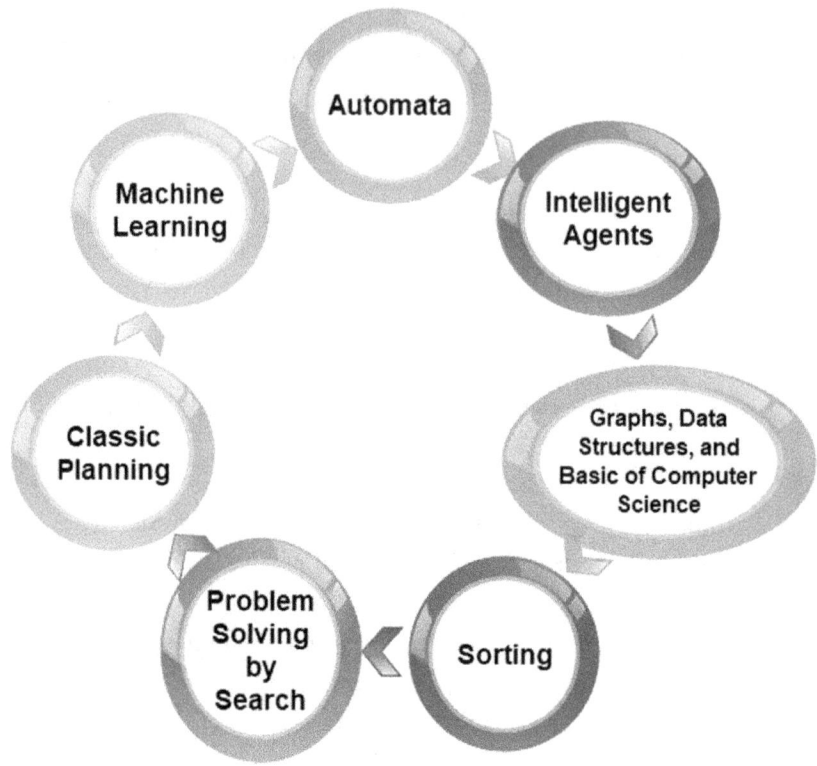

Figure 2.10 Issues that AI literacy should address.

2.9 FUTURE OF AI EDUCATION

All human actions are based on anticipated futures. Although we cannot predict the future, we can use our current knowledge to imagine the future. The better we understand the present and the history that has created it, the better we can understand the future possibilities. Many predictions about the future of AI have been based on extrapolations of historical technical development [40]. AI is impacting education in various ways, which this is expected to continue.

Two decades ago, no one had heard about Google, Facebook, YouTube, or Wikipedia. Today they are the most used digital tools on the planet. These companies have invested millions of dollars developing artificial intelligence in education (AIED) products and joining well-established multimillion-dollar funded AIED companies such as Knewton26 and Carnegie Learning.

Artificial intelligence is one of the emerging technologies that can pervade and alter every aspect of our life. AI education (AIED) has become a new trend in education.

The introduction and adoption of AI technologies in learning and teaching have rapidly evolved in recent years. Although AI is just emerging and young, there is little doubt that technology is inexorably linked to the future of education. Advances in artificial intelligence open new possibilities and challenges for teaching, learning, education organization, and governance. While some AI solutions remain dependent on programming, some have an inbuilt capacity to learn patterns and make predictions. AI solutions have the potential to structurally change educational administrative services and the realm of teaching and learning. AI has the potential to replace a large number of administrative staff and teaching assistants in higher education [41]. The impressive list of applications of AIED has made some specialists claim that teachers will not be necessary in for the future.

AI will impact education in administration, instruction, and personalized and individualized learning applications. We look towards a future when AI tools will support teachers in meeting the needs of their students. Now is the best time for educational institutions to rethink their function and future relation with AI solutions. Combining the best of humans and machines for the benefit of the students is the ultimate goal of artificial intelligence in education.

2.10 CONCLUSION

AI has produced educational tools which have attracted attention for their potential to improve education quality and enhance teaching and learning methods. As AI educational solutions mature, AI can help fill needs gaps. There is no denying the place of AI in modern teaching and learning.

Although the critical presence of teachers is irreplaceable, there will be many changes to a teacher's responsibilities.

Education might be a slower in adopting AI, but the changes will continue. In the coming decades, AI will transform education. The future of education is intrinsically linked with developments in new technologies and the computing capacities of new intelligent machines. It has been shown that AI is unquestionably superior to human intelligence in the cognitive domain. Practitioners and academicians believe that artificial intelligence is the future of our society.

A gap exists between artificial intelligence and current educational training in AI. It is expedient for educators and policymakers to explore the intersection of education and artificial intelligence and fill the gap. Since students of today today's students will work in an environment where AI is the reality, it is expedient that our academic institutions expose students to AI technology. AI skills must also be balanced with person-centered aspects of education to develop more rounded leaders of tomorrow. More information on 4artificial intelligence in education can be found in the books in [6,7,40,42-56] and the following related journals:

- *Artificial Intelligence Review*
- *Artificial Intelligence Review*
- *Journal of Artificial Intelligence and Consciousness*
- *AI Magazine*
- *AI & Society*
- *IEEE Transactions on Artificial Intelligence*
- *International Journal of Artificial Intelligence in Education*
- *International Journal of Applications of Fuzzy Sets and Artificial Intelligence*
- *Computers & Education: Artificial Intelligence*
- *International Journal of Learning Analytics and Artificial Intelligence for Education*

REFERENCES

[1] P. Dadhich, "Impact of artificial intelligence on the current education system," September 2020, https://wire19.com/impact-of-artificial-intelligence-on-education-system/#:~:text=The%20implementation%20of%20educational%20AI,more%20knowledge%20in%20multiple%20subjects.&text=The%20implementation%20of%20AI%20can,well%20as%20streamline%20administrative%20tasks.

[2] : "Future: Artificial Intelligence," https://www.rapid-city.top/ProductDetail.aspx?iid=56512769&pr=44.88

[3] "Ten facts about artificial intelligence in teaching and learning," https://teachonline.ca/sites/default/files/tools-trends/downloads/ten_facts_about_artificial_intelligence_0.pdf

[4] X. Chen et al., "Application and theory gaps during the rise of artificial intelligence in education," *Computers and Education: Artificial Intelligence,* vol.1, 2020.

[5] G. J. Hwang et al., "Vision, challenges, roles and research issues of artificial intelligence in education," *Computers and Education: Artificial Intelligence,* vol.1,2020.

[6] M. N. O. Sadiku, S. M. Musa, and U. C. Chukwu, *Artificial Intelligence in Education.* Bloomington, IN: iUniverse, 2022.

[7] M.N. O. Sadiku, S. M. Musa, and S. R.Nelatury, *Applications of Artificial Intelligence.* Sherida, NY: Gotham Books, 2022.

[8] M. N. O. Sadiku, T. J. Ashaolu, A. Ajayi-Majebi, and S. M. Musa, "Artificial intelligence in education," *International Journal of Scientific Advances,* vol. 2, no.1, Jan.-Feb. 2021, pp. 7-11.

[9] G. Singh, A. Mishra, and D. Sagar, "An overview of artificial intelligence," *SBIT Journal of Sciences and Technology,* vol.2, no. 1, 2003.

[10] "How artificial intelligence could benefit the future of education," August 2019, Unknown Source.

[11] M. N. O. Sadiku, A. E. Shadare, and S.M. Musa, "Digital natives," *International Journal of Advanced Research in Computer Science and Software Engineering*, vol. 7, no. 7, July 2017, pp. 125-122.

[12] "The role of artificial intelligence in the future of education," March 2019, https://www.getsmarter.com/blog/market-trends/the-role-of-artificial-intelligence-in-the-future-of-education/

[13] H. Burgsteiner, E. Allee, and M. Kandlhofer, "IRobot: Teaching the basics of artificial intelligence in high schools," *Proceedings of the Sixth Symposium on Educational Advances in Artificial Intelligence*, 2016, pp. 4126-4127.

[14] L. Plitnichenko, "5 Main roles of artificial intelligence in education," May 2020, https://elearningindustry.com/ai-is-changing-the-education-industry-5-ways

[15] "How AI is changing America's classrooms," https://universitybusiness.com/how-ai-is-changing-americas-classrooms/

[16] X. Chen, H. Xie, and G. Hwang, "A multi-perspective study on artificial intelligence in education: Grants, conferences, journals, software tools, institutions, and researchers," *Computers and Education: Artificial Intelligence*, vol.1, 2020.

[17] A. Schroer, "12 Companies using AI in education to enhance the classroom," March 2020, https://builtin.com/artificial-intelligence/ai-in-education

[18] https://www.educationworld.in/how-ai-in-education-can-dominate-in-2020/

[19] A. Sears, "The role of artificial intelligence in the classroom," April 2018, https://elearningindustry.com/artificial-intelligence-in-the-classroom-role

[20] S. Maghsudi et al., "Personalized Education in the AI Era: What to expect next?" https://arxiv.org/pdf/2101.10074.pdf

[21] B. Marr, "How is AI used in education -- Real world examples of today and a peek into the future," July 2018, https://www.forbes.com/sites/bernardmarr/2018/07/25/how-is-ai-used-in-education-real-world-examples-of-today-and-a-peek-into-the-future/?sh=2aea5075586e

[22] V. Rampton, M. Mittelman, and J. Goldhahn, "Implications of artificial intelligence for medical education," https://www.thelancet.com/journals/landig/article/PIIS2589-7500(20)30023-6/fulltext

[23] K. Paranjape et al., "Introducing artificial intelligence training in medical education," *JMIR Medical Education,* vol 5, no 2 (2019): July-December. 2019.

[24] S. Elhajjar, M. S. Karam, and S. Borna, "Artificial intelligence in marketing education programs," *Marketing Education Review*, 2020.

[25] M. N. O. Sadiku, A. Omotoso, and S. M. Musa, "Essence of Education 4.0," *International Journal of Trend in Scientific Research and Development,* vol. 4, no. 4, June 2020, pp. 1110-1112.

[26] M. N. O. Sadiku, S. R. Nelatury, and S. M. Musa, "AI in chatbots: A primer," *Journal of Scientific and Engineering Research,* vol. 8, no. 2, 2021, pp. 16-22.

[27] A. Lindner and M. Berges, "Can you explain AI to me? Teachers' pre-concepts about artificial intelligence," *Proceedings of IEEE Frontiers in Education Conference,* October 2020.

[28] R. Baja, and V. Sharma, "Smart Education with artificial intelligence based determination of learning styles," *Procedia Computer Science,* vol. 132, 2018, pp. 834–842.

[29] "Artificial intelligence in education: Use cases and applications," September 2020, https://pixelplex.io/blog/top-use-cases-of-ai-in-education/

[30] "The Commission publishes guidelines to help teachers address misconceptions about artificial intelligence and promote its ethical use," https://ec.europa.eu/commission/presscorner/detail/en/ip_22_6338

[31] A. Gupta, "The role of artificial intelligence in education," June 2020, https://discover.bot/bot-talk/role-of-artificial-intelligence-in-education/

[32] P. Saxena, "AI impact on India: AI in education is changing India's learning landscape," https://indiaai.gov.in/article/ai-impact-on-india-ai-in-education-is-changing-india-s-learning-landscape

[33] T. Karsenti, "Artificial intelligence in education: The urgent need to prepare teachers for tomorrow's schools," *Formation et Profession*, vol. 27, no. 1, 2019, pp. 105-111.

[34] R. Luckin and W. Holmes, "Intelligence unleashed: An argument for AI in education," https://static.googleusercontent.com/media/edu.google.com/en//pdfs/Intelligence-Unleashed-Publication.pdf

[35] Nelishia Pillay. B.T. Maharaj, and G. van Eeden, "AI in engineering and computer science education in preparation for the 4th industrial revolution: A South African Perspective," *Proceedings of World Engineering Education Forum - Global Engineering Deans Council,* November 2018.

[36] V. Kuprenko, "Artificial intelligence in education: Benefits, challenges, and use cases," https://medium.com/towards-artificial-intelligence/artificial-intelligence-in-education-benefits-challenges-and-use-cases-db52d8921f7a

[37] "The role of artificial intelligence in the future of education," March 2019, https://www.getsmarter.com/blog/market-trends/the-role-of-artificial-intelligence-in-the-future-of-education/

[38] O. Zawacki-Richter et al., "Systematic review of research on artificial intelligence applications in higher education – Where are the educators?"

International Journal of Educational Technology in Higher Education, 16, vol. 16, no. 39, 2019.

[39] M. Kandlhofer et al., "Artificial intelligence and computer science in education: from kindergarten to university," *Proceedings of IEEE Frontiers in Education Conference,* October 2012.

[40] I. Tuomi, *The Impact of Artificial Intelligence on Learning, Teaching, and Education Policies for the Future,* EUR 29442 EN, Publications Office of the European Union, Luxembourg, 2018,

[41] S. A. D. Popenici and S. Kerr, "Exploring the impact of artificial intelligence on teaching and learning in higher education," *Research and Practice in Technology Enhanced Learning,* vol. 12, November 2017.

[42] *Artificial Intelligence in Education; Building Technology Rich Learning Contexts That Work,* (Int'l Conference on Artificial Intelligence in Education, 2007, Los Angeles, CA). IOS Press, 2007.

[43] R. Luckin, K. R. Koedinger, and J. Greer (eds.), *Artificial Intelligence in Education: Building Technology Rich Learning Contexts that Work* IOS Press, 2007.

[44] M. Yazdani and R. W. Lawler (eds.), *Artificial Intelligence and Education Volume 2: Principles and Case Studies.* Ablex, 1991.

[45] Artificial Intelligence in Education: Promises and Implications for Teaching and Learning. C enter for Curriculum Redesign, 2019.

[46] R. Luckin, *Machine Learning and Human Intelligence: The Future of Education for the 21st Century.* UCL Institute of Education Press, 2018.

[47] R. W. Lawler and M. Yazdani, *Artificial Intelligence And Education: Learning Environments and Tutoring Systems.* Intellect Ltd, 1987.

[48] C. Fadel, W. Holmes, and M. Bialik, *Artificial Intelligence in Education: Promises and Implications for Teaching and Learning.* Independently published, 2019.

[40] G. Gauthier and C. Frasson (eds.), *Intelligent Tutoring Systems: At the Crossroad of Artificial Intelligence and Education*. Intellect Ltd, 1990.

[50] R. M. Cameron, *A.I. - 101: A Primer on Using Artificial Intelligence in Education*. Exceedly Press, 2019.

[51] C. Fadel, W. Holmes, and M. Bialik, *Artificial Intelligence in Education: Promises and Implications for Teaching and Learning*. Independently Published, 2019.

[52] C. K. Looi et al., *Artificial Intelligence in Education (Frontiers in Artificial Intelligence and Applications)*. IOS Press, 2005.

[53] U. Hoppe, M. F. Verdejo, and J. Kay (eds.), *Artificial Intelligence in Education: Shaping The Future of Learning Through Intelligent Technologies*. IOS Press, 2003.

[54] J. E. Aoun, *Robot-Proof: Higher Education in the Age of Artificial Intelligence*. The MIT Press, 2017.

[55] U. Kose and D. Koc (eds.), *Artificial Intelligence Applications in Distance Education*. Information Science Reference, 2015.

[56] R. J. Spiro, B. C. Bruce, and W. F. Brewer, *Theoretical Issues in Reading Comprehension: Perspectives from Cognitive Psychology, Linguistics, Artificial Intelligence and Education*. Taylor & Francis, 2017.

CHAPTER 3

ROBOTICS IN EDUCATION

"Robots have already surpassed human beings in calculation and memory, but I have no doubt that the time will come when they will surpass in wisdom as well."
—Masayoshi Son

3.1 INTRODUCTION

Education has always been a controversial subject. In a traditional learning environment, a teacher writes on the blackboard everything he knows to a group of students that records the information. New classroom approaches, methods, and techniques are continually discussed, developed, implemented, and replaced with newer, more effective ones. Access to the Internet, overhead projectors, interactive boards, comprehensive online databases, and animation software are just some of the technologies that teachers have been constantly using over the past decades. The introduction of Information and Communication Technologies (ICT) in education has completely transformed the teaching-learning process and reshaped knowledge acquisition [1].

In today's technology-driven world, preparing students for the future is important. The schools need to provide robotics education to their students to ensure they are well-equipped with the skills necessary for a bright career and future. Robotics, an offshoot of artificial intelligence, is the new kid on the block to captivate the imagination of the young generation, all for the right reasons. It is the discipline of creating robots. It is a branch of engineering that involves the conception, design, manufacture, and operation of robots. Robots are used in various areas such as manufacturing, healthcare, entertainment, military and defense, service industries, design, construction, law enforcement, education, shopping, and agriculture.

Robotics in education is a growing field where robots teach students subjects. Robots play different roles in education. These include teaching assistants, personal tutors, small group leaders, and peer learners. Robots can teach people of all ages. Early education on robotics should be made compulsory at all levels to prepare students adequately for the challenges of an increasingly digital world. Today, there are robots that can autonomously sense, reason, plan, act, move, communicate, and collaborate with other robots. The robot revolution is going to change us as humans [2,3]. Robots used in the educational system are typically known as educational robots.

This chapter explores the uses of robots in the education industry. It begins by explaining what robots are. It discusses some educational robots. It provides some applications of robots in education. It highlights the benefits and challenges of robots in education. It covers how robots are being used in education worldwide. The last section concludes with comments.

3.2 WHAT ARE ROBOTS?

The word "robot" was coined by Czech writer Karel Čapek in his play in 1920. Isaac Asimov coined the term "robotics" in 1942 and came up with three rules to guide the behavior of robots [4]:

(1) Robots must never harm human beings,
(2) Robots must follow instructions from humans without violating rule 1,
(3) Robots must protect themselves without violating the other rules.

Robotics has advanced and taken many forms, including fixed robots, collaborative robots, mobile robots, industrial robots, medical robots, police robots, military robots, officer robots, service robots, space robots, social robots, personal robots, and rehabilitation robots [5,6]. Robots are becoming increasingly prevalent in almost every industry, from healthcare to manufacturing. Figure 3.1 indicates that robotics is one of the branches of artificial intelligence.

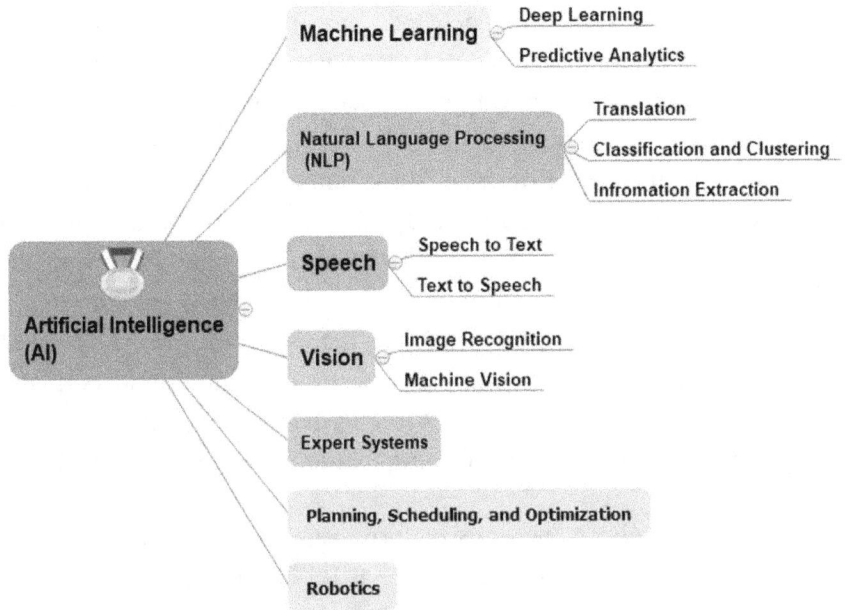

Figure 3.1 Robotics is one of the branches of artificial intelligence.

Robots include articulated robots, mobile robots, or autonomous vehicles. Other forms of robots in common use include drones and chatbots. Drones are flying robots, a type of robot that is poised to proliferate in certain commercial sectors. Drones can help utility crews quickly and safely identify areas needing repair after a storm. Drones can also help with maintenance tasks, such as surveying solar panels for damage. Chatbots–have simplified complex processes by empowering banks and other financial institutions. We interact with Facebook Messenger bots all the time. Messenger bots are revolutionizing the small business world. Messenger bots can answer customers' questions, collect users' information, organize meetings, reduce overhead costs, and engage in other business tasks. Big companies like Walmart, Alibaba, and Amazon have been benefitting from the help of bots.

3.3 EDUCATIONAL ROBOTICS

There are many robots available with some keys to promoting robotics learning in the classroom. These are known as educational robots. Educational robots (also known as pedagogical robots) teach the design, analysis, application and operation of robots. Educational robotics can be taught from elementary school to graduate programs. They are used to allow students to pick up skills in a range of Science, Technology, Engineering, and Mathematics (STEM) disciplines. Such skills are increasingly important in a world in which technology is advancing rapidly. The goal of STEM education is to help students organize information within and across disciplines. Science is the explanation of the natural world. Students that are scientifically literate can understand both the concepts and practices of science. While science describes the actions of our world, engineering involves finding solutions to a particular problem.

Educational robotics is a means of forming engineering thinking and creativity in school children. Educational robots enable students of all ages to become familiar with and deepen their knowledge of robotics and programming. The robots facilitate learning and introduce students to robotics at a young age. As students grow older, more advanced robots can be used that can perform more complex tasks and are more complicated to program. Examples of educational robots are in Figure 3.2 [7]. Educational Robotics can be an effective tool to teach computational thinking while also helping to broaden participation goals. It has flourished as teachers and schools embrace the potential of robotics to provide hands-on and engaging ways to teach design.

Educational robots often come equipped with eyes, mouths, and other facial features that can read emotions. Many companies now provide robotic building kits that educators can use to build systems thinking, learn engineering, and practice STEM concepts. Educational robots can help young students develop cognitive skills and mathematical thinking at an early age. They also give them skills that they can transfer to other areas of their learning.

ROBOTICS IN EDUCATION

Other benefits of educational robots include [8]:

- Preparing students for future career opportunities
- Helping remote students access their school
- Help the students to develop teamwork and cooperative skills
- Increases creative and innovative skills of students
- Help the students to communicate and learn different advanced technological platforms
- Simplify complex programming from a young age
- Support students with special needs
- Promote the development of cognitive skills among children and young people
- Stimulate imagination and creativity
- Help students deepen their knowledge of robotics and programming
- Make STEM simple and fun to learn

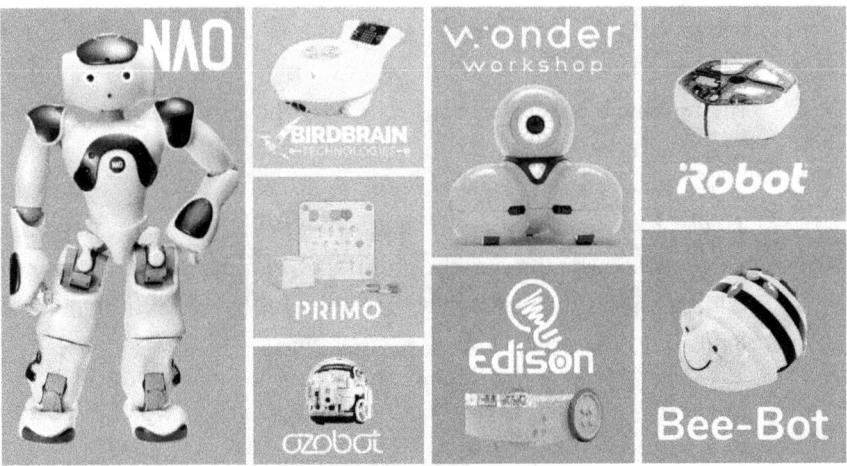

Figure 3.2 Examples of educational robots [7].

3.4 APPLICATIONS

There is a place for lessons involving robots in every grade and every subject. Teachers who want to incorporate science, technology, engineering, math (STEM), computer science (CS) into their curriculum can consider robotics. They should keep things simple and focus on fun and the intended learning. There are many potential applications for robots. Some of these application areas in education are presented as follows [9]:

- *Elementary School Education*: Robots can be used in early education since they are very popular with children. Increasing robotic literacy is crucial in the early stages of education. Therefore, K-12 educators can turn to robotics to get students excited about science, technology, engineering, arts, and math (STEM) education. Robots can be used to bring students into the classroom that otherwise might not be able to attend due to their health conditions. Robots can "bring school" to students who cannot be present physically. Teachers must identify the specific learning objective they want the robot to help them achieve and then use it accordingly. Children are generally curious and love to experiment with hands-on activities. Figure 3.3 shows how robots help children develop skills [7]. Robots can be useful for teaching language to children, and children can enjoy learning the language with a robot. Figure 3.4 shows robots and STEM kits for students [10].

- *Higher Education:* Robotics is a growing field that has the potential to significantly impact the nature of engineering and science education at all levels. For example, when receiving medical education, the use of robotics is beneficial.

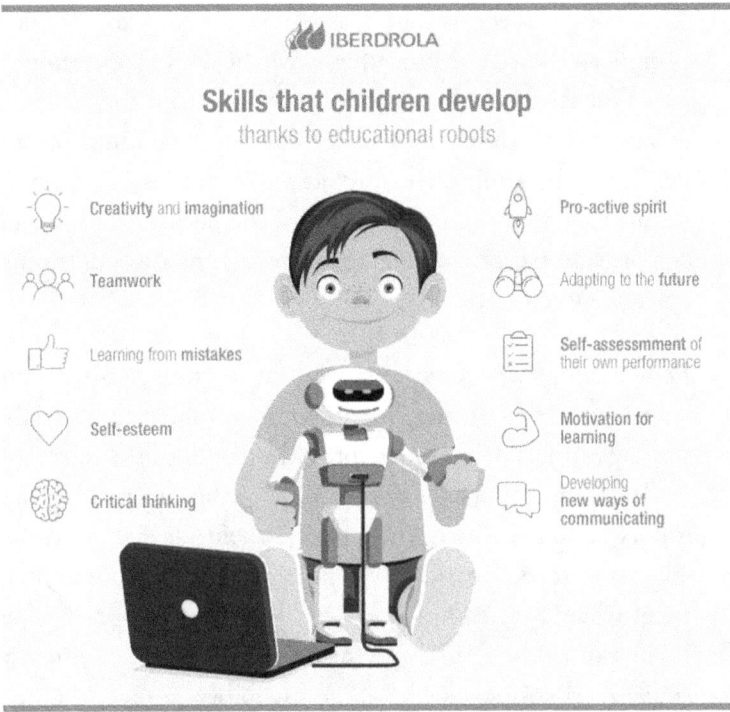

Figure 3.3 How robots help children develop skills [7].

Figure 3.4 Robots and STEM kits for students [10].

A human subject is not feasible when learning to perform complicated medical procedures. Medical educators employ the use of robots as stand-ins. Robots can be created and programmed to give off all indications of human life, including breath and heartbeat. In addition to providing medical students with the means for a thorough exploration of the human body, simulators can provide exceptional methods of crisis and disaster training for emergency response.

- *Personalized Education:* Personalized learning aims to support learning in which the learning environment is crucial.–The shortage of teachers has put pressure on educators to serve more students, but robots are easing some of the strain. The ability of robots to talk with children makes them ideal for personalized education roles. Robots have exhibited enough autonomy to the point where they can interact with kids on a one-on-one basis. A robot can act as a tutor, giving students individual attention. A single teacher does not have the capability to meet the needs of personalized learning for every student. A robot does not replace the teacher but allows students to learn at their own pace.

- *Special Education:* The appeal of robots lies in the way they can adjust to a child's learning abilities. This is feature important when it comes to teaching autistic children. Autism is characterized by people typically struggling to understand social communication and social interaction. Students with special requirements can be reached through the use of robotics in the classroom. Assistive technology is growing, and the abilities it provides to special education students are limitless.

- *Coding:* Even if students have no interest in a coding career, teachers can introduce coding into their curriculum easily through various programs. Educational robots are excellent for teaching kids fundamental engineering design and programming skills. They allow students to see and interpret code results in real-time. Dash and Dot Robots are popular for the programmable personality features of the bots, which are a big hit with elementary-aged learners. They are kid-friendly programming teaching tools and interpreters of the "programmable" units. Dash captivates children with singing and dancing while exhibiting the ability to respond to voices. Studies indicate that gender, interest, and prior experience with robots influence the level of motivation to learn more about coding.

- *Competition:* Robotics competitions are events where participants are required to design and produce robots and compete with each other. A competition for students presents a central problem and asks participants to develop a solution. Students can participate in robotics competitions across the whole world. Robotics competitions improve students' problem-solving skills. They help students of all ages see what they learn in practice. They also provide a great way to teach coding and gain universal skills. Figure 3.5 shows a design for competition [11]. Competition creates infectious excitement on the faces of participants, especially the winners.

In addition to these applications, robots can be used to learn languages and environments.

Figure 3.5 A design for robotics competition [11].

3.5 BENEFITS

Robotics is an entertaining and innovative pedagogical tool that is becoming very important in modern society. It has seen an exponential growth in the past decade. In addition to being fun, robotics includes the fundamental concepts of STEM that give an excellent platform for students to enjoy learning. Not only can robots optimize the learning experience, but they can also give students the key computer skills required in the job market. There are endless educational possibilities with robotics. Robotics offers great opportunities for teamwork and collaboration. It encourages children to learn valuable life and career skills.

Due to the incredible potential of robotic technology, application opportunities are limitless in the future. Current trends lead many people to believe they will take over the workforce in many sectors and there will be an increase in demand for automation [12]. The robotics revolution is inevitable. It is rapidly accelerating as technology advances in automation, engineering, energy storage, and artificial intelligence converge.

Robots are used extensively in schools and special-education institutions that offer higher education. Many universities are studying collaborative robots to assist doctors and surgeons in various medical procedures. Robotic teaching benefits students with special learning needs, improving their communication and social skills.

For students, the major benefits of educational robotics are as follows [13,14]:

- Develops interest in STEM (Science, Technology, Engineering, and Mathematics)
- Strengthens coding skills
- Develops problem-solving skills
- Fosters future-ready learning
- Instils team spirit and improves self-esteem
- Develops computational skills and logical thinking
- Promotes entrepreneurship

- Enhances confidence and engagement
- Encourages creativity
- Teaches soft skills
- Adapts and supports different learning levels
- It can be programmed to support individual needs

3.6 CHALLENGES

Educational robots are plagued with numerous challenges despite the benefits of education. It is essential to make the technology accessible and affordable to bridge the digital divide and ensure equal access to educational robotics. Other challenges include the following [15,16]:

(a) *Cost:* The cost of maintaining robots in education is high. Hence, educational robots are not widely deployed. Schools often have limited budgets, making it difficult to invest in expensive robotic equipment. Providing each student with actual robots may be expensive for the school.

(b) *Teacher Training:* Educators may lack the necessary time and training to effectively integrate robotics into the curriculums. Adequate training is required by teachers who want to deploy educational robots as teaching aids. Hence, learners who have not been adequately trained on in using educational robots for learning may find it difficult to use the technology for learning.

(c) *Gender Imbalances:* There must be an acknowledgment of gender imbalances to create diversity within robotics education. Many companies are now paying close attention to how their robotic devices are perceived and are trying to develop gender-neutral solutions. Companies that offer educational robotics products are putting extra effort towards engaging girls and other underrepresented populations.

(d) *Fear of Displacement:* One of the major challenges of educational robots is that students may have the feeling that their teachers have been displaced and replaced with robots.

(e) *Emotional Attachment:* Humanoid robots that look exactly like humans and are used as teachers or tutors can create emotional attachments between children and robots. This practice usually creates a form of deception in the children's minds. Thus, a loss or irreparable damage to the robot can affect the child's learning process.

(f) *Technology Reliability:* Robots are mechanical devices that can fail at anytime. Hence, the reliability and integrity of educational robots is a challenge.

(g) *Appearance of Robot:* An educational robot with the same appearance as a human might create fear in the learners' minds. This concept is referred to as an uncanny valley. This practice may, in turn, impede learning.

(h) *Safety:* Some robots are designed with sharp edges, which can cause lacerations and severe harm to children. This situation can discourage the children from learning with this form of technology.

By addressing these challenges, educational robotics can become an inclusive and effective tool for classrooms worldwide.

3.7 GLOBAL USE OF ROBOTS IN EDUCATION

Education has changed considerably in the past few years as new technologies enter classrooms worldwide. Around the world, it is common to see robots being used as educational tools in schools. But the use of educational robots in children's education is still in its infancy. Educational robots (such as NAO, OWI 535, LEGO, etc.) are used to allow students to develop skills in a range of Science, Technology, Engineering, and Mathematics (STEM) disciplines. They are used to make learning easier for students. They create an environment in which students can interact with the environment and solve real-world problems. Working with them can improve students' communication, interpersonal skills, and creativity in problem-solving. We now consider how educational robots are being used in some nations.

- *United States:* The use of robotic and simulation technologies has proven to be a worthy component of available educational resources. When applied to education, robotics and simulators can change how students learn and ultimately create a more knowledgeable and well-adjusted student.–Robots can "bring school" to students who cannot be physically present. When receiving medical education, many students find benefits in the use of robotics [17].

- *United Kingdom:* Robots and Artificial Intelligence (AI) have long been used in UK classrooms to introduce a new, more modern way of teaching children. It has been debated whether they should be a part of the classroom or how they can help education in the UK, especially in the fourth industrial revolution. Some claim that robots present a new way of teaching children, while some say that it defeats the point of having teachers. Although robots will not be replacing classroom teachers, the teachers will need to develop new skills so that this tool can be better utilized. Robots can benefit the future of education, especially in the languages department [18].

- *Europe:* Europe is incorporating robots into its education system. As education focuses more on innovation and creativity, robots continue to make their way into classrooms. Robots are proving themselves useful as teaching tool. Robots can optimize the learning experience and give students the key computer skills that have become essential in the job market. Robots can help students with specific requirements, taking some of the pressure off teachers. School should be about equipping students with the skills and knowledge they will need later in life. Robots in education can serve as a motivational and creative medium to promote a radical and innovative approach to learning [19]. Developing an active European community in educational robotics will promote further networking of researchers, educators, and students.

- *China:* China's robotic market is booming. It is home to the world's largest industrial robot base, buying and building robots faster than any other nation. It appears that robots are not just replacing human factory workers in China. Now they are being recruited to help out in school classrooms. The Chinese government has ambitious plans for its robotics industry. A robot called KeeKo interacts with the children by playing games with them, singing, dancing, reading stories, carrying out conversations, and even doing mathematics. The robot is popular with students and is part of the wave of robots sweeping China. The robot has been used in over 200 kindergartens nationwide [20]. Some Chinese educational robots are displayed in Figure 3.6 [21].

Figure 3.6 Some Chinese educational robots [21].

- *India:* With AI and robotics having penetrated the professional landscape, Indian schools have started to absorb educational robots. The advantages of promoting and inculcating robotics in the Indian education system are many. From creating an exciting learning environment to a wider range of career opportunities, robotics will play a multi-faceted role in the Indian education system. The robot is believed to be capable of teaching students of grades V. Introducing young children to robotics helps ignite creativity, invigorate critical thinking, and further permeate a collaborative mindset by opening up a world of unending career opportunities. Robotics provides a great opportunity to learn how real-world creativity reveals from students' interaction with their environments: physical, social, and cultural [22].

3.8 CONCLUSION

Robotics is a field at the crossroads of computer science, technology, and engineering. STEM and robotics will soon become inseparable components of one another. Robotics is one of the most necessary aspects of education today because children will interact with or encounter robots their entire lives. As robots replace a growing number of workers, there will be plenty of career opportunities for those who know how to design, develop, and program them. Integrating robotics into the curriculum exposes students to practical skills that could lead to a promising career. Robots could prove a huge boon to education.

Robotics education should be made compulsory since robotics is closely intertwined with our lives. Students need to learn the fundamental basis of robot programming and operation. Students can become the architects of a better future by integrating robotics into the curriculum through carefully designed courses. They can learn about robots through courses, STEM robotics camps, online programs, competitions, and kits, and by joining robotics groups.

Robotics is integral to cutting-edge careers like aerospace engineering, computer science, and hardware design. The skills in robotics is highly sought after in business and other sectors. To be a roboticist, you will need key skills such as mathematics and science. For more information about robotics in education, one should consult the books in [23-39] and the following related journals devoted to robotics:

- *Robotica*
- *Robitics and Autonomous*
- *Robotics and Computer-Integrated Manufacturing,*
- *Advanced Robotics*
- *Autonomous Robots*

- *Journal of Robotics*
- *Journal of Robotic Systems*
- *Journal of Robotic Surgery*
- *Journal of Robotics and Mechatronics*
- *Journal of Intelligent & Robotic Systems*
- *Journal of Mechanisms and Robotics-Transactions of the ASME*
- *Journal of Automation, Mobile Robotics and Intelligent Systems*
- *Journal of Future Robot Life*
- *IEEE Robotics and Automation Letters*
- *IEEE Transactions on Robotics*
- *International Journal of Medical Robotics and Computer Assisted Surgery*
- *International Journal of Robotics Research*
- *International Journal of Social Robotics*
- *International Journal of Humanoid Robotics*
- *International Journal of Advanced Robotic Systems*

REFERENCES

[1] S. Brezgov, "Robots in education: Is the educational revolution just around the corner?" January 2020, https://scholarlyoa.com/robots-in-education-is-the-educational-revolution-just-around-the-corner/

[2] M. N. O. Sadiku, S. Alam, and S.M. Musa, "Intelligent robotics and applications," *International Journal of Trends in Research and Development*, vol. 5, no. 1, January-February 2018, pp. 101-103.

[3] M. N. O. Sadiku, U. C. Chukwu. A. Ajayi-Majebi, and S. M. Musa, "Robotics in education," *International Journal of Trend in Scientific Research and Development*, vol. 6, no. 7, November-December 2022, pp. 608-613.

[4] "Human–robot interaction," *Wikipedia,* the free encyclopedia https://en.wikipedia.org/wiki/Human–robot_interaction

[5] R. D. Davenport, "Robotics," in W. C. Mann (ed.), *Smart Technology for Aging, Disability, and Independenc*e. John Wiley & Sons, 2005, Chapter 3, pp. 67-109.

[6] M. N. O. Sadiku, S. Alam, and S.M. Musa, "Intelligent robotics and applications," *International Journal of Trends in Research and Development*, vol. 5, no. 1, January-February 2018, pp. 101-103.

[7] "8 Educational robotics kits we'll always recommend," https://www.eduporium.com/blog/8-robotics-brands-well-always-recommend-for-education/

[8] "The benefits of robots in education," April 2022, https://www.euruni.edu/blog/the-benefits-of-robots-in-education/

[9] "The use of robotics and simulators in the education environment," https://www.google.com/search?q=The+Use+of+Robotics+and+Simulators+in+the+Education+Environment&rlz=1C1CHBF_enUS910US910&oq=The+Use+of+Robotics+and+Simulators+in+the+Education+Environment&aqs=chrome..69i57j69i64l2.1584j0j7&sourceid=chrome&ie=UTF-8

[10] "Top 10 robots and STEM kits for elementary, middle, and high school students," March 2021, https://sphero.com/blogs/news/top-robots-stem-kits

[11] "Why are robotics competitions important for education?" https://riders.ai/en-blog/why-are-robotics-competitions-important-for-education

[12] M. N. O. Sadiku, K. Patel, S. M. Musa, "Future of robotics," *International Journal of Trend in Scientific Research and Development*, vol. 6, no. 4, June 2022, pp.1805-1810.

[13] "6 Educational benefits of robots in the classroom," https://edtechimpact.com/news/6-educational-benefits-of-robots-in-the-classroom

[14] V. Kakumanu, "Use of robots in school education," March 2022, https://www.schoolserv.in/Use-of-Robots-in-School-Education/

[15] A. B. Iliescu, "The future of educational robotics: Enhancing education, bridging the digital divide, and supporting diverse learners," https://aiforgood.itu.int/the-future-of-educational-robotics-enhancing-education-bridging-the-digital-divide-and-supporting-diverse-learners/#:~:text=Challenges%20in%20Implementing%20Robots%20in%20Classrooms&text=The%20high%20cost%20of%20advanced,integrate%20robotics%20into%20their%20curriculums.

[16] O. G. Iroju et al., "Prospects and challenges of robotic technology in children's educational development," *The Educational Psychologist*, vol. 14, no. 1, 2021, pp. 69-76

[17] "Robotics and simulators in education," https://online.purdue.edu/blog/education/robotics-simulators-education-environment

[18] "How robots and AI will help education in the UK," https://www.desiblitz.com/content/how-robots-ai-help-education-uk

[19] "How robots are impacting education in Europe," May 2016, https://www.roboticsbusinessreview.com/rbr/how_robots_are_impacting_education_in_europe/

[20] S. Xheng, "Robots being used to teach children in China's schools ... will they replace teachers?" April 2017, https://www.scmp.com/news/china/society/article/2087341/robots-are-being-used-teach-children-chinas-schools-no-fear-they

[21] S. Wang, "AI robots are transforming parenting in China," October 2018, https://www.cnn.com/2018/09/28/health/china-ai-early-education/index.html

[22] "How is robotics framing the Indian education system," July 2021, https://www.dqindia.com/robotics-framing-indian-education-system/

[23] M. Merdan et al. (eds.), *Robotics in education: Research and practices for robotics in STEM education.* Springer, 2016.

[24] B. Siciliano and O. Khatib (eds.), *Springer Handbook of Robotics.* Berlin: Springer.

[25] J. Jacoby, *STEM Starters for Kids Robotics Activity Book: Packed with Activities and Robotics Facts.* Racehorse for Young Readers, 2020.

[26] J. Swanson, *National Geographic Kids Everything Robotics: All the Photos, Facts, and Fun to Make You Race for Robots.* National Geographic Kids, 2016.

[27] K. Ceceri and S. Carbaugh, *Robotics: Discover the Science and Technology of the Future With 20 Projects (Build It Yourself).* Nomad Press, 2012.

[28] B. Katocich, *Awesome Robotics Projects for Kids: 20 Original STEAM Robots and Circuits to Design and Build (Awesome STEAM Activities for Kids).* Rockridge Press, 2019.

[29] E. Ren, *Robot Engineer: Fun and Educational STEM (science, technology, engineering, and math) Book for Kids (STEM (Science, technology, engineering, and math) Educational Picture Book* (3books)) Lulu Books, 2021.

[30] D. Alimisis, E. Menegatti, and M. Moro, *Educational Robotics in the Makers Era.* Springer, 2017.

[31] L. Daniela, *Smart Learning with Educational Robotics: Using Robots to Scaffold Learning Outcomes.* Springer, 2019.

[32] B. S. Barker, *Robots in K-12 Education: A New Technology for Learning.* Information Science Reference, 2012.

[33] I. Gaudiello and E. Zibetti, *Learning Robotics, with Robotics, by Robotics: Educational Robotics.* Wiley, 2016.

[34] M. Kalogiannakis and S. Papadakis (eds.), *Handbook of Research on Using Educational Robotics to Facilitate Student Learning.* IGI Global, 2020.

[35] D. Alimisis, M. Moro, and M. Malvezzi (eds.), *Education in & with Robotics to Foster 21st-Century Skills: Proceedings of EDUROBOTICS 2020.* Springer, 2021.

[36] M. S. Khine, *Robotics in STEM Education: Redesigning the Learning Experience.* Springer, 2017.

[37] F. Alnajjar et al., *Robots in Education.* Routledge, 2021.

[38] M. Chang et al. (eds), *Learning by Playing. Game-based Education System Design and Development. Edutainment 2009. Lecture Notes in Computer Science.* Berlin: Springer, 2009.

[39] W. Lepuschitz et al. (eds), *Robotics in Education Methodologies and Technologies.* Springer 2021.

CHAPTER 4
CLOUD COMPUTING IN EDUCATION

> *"Cloud computing offers individuals access to data and applications from nearly any point of access to the Internet, offers businesses a whole new way to cut costs for technical infrastructure, and offers big computer companies a potentially giant market for hardware and services."*
> —Jamais Cascio

4.1 INTRODUCTION

Education plays a pivotal role in the economic growth of any nation. The world is changing rapidly. Education is consequently changing. The classroom is changing. Teaching and learning are no longer confined to textbooks and classrooms but involve using computers and mobile devices. Technology and education are closely related. The educational model in many nations has evolved with technology. Today, learners are digital natives and are always connected. They are demanding more technology services from their institutions. From lectures to assignment submissions, everything is now Internet-based. There comes the need for cloud computing [1].

Cloud computing refers to a setup of computing resources that can be shared anywhere, irrespective of the location of the users. It is an emerging new computing paradigm for delivering computing services. It is changing the way information technology services are provided. A cloud platform makes accessing educational resources easier for students and teachers. Lesson plans, coursework, and assignments can be uploaded, updated, and accessed anytime by students. It is easy for educators to monitor coursework and access students' progress without meeting face-to-face. Teachers can work from anywhere, connect their students to multiple programs and applications, and save all their lesson plans and assignments to the cloud.

Computing resources can be network servers, applications, platforms, storage, software infrastructure segments, and services. They are abstracted and provided as services on a network or Internet [2]. The data center hardware and software are what we will call a cloud. Cloud computing relies on several existing technologies, e.g., the Internet, virtualization, grid computing, web services, etc. The user does not require expertise and knowledge to control the infrastructure segment of clouds.

Cloud computing differs from other historical IT models because it focuses mainly on services rather than technology. Technology (storage, CPU, networking equipment) is not the service but the building blocks for a service. Cloud computing in education refers to moving a school system's data and IT resources to a cloud server. Several higher education institutions are already taking advantage of the many benefits the cloud offers, including cost savings, scalability, agility, and modernization [3].

This paper provides an introduction to cloud computing for education. It begins by explaining the concept of cloud computing. It provides some applications of cloud computing in education. It highlights the benefits and challenges of incorporating cloud computing in education. It covers the global use of cloud computing in education. The last section closes with comments.

4.2 CONCEPT OF CLOUD COMPUTING

Cloud computing is a new means of providing computing resources and services. It is an on-demand and self-service Internet infrastructure. It offers large scalable computing and storage, data sharing, and on-demand anytime and anywhere access to resources. Figure 4.1 depicts cloud computing [4].

Cloud computing presents several characteristics such as [5]:

- The pooling of resources
- Better use of resources
- Elasticity
- Dynamic (distributed)
- Scalability
- Virtualized

Figure 4.1 Cloud computing [4].

From a service point of view, cloud computing includes three models: software, platform, and infrastructure [6].

(1) Software as a service (SaaS): The applications are hosted by a cloud service provider and made available to customers over the Internet. As a SaaS, the cloud can offer organizations on-demand hosted services.

(2) Platform as a service (PaaS): The development tools (e.g., operation systems) are hosted in the cloud and accessed through a browser. Using a PaaS environment, Microsoft provides a service to supply providers with networks, servers, and storage.

(3) Infrastructure as a service (IaaS): Cloud service providers set up huge infrastructure like servers, storage devices, hardware, etc., to be used by potential clients.

The three models are shown in Figure 4.2 [7].

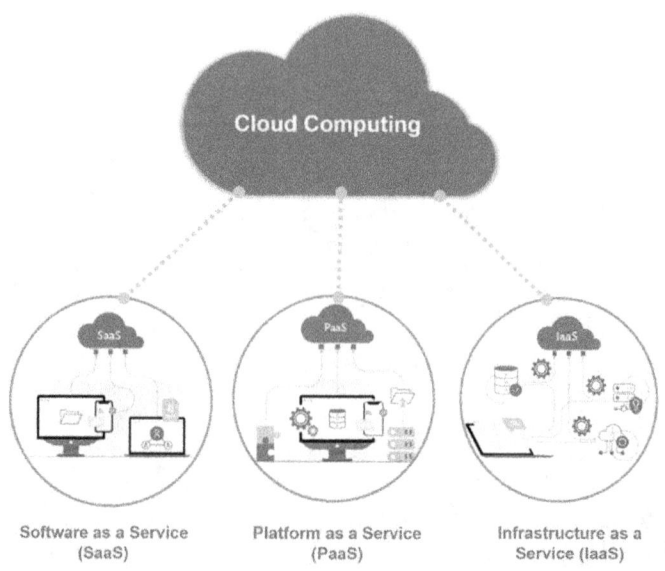

Figure 4.2 Three cloud computing models [7].

The cloud computing deployment models [8].

(1) Public cloud: A public cloud is a publicly accessible cloud environment owned by a third-party cloud provider. The service provider makes resources available to the general public over the Internet on a pay-as-you-go basis.

(2) Private cloud: A cloud infrastructure is owned and operated solely by a single organization. Organizations build their cloud infrastructure for use by their business units. They can also choose between private cloud or public cloud.

(3) Community cloud: A community cloud is similar to a public cloud except that its access is limited to a specific community of cloud

consumer. Several organizations share the cloud infrastructure with common concerns.

(4) Hybrid cloud: A hybrid cloud is a combination of a public and private cloud

Figure 4.3 illustrates these cloud computing types [9], while Figure 4.4 shows some popular cloud computing providers [9]. For example, Microsoft Azure is one of the eminent cloud computing platforms created by Microsoft.

Figure 4.3 Cloud computing types [9].

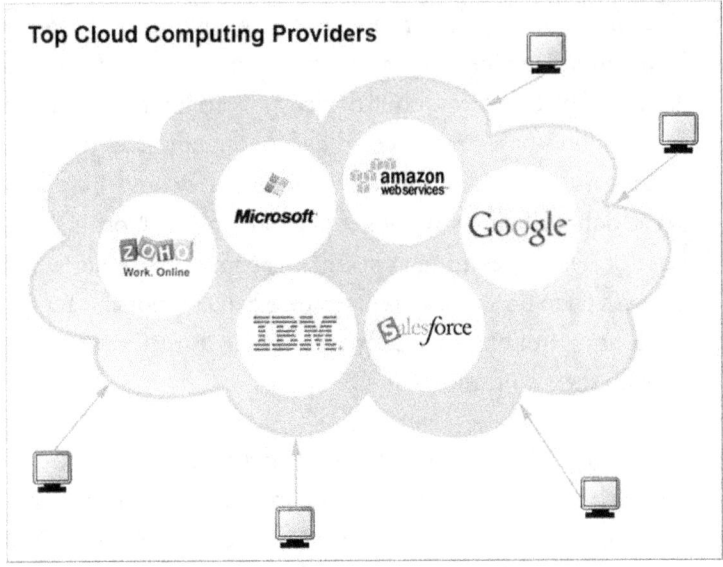

Figure 4.4 Some popular cloud computing providers [9].

4.3 APPLICATIONS OF CLOUD COMPUTING IN EDUCATION

Cloud computing is an emerging technology that relies on transferring computer data storage and processing power to the cloud (or Internet). It refers to the physical structure of a communications network, where data is stored in large data centers and can be accessed anywhere, at any time, using different devices. It offers many advantages to education, from K-12 schools to university students. Common applications of cloud computing in education include the following [10,11]:

- *Teaching:* Cloud-based services offer an ideal platform for hosting lectures and providing feedback to students. Cloud-based technologies can significantly change how education works, whether in traditional classrooms, online courses, or blended learning. Teachers can use cloud-based technologies to aid understanding of course materials and engage students in the learning process. They can also keep track of their student's progress at any time, creating personalized learning opportunities. They may also use cloud computing to create new and creative classroom structures.

- *Learning:* Today, learners and teachers have access to computers and mobile devices that are always connected. Students need a laptop, tablet, or any mobile device, plus an internet connection to access cloud-based resources. The cloud guarantees that students, educators, personnel, guardians, and staff would have access to basic data utilizing any gadget from any place. Nothing beats the ease of having learning at your fingertips, and cloud technology allows you to do so. Cloud computing makes it possible for students who have trouble attending traditional learning institutions to pursue their education.

- *E-learning:* This is a concept that integrates information technology in teaching and learning. It is an Internet-based learning system that uses technology to develop, execute, choose, manage, facilitate, and enhance learning. Cloud-based technologies supported e-Learning during the emergence of the COVID-19 pandemic. They are essential for e-learning, especially mobile learning, distance learning, and web-based collaborative learning. Instead of traditional classrooms, cloud computing facilitates online learning through virtual classrooms.

- *E-textbooks:* The problem with printed textbooks is that schools and students need to constantly purchase new books to get updated editions. E-textbooks are beneficial, particularly in subjects that continuously change, such as technology. Cloud-based materials can reduce the volume of paper that schools have to print for handouts and assignments and consequently reduce the cost of education. Users of cloud-based materials can highlight and edit text and write notes easily.

- *Higher Education:* Today's higher education students come to campuses with many digital devices, looking for opportunities to use them. Cloud computing creates endless possibilities to transform education through innovation and drive student success. Colleges and universities need a solid technology partner that is preferably "on-cloud" to manage its complexity and keep the stakeholders connected, productive, innovative, and efficient. Cloud computing in higher education provides an online platform for educational institutes through various applications and subscription models. It transforms the way higher education institutions run and serve their community. Higher education institutions are rapidly embracing the power of cloud computing technology to augment the way it serves their constituents. Figure 4.5 shows why higher education should adopt cloud computing [12]. Coursera offers a variety of online courses from established universities and instructors through its cloud platform. Massive Open Online Courses (MOOCs) are cloud-based educational platforms promising to transform higher education. Figure 4.6 displays a cloud-based higher education system [13].

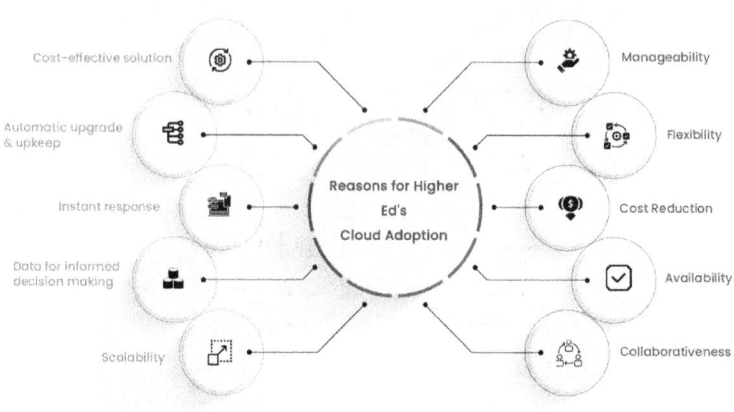

Figure 4.5 Reasons higher education should adopt cloud computing [12].

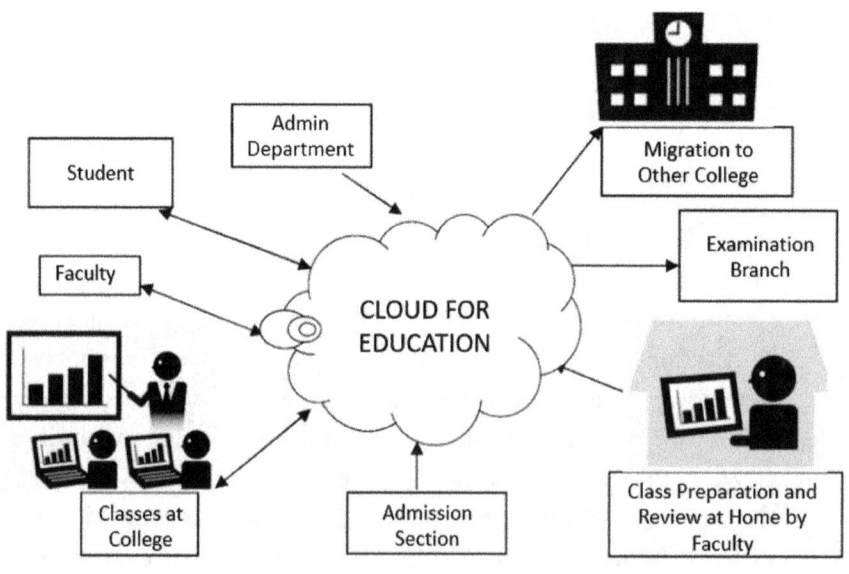

Figure 4.6 Cloud-based higher education system [13].

4.4 BENEFITS

Education providers and seekers can greatly benefit from the cloud. The 21st-century classroom needs more flexibility in terms of design and layout. Cloud computing can make learning more convenient, cost-efficient, agile, and flexible for students and teachers. Easy accessibility, collaboration, and community development in a safe environment are easy with a cloud-enabled educational model. The 21st-century classroom needs more flexibility in terms of design and layout.

The benefits of cloud computing for the education sector are many. They include [14-16]:

- *Accessibility:* The potential of the cloud is unmatched when it comes to accessibility. Users can access it anytime, anywhere, making life much easier and more convenient. With learning materials residing in the cloud, students can have 24/7 access to their courses through multiple devices such as desktops, laptops, tablets, or smartphones anytime. They have access to their files from anywhere there is an Internet connection. This feature adds an element of convenience to the whole learning process and eliminates spatial and temporal limitations.

- *Convenience*: Cloud-based applications can be accessed by users anywhere and with any device, making them convenient and easy to use. The only requirement is a digital device that can access the Internet.

- *Cost:* A major advantage of cloud computing is the capacity to increase storage for less cost. Cloud computing can improve efficiency, cost, and convenience for the educational sector. It reduces the IT cost to organizations, freeing them from the hassle of installing and maintaining applications locally. Users of cloud computing are more likely to reduce their carbon footprint. With digital materials stored on the cloud, schools can save tremendously on paper, ink, and toner.

- *Collaboration:* Real-time collaboration is an important aspect of cloud computing education. Cloud computing enables effortless collaboration, sharing, and transmission of ideas in real time. It allows multiple users to work on and edit documents simultaneously. Teachers can easily share lesson plans and work on them together at any place or time. They can set up student groups to work on projects and assignments in the cloud. Cloud software helps to support student communication and create teacher management portals.

- *Scalability:* As a business grows, so will its technical requirements. Scalability refers to the ability of cloud computing applications to match the growing numbers of users. The cloud allows users to scale their resources in real-time with no hidden costs. Regardless of how many students you have or the higher education facilities you manage, your cloud system can grow alongside you.

- *Minimal Hardware:* Once all the learning resources are moved to the cloud, educational institutions handle minimal hardware on campus. With cloud-based applications, the requirements of hardware resources are minimal.

- *Security:* Security is one of the most important advantages of cloud computing technology. Service providers invest heavily in securing their cloud-based solutions from any intrusion. Whatever you store in the cloud usually requires authentication (ID and password, for example). Students can be assured that their data is secure. The cloud platform will offer authentication and security features to ensure that learning materials are only available to the right users. Cloud computing helps academic institutions meet data protection obligations to keep student and staff information safe.

- *Flexibility:* Users can create, edit, and save files in the cloud according to their needs, like a self-service. The disruptions due to COVID-19 have shown the necessity of flexible technology.

- *Stability:* Cloud computing is a stable technology that one can rely on.

- *Trackability:* Cloud computing will save multiple revisions and versions of a document so you can chronologically trace its evolution.

- *Affordable Education:* The cloud can make education much more affordable for the masses.

- *Long-Term Cost Savings:* Cost reduction is a major benefit of cloud education software. Cloud computing causes reduced data storage costs and minimal data center maintenance.

- *Quick Deployment:* Cloud computing gives you the advantage of quick deployment. Your entire system can be fully functional in a matter of minutes.

Some of these benefits are displayed in Figure 4.7 [17].

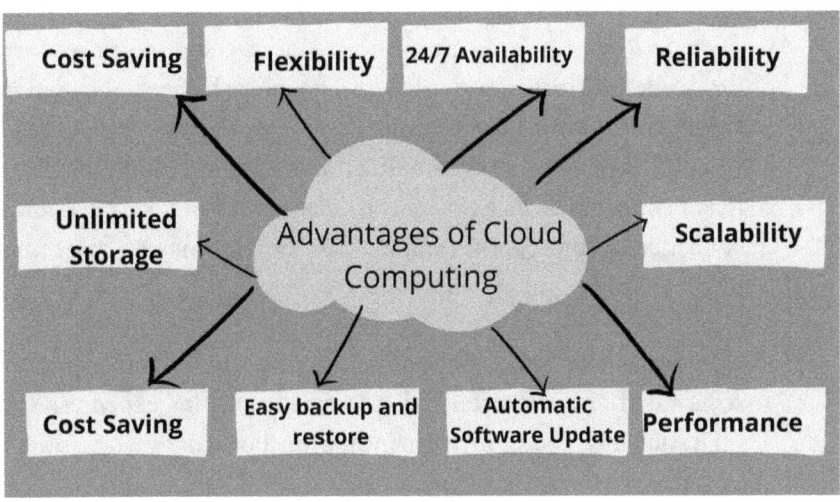

Figure 4.7 Some of the benefits of cloud computing [17].

4.5 CHALLENGES

Despite the benefits, cloud computing in education has several drawbacks and obstacles. As an emerging computing service, there are fears, uncertainties, and concerns about the technology's maturity. The major concerns are related to control, up-front costs, vendor lock, performance, latency, security, privacy, and reliability. Cloud computing's dependency on an Internet connection is inconvenient. Other challenges include [14,18]:

- *Big Leap:* We are becoming a paperless society. But by nature, human beings are conservative. Going from paper to digital requires a big leap of faith. We can feel, see, and touch paper but not digital object objects.

- *Less Control:* Users have less control over updates, training, and other features. The cloud service provider handles these and cannot easily switch between service providers. Everything is hosted off-site so you will have less control over the infrastructure and the system setup.

- *Data Security:* Data security in the cloud is the primary concern for academic institutions due to the non-efficient encryption algorithms of cloud computing. There are inherent security risks when all assets are hosted online, and data security becomes a major concern. Securing parents, students, staff, and teachers' data is a concern. Improperly-secured cloud systems may be vulnerable to cyberattacks.

- *Up-Front Costs:* There are some up-front costs. IT infrastructure costs are often substantial and are treated as capital expenses. The migration may be costly, depending on how many applications or services you are moving to the cloud. There is also the cost required to train staff on the new system.

- *Reliability:* This is an issue for academic institutions using the cloud. In the event of service failure, data recovery becomes a major concern.

4.6 GLOBAL USE OF CLOUD COMPUTING IN EDUCATION

Cloud computing in education is on the rise globally. The education industry has greatly improved with the advent of cloud computing. Educators throughout the spectrum, from early years professionals to those in higher education, have been looking for ways to build a cloud infrastructure that helps lower costs and improve learning experiences for the generation of digital natives. We now consider how cloud computing is incorporated into the educational systems of some nations.

- *United States:* The government's mandate for a cloud-first public sector pressures education professionals to explore new technologies. Some universities in the US offer bachelor of science (BS) degree programs in cloud computing. The program covers core areas such as networking, security, and architecture. It is designed to give students a strong foundation and advanced understanding of information technology/computer science core areas relevant to cloud computing. It prepares students for entry-level and mid-level positions in several cloud computing areas, such as SysOps, support, operations, architecture, and development [19]. Some universities offer online masters programs on cloud computing. The program is designed to help graduates deal with increasingly complex business technology environments. It will give students the technical and management skills they need to design, operate, and maintain cloud computing systems. Graduates will be equipped to guide migration strategies, manage multi-cloud environments, and optimize cloud architecture for performance, security, and reliability [20].

- *United Kingdom:* Although there can be many benefits of using cloud computing services in the UK education sector, schools and other public sector departments are holding back on this. Many schools may have competent IT technicians but the cultural difficulties in academic environments can be challenging. Some schools usually regard IT as a "necessary evil," to be tolerated, not embraced. A fundamental shift in thinking is necessary for schools to see the key benefits of using cloud data storage and virtualization services. Moving to the cloud is a huge consideration for any institution. One way to get cloud computing into schools is to build it into the curriculum [21]. Some academic institutions in the US offer masters programs in cloud computing, giving students the highly sought-after skills they need to launch their digital careers.

- *China:* Chinese cloud services provider, 3Tcloud, is implementing the country's biggest education cloud project. Alibaba is helping rural students in China via cloud computers. China launched a national cloud learning platform for millions of students restricted to their homes and ensures that 50 million students can access the cloud learning platform simultaneously. The cloud learning platform is open to students in elementary and secondary schools, providing them with free education resources until they can return to their normal classrooms. The national platform provides learning resources of six modules: Epidemic prevention education, moral education, special-theme education, curriculum learning, electronic teaching materials, and education via film and television. The curriculum learning module was supplemented by courses newly recorded by teachers in Beijing and other cities and e-learning programs. Online education companies and platforms provide numerous free online courses to meet school plans [22].

- *India:* Although technological innovations have taken the Indian education sector by storm, the Indian education sector is rapidly embracing digital technologies. Technological advancements have completely transformed the Indian educational system. Cloud computing has been implemented in India, making it easier for students to share information and learn. Cloud infrastructure is addressing the challenges of the Indian education sector, offering a seamless collaboration between students and teachers. Cloud computing has enhanced the education sector by drastically transforming it from student email to distance learning platforms. It is also enhancing the quality of education. Since the education sector is becoming more crucial in India, cloud computing has been adopted to ease information sharing and the learning process. Cloud computing allows easy access to learning tutorials and makes learning material easily accessible to students with lower incomes. It overcomes the challenge associated with the lack of skilled teachers or school infrastructure in remote area [23].

4.7 CONCLUSION

Cloud computing is essentially accessing computing services through the Internet. It uses virtualization as its key technology. Its success lies in its easy-to-use computing model and the benefits it brings to the users. While cloud computing is a relatively new concept, it is becoming increasingly popular and an integral part of the lives of many students. Using mixed media may engage students more effectively and improve classroom performance.

The importance of cloud computing in education cannot be overemphasized. Nothing beats the convenience of education at your fingertips. Everyone in the education sector is experiencing the positive impact of cloud computing technology [24]. After the rapid adoption of cloud computing in the education industry, education has become more accessible, and educational institutions can now stay relevant. One should consult the books in [25-42] for more information about cloud computing in education.

REFERENCES

[1] "Cloud computing for education," http://cappadocia-education.com/cloud-computing-for-education/

[2] A. D. Baharuddin et al., "Implementation of cloud computing system in learning system development in engineering education study program," *International Journal of Education in Mathematics, Science, and Technology*, vol. 9, no. 4, 2021, pp. 728-740.

[3] M. N. O. Sadiku, U. C. Chukwu, and J. O. Sadiku, "Cloud computing in education," *International Journal of Human Computing Studies,* vol. 5, no.3, May 2023, pp.167-175.

[4] "Cloud computing," http://www.contrib.andrew.cmu.edu/~dyafei/CC.html#

[5] H. Jemal et al., "Cloud computing and mobile devices based system for healthcare application," *Proceedings of IEEE International Symposium on Technology in Society,* 2015.

[6] M. N. O. Sadiku, S. M. Musa, and O.D. Momoh, "Cloud computing: Opportunities and challenges," *IEEE Potentials,* vol. 33, no. 1, Jan/Feb. 2014, pp. 34-36.

[7] "Why cloud computing is a key enabler for digital government," https://development.asia/explainer/why-cloud-computing-key-enabler-digital-government

[8] F. Alharbi et al., "Strategic value of cloud computing in healthcare organisations using the balanced scorecard approach: A case study from a Saudi hospital," *Procedia Computer Science,* vol. 98, 2016, pp. 332 – 339.

[9] "Cloud computing, why and future!" Unknown Source.

[10] J. Obana, "Cloud computing in education," May 2016, https://www.linkedin.com/pulse/cloud-computing-education-jesus-obana-cpa-mba

[11] N. Samyan and P. O. St Flour, "The impact of cloud computing on e-Learning during COVID-19 pandemic," *International Journal of Studies in Education and Science (IJSES),* vol. 2, no. 2, 2021, pp. 146-172.

[12] C. Suvin, "The ultimate guide to higher education cloud computing," June 2021, https://www.creatrixcampus.com/blog/ultimate-guide-higher-education-cloud-computing

[13] https://www.researchgate.net/figure/Figure2-Cloud-Computing-in-Higher-Education-systems-12_fig1_318817076

[14] "The main benefits & challenges of cloud computing in education," https://www.buchanan.com/benefits-cloud-computing-education/

[15] "12 Ways cloud computing is transforming education," https://www.dincloud.com/blog/how-cloud-computing-transforming-in-education-sector

[16] A. M. Mansuri, M. Verma, and P. Laxkar, "Benefit of Cloud Computing for Educational Institutions and Online Marketing," *Information Security and Computer Fraud*, vol. 2, no. 1, 2014, pp. 5-9.

[17] B. X. Hien, "13 Advantages of cloud computing to boost your business," January 2023, https://biplus.com.vn/advantages-of-cloud-computing/

[18] "Cloud computing in education – Benefits, challenges and future," February 2022, https://www.rapyder.com/blogs/cloud-computing-in-education-benefits-challenges-and-future/

[19] "Cloud computing," https://www.tesu.edu/ast/programs/bs/cloud-computing?gclid=EAIaIQobChMI79Ldn-2k_wIVrnxMCh3mngotEAAYAiAAEgI_G_D_BwE&gclsrc=aw.ds

[20] "Online Master's in cloud computing management," https://onlinecybersecurity.seas.gwu.edu/online-masters-cloud-computing/?ace_campaign=google_search&cid=1985&.source=google&.medium=cpc&.campaign={campaign}&.term=cloud%20computing%20masters%20degree%20online&.content=468148979277&.device=c&.campaign_id=10747746136&.adgroup_id=1087313123348&.target_id=kwd-962991449749&.matchtype=b&.network=g&.loc_physical=9012004&.loc_interest=&.feeditemid=&.target=&.placement=&trkid=V3ADW379364_1087313123348_kwd-962991449749__468148979277_g_c__&gad=1&gclid=EAIaIQobChMI79Ldn-2k_wIVrnxMCh3mngotEAAYBCAAEgLLc_D_BwE

[21] "The growth in the use of the cloud in UK education," https://www.safedatastorage.co.uk/blog/the-growth-in-the-use-of-the-cloud-in-uk-education

[22] H. Yabin, "China launches national cloud learning platform as teaching goes online amid epidemic," February 2020, https://news.cgtn.com/news/2020-02-19/China-launches-national-cloud-learning-platform-for-online-education-Ods9XruOR2/index.html

[23] "How the Indian education sector is embracing cloud computing," https://www.esds.co.in/blog/how-the-indian-education-sector-is-embracing-cloud-computing/#:~:text=With%20the%20education%20sector%20becoming,grow%20to%2026%25%20by%202021.

[24] "Here are the reasons why we need cloud computing in schools in Nigeria," https://edufirst.ng/education-in-nigeria/the-importance-of-cloud-computing-in-education/

[25] M. Despotovi-Zraki, *Handbook of Research on High Performance and Cloud Computing in Scientific Research and Education*. IGI Global, 2014.

[26] G. C. Delta, *Prospects of Cloud Computing in Education and e-Governance: An Analytical Study*. LAP LAMBERT Academic Publishing, 2012.

[27] D. Srivastava, *Cloud Computing in Indian Education*. BlueRose Publishers, 2020

[28] L. Chao, *Cloud Computing for Teaching and Learning: Strategies for Design and Implementation*. Information Science Reference, 2012.

[29] K. C. Koutsopoulos, K. Doukas, and Y. Kotsanis, *Handbook of Research on Educational Design and Cloud Computing in Modern Classroom Settings*. IGI Global, 2017.

[30] G. C. Deka, *Prospects of Cloud Computing in Education and E-Governance*. LAP LAMBERT Academic Publishing, 2012.

[31] N. Kishor et al. (eds.), *Digitalization of Higher Education Using Cloud Computing: Implications, Risk, and Challenges*. Boca Raton, FL: CRC Press, 2021.

[32] A. Belić, M. Despotović-Zrakić, and V. Milutinović, *Handbook of Research on High Performance and Cloud Computing in Scientific Research and Education*. IGI Global, 2014.

[33] H. Yang et al. (eds.), *Technology for Education in Cloud*. Springer, 2013.

[34] L. Chao (ed.), *Handbook of Research on Cloud-Based STEM Education for Improved Learning Outcomes*. IGI Global, 2016.

[35] N. Cavus and M. R. Munyavi, *Adoption of Cloud Computing in Higher Education*. LAP LAMBERT Academic Publishing, 2016.

[36] E. S. C. Rodríguez et al. (eds.), *Workshop on Learning Technology for Education in Cloud (LTEC'12)*. Springer, 2012.

[37] R. N. Katz, *The Tower and the Cloud: Higher Education in the Age of Cloud Computing*. EDUCAUSE, 2010.

[38] D. Srivastava, *Cloud Computing in Indian Education System: Step-up Guide*. Kindle Edition, 2019.

[39] P. Korzeniowski, *Profiles of the Use of Cloud Computing in Higher Education*. Primary Research Group, 2013.

[40] T. Erl, R. Puttini, and Z. Mahmood, *Cloud Computing: Concepts, Technology & Architecture*. Pearson, 2013.

[41] P. M. Parker, *The 2023-2028 Outlook for Cloud Computing in Education in Japan*. ICON Group International, 2022.

[42] P. M. Parker, *The 2023 Report on Cloud Computing in Education: World Market Segmentation by City*. ICON Group International, 2022.

CHAPTER 5

SOFT COMPUTING IN EDUCATION

"The purpose of computing is insight, not numbers."
—Richard W. Humming

5.1 INTRODUCTION

Education is a process where teachers give systematic instructions while students receive them. Traditional educational systems are known to be inflexible but are now changing to adapt to the technological advancements of today's world. Therefore, efforts have been made to evolve the educational system to the requirements and needs of students in the 21st century. One key technology that is poised to transform education is soft computing. The use of computers and soft computing techniques has influenced a revolution in the quality of education in the past few decades. They are powerful tools for building learning, education, or training materials that provide a good learning experience for the students. However, effectively integrating these tools requires properly handling their variables, which contain imprecision and uncertainties.

An educational process is a continuous improvement of the knowledge and skills of students. There are four types of activities related to scientific advancement through education: Teaching, Research, Transfer, and Dissemination, as illustrated in Figure 5.1 [1]. A significant amount of money is spent on technology (computers, software, Internet, mobile devices, etc.) by the government, schools, and families to improve the quality of education. Technology helps both students and teachers to interact and collaborate efficiently. There are two ways by which technology may be used for educational purposes: classroom use in schools and home use by students [2]. To keep up with the technological trend and be more competitive, several universities worldwide have started offering courses on artificial intelligence (AI) and soft computing (SC) since these techniques are applied in different areas of our lives to solve real-life problems. Education in soft computing is a means for promoting science and innovation in a changing society [3].

This chapter is a primer on the applications of soft computing in education. It begins by providing an overview of soft computing. It presents some applications of SC in education. It highlights some benefits and challenges of SC in education. It covers the use of SC in education around the world. The last section concludes with comments.

5.2 OVERVIEW OF SOFT COMPUTING

Technologies have been an essential part of human progress. They have become intrinsic to the evolution of education in the 21st century. Soft computing is markedly impacting the education sector. In fact, soft computing is poised to make revolutionary changes in the field of education to facilitate teaching, research, learning, or decision-making. It is revolutionizing schools and classrooms and making the educator's job much easier. As a result, it has penetrated elementary schools, high schools, and higher institutions and is expected to take center stage in global education. It is the future of education.

Figure 5.1 Four types of activities related to the scientific advancement through education [1].

Soft computing (SC) is a newly emerging multidisciplinary field. The principal premise of soft computing (SC) is that we live in an imprecise and uncertain world. Soft computing refers to using "inexact" or approximate solutions to computationally hard tasks. The role model for soft computing is the human mind. As shown in Figure 5.2 [4], SC differs from traditional (hard) computing in that it tolerates imprecision, uncertainty, and approximation. It deals with partial truth to generate practical, low-cost (in space and time complexity), low-precision (approximate), and good solutions [5].

The term "soft computing" was coined in 1991 by Professor Lofti A. Zadeh of the University of California, Berkeley. Since then, the area has experienced rapid development. Soft Computing became a discipline within Computer Science in the early 1990s. The terms "machine intelligence" and "computational intelligence" have been used to have close meanings as soft computing. As shown in Figure 5.3 [6], soft computing is a consortium of techniques, including artificial neural networks (ANNs), evolutionary computation (EC), genetic algorithms (GAs), machine learning (ML), fuzzy logic (FL), cellular automata (CA), chaos theory (CT), swarm intelligence (SI), probabilistic reasoning (PR), support vector machines (SVMs), and their hybrids [7]. These techniques provide information processing capabilities to solve complex practical problems.

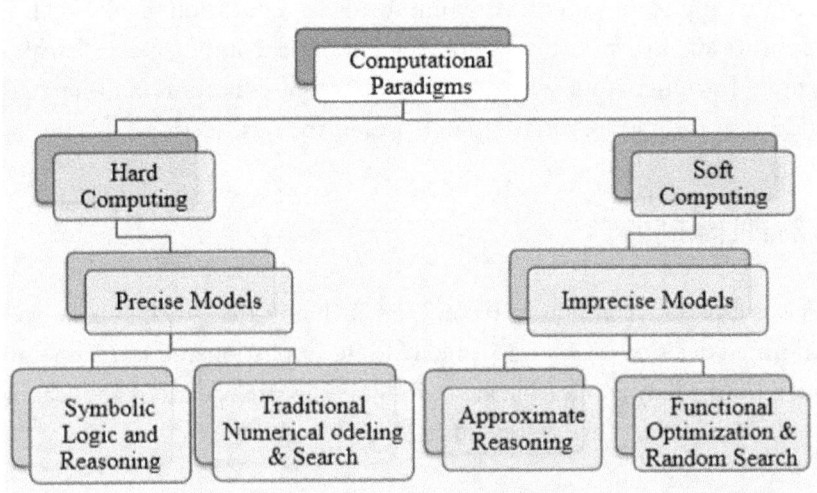

Figure 5.2 Hard and soft computing [4].

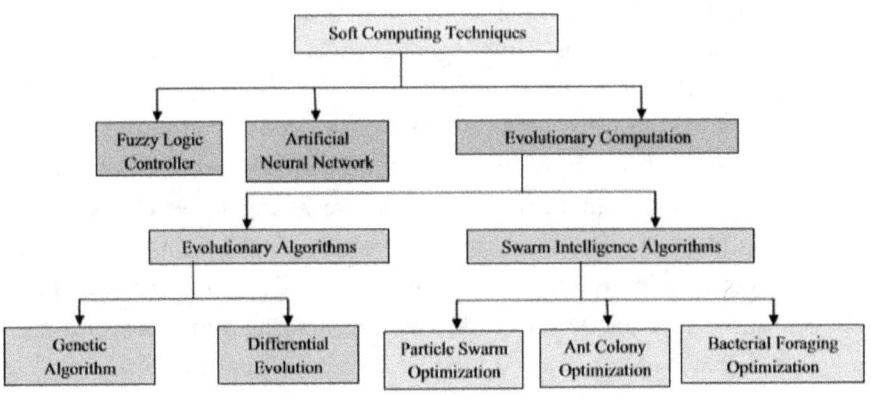

Figure 5.3 Principal constituents of soft computing [6].

SC technology in education allows a degree of flexibility and customization that was never possible. This feature is useful for both students and educators alike. Early exposure of the digital natives to the applications of soft computing will fundamentally change the way they learn, behave, and operate. SC is expected to have a significant impact on higher education. Hence, SC promises a far-reaching application at all levels of education.

Various applications of soft computing in education exist, such as applications in education management, e-learning, smart learning, remote learning, student evaluation, quality of education, and language education—these are discussed in detail in the next section.

5.3 APPLICATIONS

The use of soft computing techniques in many fields helps make well-informed decisions easily and quickly [8,9]. Education and learning stand out among many application areas of soft computing. Various applications of SC in education are presented as follows.

- *Education Management:* This is an area that involves the administration of education and academics. Since a classroom is a place where the future foundation of any child is developed, issues related to classroom management are important. Effective classroom management is the effective and wise usage of resources to attain the consummate goal of the teaching-learning process.

    Technology helps both students and teachers interact and collaborate more efficiently. Many SC techniques have been employed in education management, such as forecasting student enrolment, student and faculty performance evaluation, forecasting student grade point average, etc. SC techniques like neural networks are used to evaluate the student course grading and evaluation and fuzzy logic for efficient learning and performance [10].

    Along with the basic equipment, the following things provide a conducive classroom scenario [11]:

    ➢ Introducing of Multimedia Centre for constant support.

> The classroom should be equipped with LED panels for using 3D animation graphics to provide students the real-world scenarios.

> Digital library facilities should be provided to the students.

> E-games can assist students in enhancing the capability of critical thinking and learning capabilities.

> Soft computing should be assembled with a classroom management process, and evaluation of them should be done with the help of this software.

> School campus should be upgraded to a Wi-Fi campus to avail those facilities.

- *E-Learning:* E-Learning (also referred to as web-based education, computer-based training, online learning, or e-teaching) is essentially an electronic teaching strategy in which guidelines are created or configured to facilitate student learning and then distributed to targeted recipients by smart devices. It is a new concept for education where large amounts of information describing the continuum of teaching-learning interactions are endlessly generated. It has experienced rapid growth, mainly in higher education and training. E-Learning can be categorized in two ways: teacher-based learning called synchronous e-Learning, and self-based asynchronous e-learning is a form of individual research. E-Learning course offerings are now available, and many new e-Learning platforms have been developed and implemented with varying degrees of success. The educational community believes that half of the world's higher education courses will soon be delivered through e-Learning. There is the basic role of e-tutors and e-trainers in guaranteeing educational quality. Using soft computing techniques, knowledge can be extracted from the data produced and stored by e-Learning systems, allowing the classification, analysis, and generalization of the extracted knowledge. The educational community is divided as to the role of e-learning in the future. It was predicted that by 2019 half of the world's higher education courses will be delivered through e-Learning [12]. Figure 5.4 shows students applying e-textiles and soft computing in education [13].

Figure 5.4 Students applying e-textiles and soft computing in education [13].

- *Smart Learning:* Smart education is an implementation of the Internet of things (IoT) in higher education. This practice denotes a new way of interaction between the students and the teachers to generate a smart-based academic environment. Smart learning (S-learning) is an advanced form of education. It focuses on the content of learners based on advanced computing technologies. The overall structure of a smart learning environment is shown in Figure 5.5 [14]. Mobile devices such as laptops, personal digital assistants, tablet personal computers (PCs), cell phones, and e-book readers have become learning tools, especially for digital natives. This feature has led to the close integration of mobile devices and the curriculum. Mobile devices are expected to encourage innovation in education, communication, and cooperative skills [15].

- *Remote Learning:* Recent developments in remote learning offer increasing possibilities for improving learning processes in education. A powerful social impact of remote learning is observed as a result of globalization, international standardization, and rising requirements of teaching qualifications. A remote distribution of resources changes the structure, strategy, and performance of learning processes. Some advantages of remote learning include (1) Flexible freedom of choice of disciplines, programs, and courses that are offered in learning cyberspace. (2) Possibilities to use the most advanced achievements in every field of consideration. (3) Convenience with respect to scheduling of learning preferences, personal user choice, individual mental abilities, and studying time. (4) Continuous control of learning levels using the best virtual Internet controllable mentors. Soft computing decisions may be successfully integrated with existing mobile agents [16].

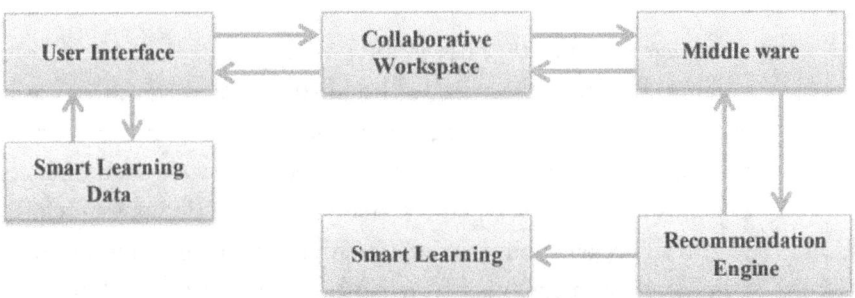

Figure 5.5 The overall structure of a smart learning environment [14].

- *Student Evaluation:* To maintain quality in higher education, there is a need to do students' regular assessments. Many institutions have used traditional grading methods to evaluate student academic performance for several decades. Soft computing can help evaluate students in a classroom in a very efficient manner. It can also help the teachers do nonacademic tasks such as scheduling, preparing, grading, etc. The Fuzzy Logic (FL) approach is a new idea for students' academic performance evaluation in the educational field. The evaluation of students' performance using fuzzy techniques is adapted for evaluation based on obtained numerical scores in the assessment. FL, with a fuzzy expert system, gives the interesting results for evaluation based on qualitative and quantitative facts or data to measure students' performance. The results of FL are more realistic than the traditional method of grading [17].

- *Quality of Education:* This has awakened the interest of investigators worldwide because they can answer education problems. Researchers of education believe that the expectations and needs of human beings depend on factors like the quality of curricula for which they are prepared, the infrastructure of the country in education, the academic environment which is developed, the faculty and the relationship between teachers and students, etc. Fuzzy logic can be used to measure the quality of education by using quantitative and qualitative values. The major advantage of fuzzy logic is that one can handle an unlimited number of indicators expressed in any unit of measurement [18].

- *Language Education:* This is an important application of soft computing. From the point of linguistic perspective, three basic approaches of corpus linguistics (bottom-up, top-down, and mixed) are regarded as quality keepers for the process of automated system designs. It is expedient that the system designers include features that overcome major classroom challenges like teacher-commenting mechanisms, reliable scoring systems, language education and research. Such systems can also enhance the quality of intelligent systems used for language education, and research if used appropriately. They can integrate lexical approach with corpus linguistics to enrich students working the lexicon [19].

5.4 BENEFITS

Soft computing is a science of thinking and reasoning that helps to deal with complex systems. It is a newly emerging computing method that combines various knowledge, technology, and methods to set up an intelligent or automated system to solve complex problems under uncertain and inaccurate circumstances. It often accompanies various techniques (such as fuzzy logic, machine learning, and artificial neural networks) to apply to a broad range of disciplines. It does not require any mathematical modeling to solve any problem.

The main aim of soft computing is to display the psychological conduct of the human brain and develop intelligent machines that will solve real-world problems. For example, soft computing can be used to design intelligent systems relevant to language education. Like a human brain, to solve complex problems, SC uses multiple techniques simultaneously in the computation in a harmonious manner [20]. It is amazing to note that machines can now think and function like humans. For example, it has become possible to make computers read text, hear speech, interpret it, and identify some important parts. Soft computing-based systems can manage extremely large data to extract insights for decision-making process. SC techniques are useful in identifying hidden patterns in data and doing the classification for making intelligent decisions.

In the field of education, soft computing techniques are used to improve the performance of students in academics. Students' evaluation systems can be improved by using soft computing. Delivering techniques of lessons can also be assessed with soft computing. Intelligent systems consistent with Natural Language Processing (NLP) can enhance the quality of teaching, meet the urgent needs of language students, and provide automated tutoring systems to assist the academic community [19].

5.5 CHALLENGES

Soft computing gives an approximate output value. One of the major challenges to implementing effective mobile learning programs is the insufficient preparation of the teachers. This gap requires the professional development of teachers before the adaptation to mobile-device-based teaching. Soft computing needs well-established Internet services and a lot of funds to run the program successfully. Without government assistance, it is quite impossible for educational organizations to set up and maintain the infrastructure. Exerting the maximum effect of information technology in the educational field requires reconciling connection among technology components, educational missions, and users (teachers and students). The machine cannot be too precise to remove humans and their assumptions. There are also concerns about privacy, protection, and ethical practices of using intelligent systems.

5.6 SOFT COMPUTING IN EDUCATION WORLDWIDE

The use of technology is ubiquitous in the educational system in most developed countries. A significant amount of money is spent on technology by the government with the hope of improving educational outcomes. Although school children have high access to home computers and Internet connections, access is not evenly distributed across the nations. Soft computing can be used for fixing real international troubles that entail uncertainty, approximation, and imprecision. We consider how some nations use soft computing in education.

- *United States*: The need for technology in education and research has become increasingly popular. Motivated by this need, many educational researchers have developed automated tutoring systems to assist the academic community. One typical example is the research-writing tutor developed by Iowa state university faculty. All instructional classrooms in US public schools have computers with Internet access. An increasing number of schools are providing one-to-one laptops, or tablets to each student and often allowing the students to take the computer home [2]. Most learning activities using mobile devices have been controlled by the teacher. Different teaching methods did not designate or implement specific teaching scenarios for students to follow. Students use mobile devices for self-paced learning. Another main accomplishment is the development of soft computing-based data summarization systems for NLP tasks [19].

- *Europe:* The European Centre for Soft Computing is involved in different educational activities. It has been involved since its creation in different activities devoted to promoting SC. The center believes that education in soft computing is a means of promoting science and innovation in a changing society. The center broadened its educational offer by launching dissemination activities [1].

- *United Kingdom:* The current debate on computing in UK schools is based on a specific issue: what should form the basis of a modern computing education? Currently, the mandatory educational component of computing (from years 11 to 16) is taught as Information and Communication Technologies (ICT), which sees computing as a tool that drives society. Digital Literacy is an important topic taught well in the UK. Computing is a young discipline, and we are still exploring its core generative problems, which are needed to inspire a new generation of thinkers and doers. Without core generative problems, a student cannot understand the real-world relevance of what they are taught and the sustainability of computing [20].

- *India:* In India, higher education has become competitive. The government and higher education organizations focus on quality improvement and change in the traditional evaluation methods. Due to the keen competition among public and private universities, evaluation standards are different. Traditional methods for student evaluation have limitations because they are based on absolute grading and crisp boundaries. Soft computing helps to evaluate students in a classroom scenario in a very effective way. The fuzzy logic approach is used to analyze multicriteria-based student performance evaluation methods. Fuzzy logic is a soft computing approach. It essentially uses natural language, which does not contain only 0 and 1 but has multi-valued logic, which contains and works with approximate reasoning. The fuzzy logic technique gives the more realistic, suitable, and reliable results [17]. Figure 5.6 shows the general architecture of the fuzzy logic system [22].

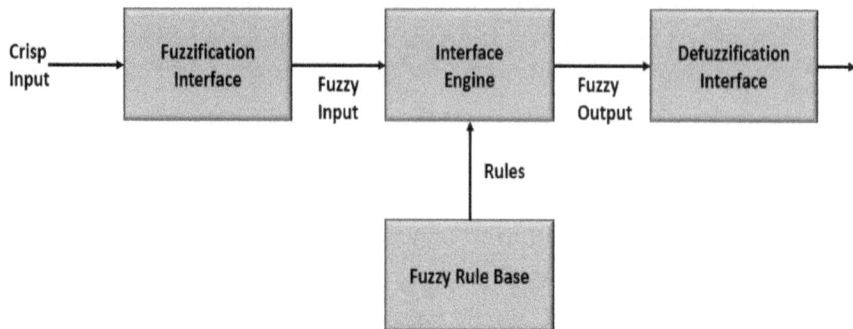

Figure 5.6 The general architecture of fuzzy logic system [22].

- *China:* The economic contribution rate of education (ECRE) is the increase in GDP induced by a one-unit investment in education. It identifies the effect of education on economic growth. The amount of ECRE is attained as the remainder after subtracting the total number of simple from the aggregate social work. Based on the level of science (S) and technology (T) progress, 31 provinces in China could be classified into three clusters. The first cluster (Developed S & T) has an ECRE of 11.60% and contains two provinces; the second cluster (developing S & T) has an ECRE of 8.84% and contains 11 provinces; the third cluster (underdeveloped S & T) has an ECRE of 1.49% and contains 18 provinces. The traditional computing methods follow along the education–human capital–economic growth chain, but they ignore education's long-term and lagging effect on economic growth. In contrast to traditional computing, soft computing is open-minded toward imprecision, vulnerability, incomplete truth, and estimation. Soft computing is a newly developed computing method that combines various knowledge, technology, and methods to set up an intelligent system for solving complicated problems. Like human, SC uses multiple techniques simultaneously in the computation in a harmonious manner [20].

- *Pakistan:* Due to the need to effectively manage education and educational institutions, several universities worldwide including countries such as Pakistan, have started and MBA education management as well as Master of Education Management programs. Artificial intelligence (AI) and soft computing (SC) techniques are applied to solve real-life problems in different areas. The major advantage of using these techniques is to achieve human decision-making ability to handle physical world situations [6].

- *Kenya:* Education and research are key sectors targeted by Kenya's Vision 2030 blueprint, which closely relates to the Millennium Development Goals (MDGs). Science, Technology, and Innovation constitute the key aspect of Vision 2030 because of the role they play in attaining other pillars of the vision. In Kenya, researchers work in isolation, while education suffers from classroom shortages, few qualified teachers, and the absence of appropriate teaching aids. With e-learning, education can be delivered and received anywhere and anytime. Students will benefit greatly from e-Learning because it will address the dwindling instructors-student ratios and enable collaboration between researchers at different universities and research institutes [23].

5.7 CONCLUSION

The pervasiveness of the Internet has enabled online distance education to become far more mainstream than it used to be, and that has happened in a surprisingly short time.

Education stands out among many application areas of soft computing. Soft Computing does not require strict mathematical definitions and distinctions for the system components. Soft computing is one of the influential technologies which have attracted researchers in the education field worldwide because it offers new ways of learning and teaching.

Soft computing has emerged as the only way to detect, analyze, and solve real-world problems with utmost excellence. Some institutions are now offering soft computing in their curriculum. With the ever-increasing integration of technology in all aspects of life, efforts should be made to teach the essence of computing knowledge to the general public. The essence of computer science (computing fundamentals, such as algorithmic thinking, tool use, coding skills, and data storage) should also be taught to students in other disciplines. Such knowledge is necessary to be successful and thrive in the workforce of the 21st century. It will help them collaborate more easily [24]. More information about soft computing in education can be found in the books in [25-32] and the following related journals:

- *Computers & Education*
- *Applied Soft Computing*
- *Computer Applications in Engineering Education*
- *International Journal of Educational Technology in Higher Education*
- *International Journal of Instructional Technology and Educational Studies*

REFERENCES

[1] L. Magdalena, "Soft computing for students and for society," *IEEE Computational Intelligence Magazine*, February 2009, pp. 47-50.

[2] G. Bulman and R. W. Fairlie, "Technology and education: Computers, software, and the Internet," Working Paper 22237, http://www.nber.org/papers/w22237

[3] M. N. O. Sadiku, U. C. Chukwu, A. Ajayi-Majebi, S. M. Musa, "Soft computing in education: A primer," *International Journal of Trend in Scientific Research and Development*, vol. 6, no. 2, January-February 2022, pp. 536-540.

[4] "Chapter 1: Introduction," Unknown Source.

[5] "Soft computing," *Wikipedia,* the free encyclopedia https://en.wikipedia.org/wiki/Soft_computing

[6] M. Balamurugan, S. K. Sahooa, and S. Sukcha,"Application of soft computing methods for grid connected PV system: A technological and

status review," *Renewable and Sustainable Energy Reviews*, vol. 17, 2017, pp. 1493-1508

[7] M. Ko, A. Tiwari, and J. Mehnen, "A review of soft computing applications in supply chain management," *Applied Soft Computing*, vol. 10, 2010, pp. 661-674.

[8] S. B. Gupta and Shivani, "A review of soft computing techniques and applications," *International Journal of Engineering Research & Technology*, vol. 9, no. 5, March 2021.

[9] K. Taylor, "What is soft computing?" https://www.hitechnectar.com/blogs/applications-soft-computing/

[10] M. Khan et al., "Soft computing applications in education management – A review," *Proceedings of the IEEE International Conference on Innovative Research and Development*, Bangkok Thailand May 2018.

[11] S. Pal, S. Bhattachary, and P. Sarkar, "Scope for applications management in India of soft computing in effective classroom," *International Journal of Instructional Technology and Educational Studies*, vol. 3, no. 1, January 2022, pp. 16-25.

[12] F. A. C. Espinoza, "A soft computing decision support framework for e-learning," *Doctoral Dissertation*, Universitat Politècnica de Catalunya – BarcelonaTech, https://upcommons.upc.edu/bitstream/handle/2117/120998/TFACE1de1.pdf;sequence=1

[13] V. Borsotti, "E-textiles and soft computing in education," http://www.valeriaborsotti.com/etextiles-and-soft-computing-in-education

[14] F. Khan and S. R. Alotaibi, " A novel architecture for smart learning based on soft computing," *International Transaction Journal of Engineering, Management, & Applied Sciences & Technologies*, vol. 2, no. 6, 2021, pp. 1-10.

[15] Y.T. Sung, K. E. Chang, and T. C. Liu, "The effects of integrating mobile devices with teaching and learning on students' learning performance: A

meta-analysis and research synthesis," *Computers & Education,* vol. 94, March 2016, pp. 252-275.

[16] D. V. Lakov and M. V. Vassileva, "Decision making soft computing agents," *International Journal of Systems Science,* vol. 36, no. 14, 2005, pp. 921-930.

[17] O. K. Chaudhari et al, "Soft computing model for students' evaluation in educational institute," *Journal of Physics: Conference Series,* 2021.

[18] S. Valdés-Pasarón, B. Y. Márquez, and J. M. Ocegueda-Hernández, "The use of soft computing for measuring the quality of education," *International Journal on New Computer Architectures and Their Applications,* vol. 1, no. 2, 2011, pp. 282-291.

[19] O. A. Eshbayev, A. X. Maxmudov, and R. U. Urokovich Rozikov, "An overview of a state of the art on developing soft computing-based language education and research systems: A survey of engineering English students in Uzbekistan," *Proceedings of the 5th International Conference on Future Networks & Distributed Systems,* Dubai, United Arab Emirates, December 2021.

[20] K. Zhu, S. Yu, and F. Diao, "Soft computing applications to estimate the quantitative contribution of education on economic growth," *Applied Mathematics and Computation,* vol. 187, 2007, pp. 1038–1055.

[21] J. G. Hall, "Computing education that doesn't compute," July 2012, https://onlinelibrary.wiley.com/doi/full/10.1111/j.1468-0394.2012.00628.x

[22] D. Ibrahim, "An overview of soft computing," *Procedia Computer Science,* vol. 102, 2016, pp. 34-38.

[23] D. Waga, E. Makori, and K. Rabah, "Utilization of cloud computing in education and research to the attainment of millennium development goals and Vision 2030 in Kenya," *Universal Journal of Educational Research,* vol. 2, no. 2, 2014, pp. 193-199.

[24] "CRA Report on innovative approaches to computing education," December 2015, https://computinged.wordpress.com/2015/12/21/cra-report-on-innovative-approaches-to-computing-education/

[25] S. Borah and R. Panigrahi (eds.), *Applied Soft Computing: Techniques and Applications*. Apple Academic Press, 2022.

[26] P. Debnath and S. A. Mohiuddine (eds.), *Soft Computing Techniques in Engineering, Health, Mathematical and Social Sciences*. Boca Raton, FL: CRC Press, 2021.

[27] A. Xie and X. Huang (eds.), *Advances in Computer Science and Education (Advances in Intelligent and Soft Computing*. Springer, 2012.

[28] D. K. Chaturvedi, *Soft Computing: Techniques and its Applications in Electrical Engineering*. Springer, 2008.

[29] N. Dey et al., *Soft Computing Based Medical Image Analysis*. Elsevier, 2018.

[30] V. Kecman, *Learning and Soft Computing: Support Vector Machines, Neural Networks, and Fuzzy Logic Models*. A Bradford Book, 2001.

[31] D. Aleksendric and P. Carlone, *Soft Computing in the Design and Manufacturing of Composite Materials: Applications to Brake Friction and Thermoset Matrix Composites*. Woodhead Publishing, 2015

[32] A. Konar, *Artificial Intelligence and Soft Computing: Behavioral and Cognitive Modeling of the Human Brain*. Boca Raton, FL: CRC Press, 2018.

CHAPTER 6

BIG DATA IN EDUCATION

"Big data is at the foundation of all of the megatrends that are happening today, from social to mobile to the cloud to gaming."
—Chris Lynch

6.1 INTRODUCTION

The world is changing rapidly due to the emergence of innovative technologies.. Individuals and organizations use a large number of technological devices. An enormous amount of data is produced through these devices, making our lives revolve around huge data sets.. Data generation has increased drastically with the advent of various social media platforms and multinational companies. There has been a rapid emergence of technology in response to the huge amounts of data generated. With the world witnessing a digital revolution, data is now the fuel that drives forward the 21st century.

Data is generated in vast amounts from every sector, be it sports, industry, government, healthcare, banking, social media, or education. Over the years, big data and analytics have slowly crept into the education system. Online courses are becoming explicit data platforms. The Massive open online courses (MOOC) generate large amounts of data. This educational data can now be stored, analyzed, and shared. Although skeptics do not see the point, big data in education has become a hot topic. Big data refers to the high volume of varied information our societies produce daily. The education industry has always had the capacity to produce a lot of data, perhaps more than any other industry. The amount of data is so vast that processing it with conventional means is difficult. Big data influences how decisions are made everywhere, and education is no exception [1].

Education systems produce a huge amount of data about students and schools. This information includes data such as registration, attendance, grades, disciplinary records, socioeconomic background, and instruction times. With thousands of students participating in a MOOC, big data will allow universities to find the best students from worldwide. The main goal of big data in the educational sector is to improve student performance. Better students are beneficial to society, organizations, and the business community. Big data can be used to determine how each student learns. This approach can reduce dropout rates for the benefit of the student and society [2].

This chapter briefly introduces how big data is used in education. It begins by explaining the characteristics of big data. It provides some applications of big data in education. It highlights the benefits and challenges of big data. It covers how big data is applied in some nations. It concludes with some comments.

6.2 CHARACTERISTICS OF BIG DATA

Big data refers to massive data that the conventional database system cannot process. While most traditional data sources are structured, big data may be structured, semi-structured, or unstructured. BD is often characterized by the five "Vs": volume, velocity, variety, veracity, and value [3] as illustrated in Figure 6.1 [4].

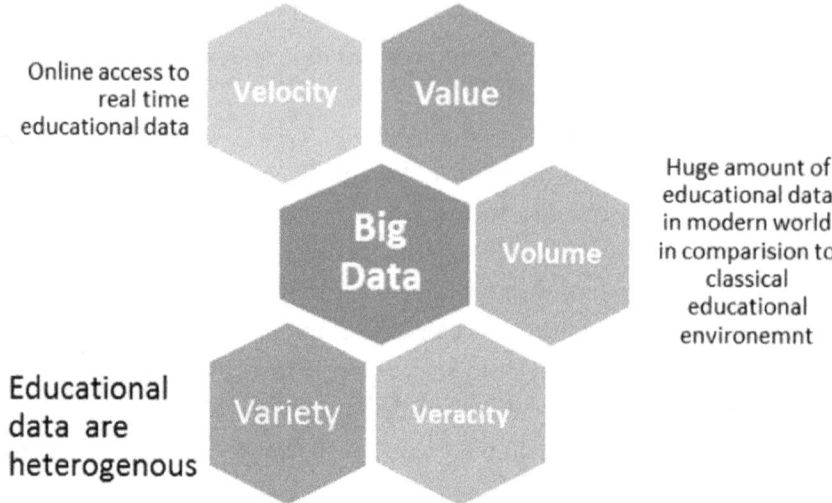

Figure 6.1 Five V's of big data [4].

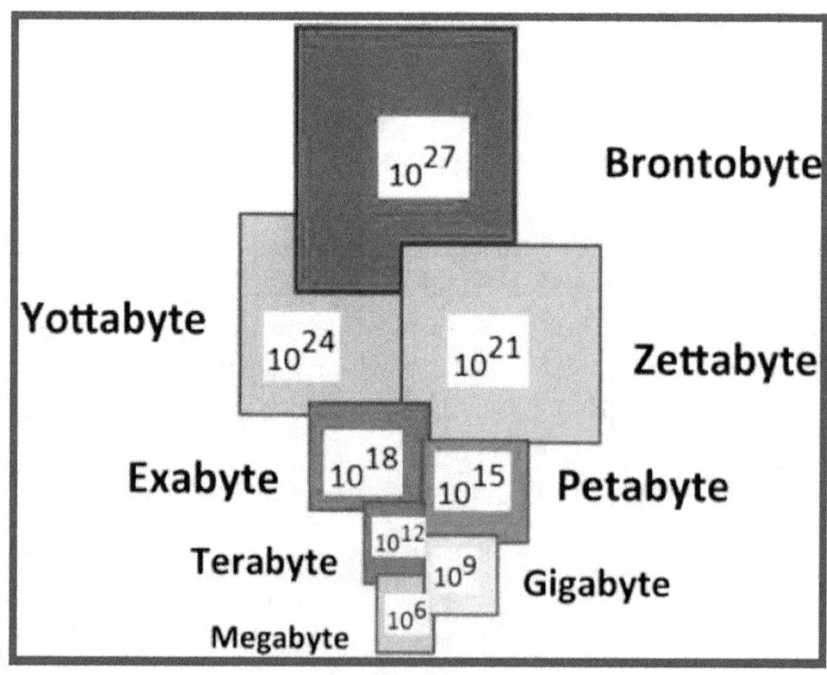

Figure 6.2 Data units in bytes [5].

- *Volume*: This refers to the size of the data generated inside and outside organizations and is increasing annually. Some regard big data as data over one petabyte in volume. The volume of data available today is measured in zettabytes (ZB), which is equal to 1 trillion gigabytes (GB). The units of data in terms of bytes are shown in Figure 6.2 [5].

- *Velocity*: This depicts the unprecedented speed at which data are generated by Internet users, mobile users, social media, etc. Data are generated and processed in a fast way to extract useful, relevant information. Real-time information makes it possible for an institution to be much more agile than its competitors.

- *Variety*: This refers to the data types since big data may originate from heterogeneous sources and is in different formats (e.g., videos, images, audio, text, logs). BD comprises of structured, semi-structured, or unstructured data. Mobile phones, e-commerce, GPS, and social media generate torrents of data daily.

- *Veracity*: By this, we mean the truthfulness of data, i.e., whether the data comes from a reputable, trustworthy, authentic, and accountable source. It suggests the inconsistency in the quality of different sources of big data. The data may be less than 100% correct.

- *Value*: This is the most important aspect of the big data. It is the desired outcome of big data processing. It refers to the process of discovering hidden values from large datasets. It denotes the value derived from the analysis of the existing data. If one cannot extract some business or educational value from the data, there is no use managing and storing it.

On this basis, small data can be regarded as having low volume, velocity, variety, veracity, and value. Big data analytic techniques are used in analyzing BD. They include data mining, data analytics, learning analytics web dashboards, web mining, machine learning, social network analysis, and visualization methods [6].

6.3 APPLICATIONS

The availability of huge amounts of data in the education system has stimulated the application of big data in education. The big data concept can be applied in various educational aspects such as recruitment, admission, financial planning, student performance, feedback, monitoring, and donor tracking. Some of these applications are shown in Figure 6.3 and explained as follows [7].

- *Personalized Learning*: This has become the most notable application of big data in education. Since students have different personalities, they learn differently. Personalized learning customizes one's learning to maximize their learning potential. Big data allows for customization at educational institutions. Algorithms make it possible to track and assess each student. Designers can personalize courses by adjusting learners' individual needs. Students at different levels can work online and by themselves through customized learning programs.

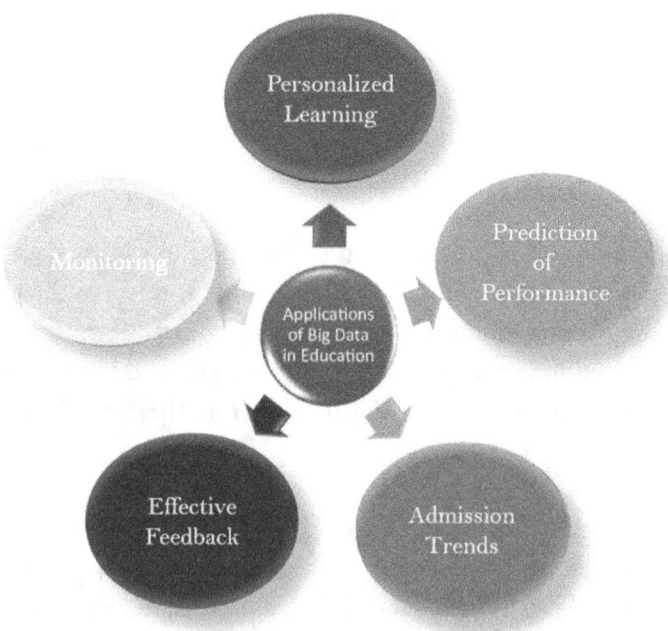

Figure 6.3 Some applications of big data in education.

- *Prediction of Performance*: The goal of predicting students' performance is to know how well a student will perform on a given learning task. Big data can be used to predict students' performance, particularly for course grades and standardized testing scores. The prediction may help to improve student retention, assessment outcomes, and satisfaction. The better we understand students through their performance, the better accomplishment they can achieve [8].

- *Admission Trends*: Big data can be used for admission. Big data can be used to predict new students by developing interest patterns of already admitted students. Admission committees use algorithms that analyze big data to guide admission decisions. Such admission decisions will be fairer than traditional decision-making [9].

- *Effective Feedback*: Big data can provide a more intelligent and effective feedback loop, where students receive information in a short time in response to their input.

- *Monitoring:* In an education system, there are multiple creators and users of information relevant for monitoring. Data is being produced for monitoring purposes. Internationally standardized tests are currently used for international comparative monitoring at the school level. Big data monitoring of the achievement levels of learners can provide focused individual learning that maximizes the value-adding activity in learning [10].

Big data tools can potentially revolutionize education as the applications are endless. They could free the students and the educators up to do stuff that matters. The ability to handle and analyze massive data is becoming important in an online environment [11]. The ultimate goals of big data applications in education are personalized learning and adaptive learning.

6.4 BENEFITS

Big data has the potential to transform education at all levels. It is reshaping the way students think and learn. With the help of big data, educational institutions can effectively classify students' responses, results, and performances to use as reference points for evaluating big policy changes. Big data can also exacerbate existing social and educational inequalities. Here are some other ways that the education industry can benefit from big data analytics [12]:

1. *It helps you find answers to complex questions*: The benefits of big data lie in how you use it. With big data, you have the context clues necessary to determine the problem.

2. *It's accessible:* Since big data relies on a technological infrastructure to capture, store and manage information, it is much easier to find what you seek. Since data is available in one centralized location, you only need internet access to find what you need. Data is important for the administration of education systems. Giving students access to data can help them define their learning goals and strategies. It can help their *families make informed decisions and support their children.*

3. *It can save costs:* Proper resource allocation is important in higher education, and your data is the key to efficiency. An analytics program will automate a lot of this tedious work, and the luxury of digital information makes accessing data quick and easy, which can save you money in the long run.

4. *It's quick:* With all of your school's information available in one centralized location, you will save an incredible amount of time weeding through data to find one specific report or information about a particular student. Big data helps you make decisions quicker than ever before.

5. *It helps you adapt*: By identifying trends, you can develop new classes, teaching strategies, and other methods to give students what they need and want. You can adjust your course offerings accordingly to ensure you always offer your students the best options.

6. *It provides individualized learning*: People learn differently and at different rates. Some students are visual learners, while others are hands-on. Standardized tests are not the best way to judge students. A major benefit of big data in education is that it individualizes learning and improves teaching and student academic performance.

   Big data analysis enables educators to determine areas where students struggle or thrive and develop strategies to assist with personalized education.

7. *It tracks student activities:* Activities such as how long they take, what sources they use to prepare, what topics are ignored, and more can be tracked. Big data can also be used to track students' careers after graduation. It will also render them an invaluable service in choosing the right college and course of study.

Some of these benefits are shown in Figure 6.4 [13].

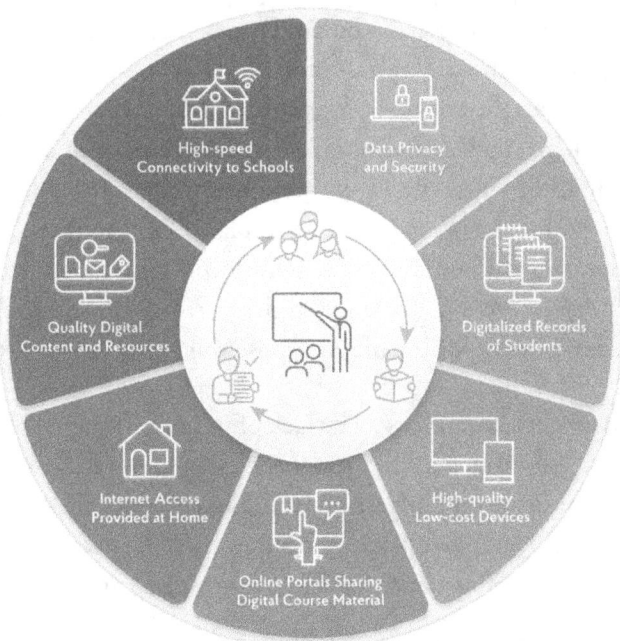

Figure 6.4 Some of the benefits of big data in education [13].

6.5 CHALLENGES

The big data era has just begun, and there are many challenges due to unanswered questions that must be addressed for its use and full adoption to be effective.

With online courses becoming increasingly popular today, competing with famous universities worldwide is very tough. Other challenges of big data in education are the following [14]:

1. *Unwillingness to Change:* Schools and universities need to change dramatically to benefit from big data. With new technologies introduced into classrooms, teachers have been slow to change how they teach, and academic institutions are still lagging in adopting big data. Not all educationists and administrators are ready for big data.

2. *Security and Privacy*: One of the most important problems is the challenge posed to privacy through the ability to collect, integrate, and analyze personal student data. Security for big data projects is not just about making information accessible. Violating of the confidentiality of working with such data can turn into serious problems, including fines from regulators, loss of customers, loss of market value, etc. Parents and privacy advocates are concerned that student information can be placed in unreliable hands, and such sensitive information may limit future opportunities for students. We must balance student privacy on the one hand and access to data for learning purposes on the other.

3. *Lack of Understanding*: The lack of understanding of how to work with big data may be a major challenge. When companies or institutions start migrating to digital products that use big data and their employees are not ready to work with such advanced solutions, implementation can be slowed down.

4. *Variety of Big Data Technologies:* One can use different data science solutions to implement big data. If one has never dealt with these before, it can be difficult for you to decide on the approach to implementing a big data system.

5. *Heavy Expenses*: When institutions implement complex big data systems, they need to be prepared for serious financial costs. These costs start from the development planning stage and end with maintenance and further modernization of systems, even if you implement free software.

6. *Lack of Expertise:* The demand for employees or staff specializing in big data exceeds the pool of existing specialists.

7. *Organizational Resistance:* Resistance to organizational change or organizational inertia is the ability of the academic community to resist innovations, which is expressed in actions aimed at maintaining the existing state of the enterprise or its separate system.

Some of these challenges are global and external to the education system. Some of them are displayed in Figure 6.5 [14].

6.6 GLOBAL USE OF BIG DATA IN EDUCATION

Big data is a state-of-the-art technique to collect, allocate, accomplish, and discover huge datasets. Big data and analytics have been powering the consumer giants in the global marketplace. It has recently gained the attention of academics and practitioners worldwide. Big data in education can play a central role in improving the financial and business operations systems of institutions. It is no surprise that institutions of higher learning expect positive outcomes from big data in education since they have been entrusted with the responsibility of educating children by shaping their skills, values, and knowledge. We now consider how big data is being applied in the education field.

Figure 6.5 Some of the challenges of big data [14].

- *United States:* Big data is a transformative tool for all aspects of education. It transforms how schools analyze information and make decisions in areas such as academic performance, faculty effectiveness, and technology efficiency. It is also transforming how administrators, professors, and students interact. It allows professors to create customized curricula through online resources, textbooks, e-books, and software programs. It also allows them to craft personalized lesson plans, identify areas where students struggle, understand the individual needs of students, predict learning outcomes, and develop strategies for personalized learning [15]. Although the US Department of Education was the first to release the education data mining, strong emotions have created a polarized debate surrounding student data use in the US.

- *United Kingdom*: Big data has the power to transform education and educational research. Online teaching can use BD to reform educational delivery and enhance learning in numerous ways. For example, big data analytics can help adapt and improve delivery by personalizing learners' experience and standardizing knowledge presentation. There are considerable opportunities for using BD in higher education. It is important that universities use BD to continue to deliver the very best learning environments for the good of society [16].

- *Europe:* Data has become a key asset for Europe's economies. However, big data has been more of a priority in the scientific, industrial, and public sectors than the education sector. European schools increasingly rely on vendors to collect, process, analyze, and make decisions based on huge student data through big data tools. Schools have come under increased pressure to rely on vendors of commercial technology in the so-called "EdTech" industry for the mining, collecting, processing, and analyzing of student data and even for applying data-driven decision-making processes. Student data may include basic academic and administrative information. It can range from online test scores to session times to records of where a student has touched while working on a problem [17]. A major challenge for education systems in Europe is to implement student tracking in ways that enable us to extract meaning from large datasets being generated through student activity; and convert this data into usable information for students, teachers, and governments.

- *China:* China has rapidly entered the era of big data with the rapid development of the Internet. Big data has significantly impacted finance, business, medical care, and other fields. Big Data China was recently launched as a new project aimed at bridging the gap between cutting-edge academic research on China and the Washington policy community. Chinese researchers pay more attention to the technology and application research of education big data. They explore the techniques of collecting, mining and analyzing educational big data [18].

- *India*: Education is crucial to forming the lives of individuals. It holds the ability to change and improve the lives of individuals. Today, data analytics and big data are popular expressions and core tools for each business ecosystem. Because of rising competition in the education sector, the Indian education system is constantly upgrading itself. Using big data systems, educators can evaluate student performance persistently and advance students as needs be. Leveraging analytics and big data in the Indian education sector can help rebuild academic processes to suit the prerequisite of modern learners. As more and more academic institutions begin harnessing the power of big data, the future of education in India will be bright [19].

6.7 CONCLUSION

Online learning tools have been used increasingly in education in recent times. This movement has resulted in an explosion of data, which can now be used to improve educational effectiveness. The age of big data will be that of continuous learning. As the data in the education system becomes larger, applying big data tools becomes necessary.

Big data has made a huge impact on the education system. It will inevitably impact education in a big way. It will dictate what we teach and how we teach it. Educators must understand the value of a data-driven approach to education. To remain relevant and competitive, every education organization must embrace big data in its vision and take full advantage of it. The future is bright for institutions willing to embrace big data analytics in their decision-making process. One should consult the books in [20-26] for more information about big data in education.

REFERENCES

[1] M. N. O. Sadiku, Y.P. Akhare, A. Ajayi-Majebi, and S. M. Musa, "Big data in education," *Journal of Scientific and Engineering Research*, vol. 7, no. 6, 2020, pp. 93-97.

[2] "Four ways big data will revolutionize education," https://datafloq.com/read/big-data-will-revolutionize-learning/206

[3] M. N. O. Sadiku, M. Tembely, and S.M. Musa, "Big data: An introduction for engineers," *Journal of Scientific and Engineering Research*, vol. 3, no. 2, 2016, pp. 106-108.

[4] J. T. Wassan, "Discovering big data modeling for educational world," *Procedia – Social and Behavioral Sciences*, vol. 176, 2015, pp. 642-649.

[5]. H. E. Pence and A. J. Williams, "Big data and chemical education," *Journal of Chemical Education*, vol. 93, 2016, pp. 504-508.

[6] I. Yaqoob et al., "Big data: From beginning to future," *International Journal of Information Management*, vol. 36, 2016, pp. 1231–1247.

[7] A. G. Picciano, "The evolution of big data and learning analytics in American higher education," *Journal of Asynchronous Learning Networks*, vol. 16, no. 3, June 2012, pp. 9-20.

[8] X. Yu and S. Wu, "Typical applications of big data in education." *Proceedings of the International Conference of Educational Innovation Through Technology*, 2015, pp. 103-106.

[9] T. H. B. Shahar, "Educational justice and big data," *Theory and Research in Education*, vol. 15, no. 3, 2017, pp. 306-320.

[10] B. Berendt et al., "Big data for monitoring educational systems," 2017, https://oro.open.ac.uk/50930/1/Big%20data%20EU.pdf

[11] P. Schwerdtle, "Big data in nurse education," *Nurse Education Today*, vol. 51, 2017, pp. 114-116.

[12] E. Spear, "5 Big benefits of big data analytics in education," https://precisioncampus.com/blog/benefits-big-data-education/

[13] "Big data in education: How data science transforms," June 2020, https://nix-united.com/blog/how-big-data-is-transforming-the-education-pr/

[14] "12 Big data issues growing companies face," January 2022, https://nix-united.com/blog/12-big-data-issues-growing-companies-face/

[15] "Big data in education," https://online.maryville.edu/blog/big-data-in-education/#:~:text=The%20Benefits%20of%20Big%20Data,develop%20strategies%20for%20personalized%20learning.

[16] " Big data and education: What's the big idea?" September 2014, https://www.ucl.ac.uk/public-policy/sites/public-policy/files/migrated-files/big_data_briefing_final.pdf

[17] Y. H. Carmel, "Regulating 'big data education' in Europe: Lessons learned from the US," *Internet Policy Review*, vol. 5, no. 1, March 2016.

[18] C. Jiang et al., "The present of education big data research in China: Base on the bibliometric analysis and knowledge mapping," *Journal of Physics: Conference Series*, 2019.

[19] "The state of data science and big data education in India," February 2022, https://www.analyticsinsight.net/the-state-of-data-science-and-big-data-education-in-india/

[20] B. Williamson, *Big Data in Education: The Digital Future of Learning, Policy and Practice*. London, UK: Sage Publications, 2017.

[22] A. Azevedo et al. (eds.), *Advancing the Power of Learning Analytics and Big Data in Education*. IGI Global, 2021.

[23] B. K. Daniel, *Big Data and Learning Analytics in Higher Education: Current Theory and Practice.* Spinger, 2016.

[24] H. Y. Zheng and K. L. Webber (eds.), *Big Data on Campus: Data Analytics and Decision Making in Higher Education.* Johns Hopkins University Press, 2020.

[25] V. Mayer-Schonberger and K. Cukier, *Learning With Big Data: The Future of Education.* New York: Houghton Mifflin Harcourt Pub., 2014.

[26] T. Prodromou (ed.), *Big Data in Education: Pedagogy and Research.* Springer, 2021.

CHAPTER 7

EDUCATION 4.0

"If a man empties his purse into his head, no man can take it away from him. An investment in knowledge always pays the best interest."
—Benjamin Franklin

7.1 INTRODUCTION

Education is no longer the privilege of the few. The purpose of education is mainly to prepare us for tomorrow. As shown in Figure 7.1, how the purpose of education is achieved differs slightly depending on whether you take the view of society, the educator, or the parents [1]. Education is a complex process that demands the best from parents, teachers, and students.

	1.0	2.0	3.0
PARENTS	Care	Capability	Competitive
EDUCATORS	Impose	Imprint	Inspire
SOCIETY	Driven by Religion	Driven by Government	Aiming for Advantage

Figure 7.1 The purpose of education through three lenses [1].

Education is rapidly evolving in response to the changes in the society. Today literacy is significantly fueled by media, the Internet, and social media technologies. Education 4.0 seeks to align with Industry 4.0 and prepare students for the next industrial revolution.

Universities should be at the forefront of innovation and knowledge creation to be relevant in the new age of Education 4.0. The basic mission of universities includes three main factors [2]: (1) the training of professionals who can face technological, social, political, and economic challenges, (2) the creation of knowledge through scientific research, and (3) sharing the knowledge and experience with the society to improve the quality of life. Educational activities are increasingly moving online to carry out this mission, and course contents are becoming available in digital format. Taking advantage of this situation requires a change in mindset [3]. Today's students grow up in a digital society and have been transformed by the Internet and mobile-related technologies into digital natives.

The Internet or the World Wide Web has become an integral component of our society and around the world. The web influences people's way of life, while people influence the development and content of the web. Consequently, one would expect schools to follow web evolution.

Education 4.0 requires a new way of thinking for teachers and students. Being a good teacher requires acquiring a large set interdisciplinary skills. Today's student is a digital native comfortable with mobile and computing devices. New skills, curricula, teaching, learning, training, and flexibility in education are necessary. Due to rapid economic and technological changes, students need to be prepared for jobs that have not yet been created. Education 4.0 also needs a strong partnership between industry and academia in developing human resources for Industry 4.0 [4].

This chapter briefly introduces the continuum described from Education 1.0 through 2.0 towards 3.0/4.0. It begins by explaining what is lacking in traditional education. It goes over three generations of education. It discusses the emergence of Industry 4.0 and Education 4.0. It highlights the benefits and challenges of Education 4.0. It covers the global adoption of Education 4.0. The last section concludes with comments.

7.2 TRADITIONAL EDUCATION IS LACKING

Several scholars, researchers, politicians, and educators lament that education is not keeping up with our rapidly changing world. Due to competition, institutions are asked to become more efficient, adaptive and strive for excellence. For universities to continue to produce successful future graduates, they must align their teaching and processes with technological advancements. Leaders in educational institutions need to be aware of what is happening, recognize that the world is changing, and understand how to shape their institutional participation for the future.

Traditional education is well established but is no longer fit-for-purpose. Traditional formal education was designed for mass distribution. It is obsessed with tests. It has yet to be integrated with the industry's needs. The new educational model is called Education 4.0 (or E4.0). Education 4.0 is a response to the needs of Industry 4.0 or the fourth industrial revolution. Education is now regarded as a life-long process rather than a classroom-oriented experience.

7.3 THREE GENERATIONS OF EDUCATION

The evolution of the web from Web 1.0 to Web 2.0 and Web 3.0 dictates how education should also be moving, developing, and evolving from Education 1.0 towards Education 4.0. Figure 7.2 shows Education 1.0, 2.0, and 3.0 framework [5].

The three generations of education are discussed as follows [6,7].

- *Education 1.0:* This is like Web 1.0, essentially a one-way process. Education 1.0 is essentialist, behaviorist, and instructivist education based on the three Rs – receiving by listening to the teacher; responding by taking notes and studying text; and regurgitating by taking the same assessments as all other students. It is authoritarian and teacher-centered, with the student as the passive recipient. Students go to school to receive education from professors, who supply knowledge using class notes, handouts, textbooks, videos, and recently World Wide Web. They are largely consumers of information resources that are delivered to them. Most schools are still working with Education 1.0 model. The curriculum is based on traditional disciplines such as mathematics, natural science, history, languages, and literature. Classrooms are teacher-oriented with little regard for the student's interests. Students are taught in masses and learn passively by listening to the teacher. Other than libraries and news outlets, students depended on the educator to provide them with content knowledge in a one-way, often didactic format. The most dominant form of instruction in Europe and America is didactic, traditional, or teacher-directed approaches. Figure 7.3 illustrates Education 1.0 [8].

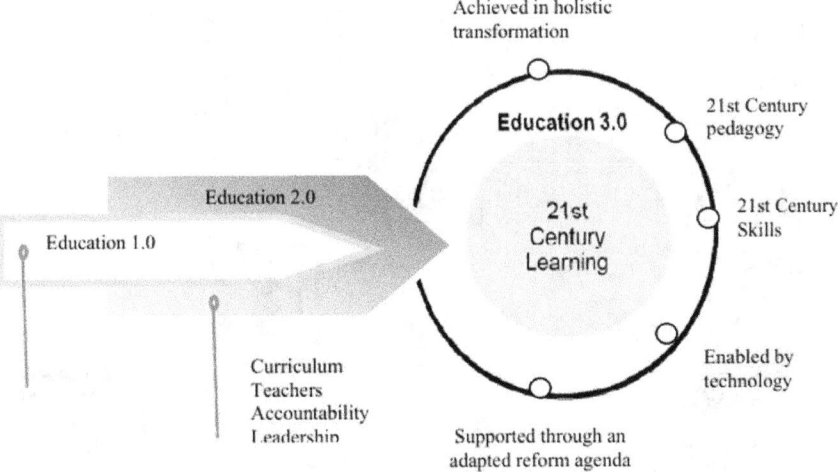

Figure 7.2 Education 1.0, 2.0, and 3.0 framework [5].

- *Education 2.0:* This uses the technologies of Web 2.0 to enhance traditional approaches to education and create more interactive education. Like Web 2.0, Education 2.0 permits more interaction between the teacher and students and between students themselves. It is an exam-based approach. The classmates communicate faster and smarter. Education 2.0 refers to the use of the technologies and social engagements of Web 2.0, which has replaced an *access* technology with a participation technology. Education 2.0 is about three Cs – communicating, contributing, and collaborating. The principles of active, experiential, authentic, relevant, and socially-networked learning experiences are built into the learning environment. Educators use educational software, online tools, global learning projects, Skype, shared wikis, blogs, and other social media in the classroom. Teachers and students can choose from a variety of digital tools that enable a new level of interaction, collaboration, analysis, and presentations. Collaboration and social negotiation are encouraged among learners. Although the groundwork for broader transformation is being for Education 3.0, the educational process is not transformed much. Figure 7.4 portrays Education 2.0 [8].

Figure 7.3 Education 1.0 [8].

- *Education 3.0:* This creates a much more free and open system focused on learning. It is characterized by rich, cross-institutional, cross-cultural educational opportunities within which the learners play a key role as creators of knowledge. Education 3.0 is based on personalized, self-determined education. It is self-determined, interest-based learning where problem-solving, innovation, and creativity drive education. It is characterized by educational opportunities where social networking and social benefits play a strong role in learning. Education 3.0 focuses on three Cs – connectors, creators, and constructivists. Students today choose differently from past students, and abundant open content facilitates their choices. They are taking their educational destiny into their own hands. Education 3.0 believes that content is freely and readily available. It has been called user-generated education. The teachers, learners, networks, connections, media, resources, and tools create a unique environment that can meet the needs of individual learners. Today, students enjoy a wealth of technology-driven educational resources such as Massive Open Online Courses (MOOCs), YouTube videos on any subject, and Google Hangouts.

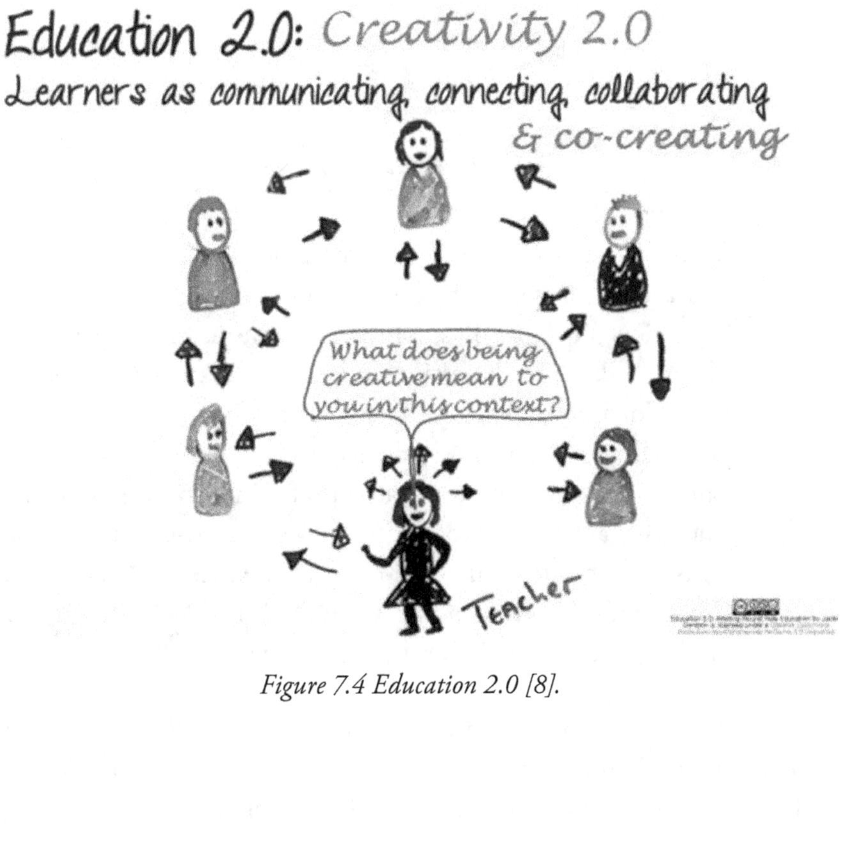

Figure 7.4 Education 2.0 [8].

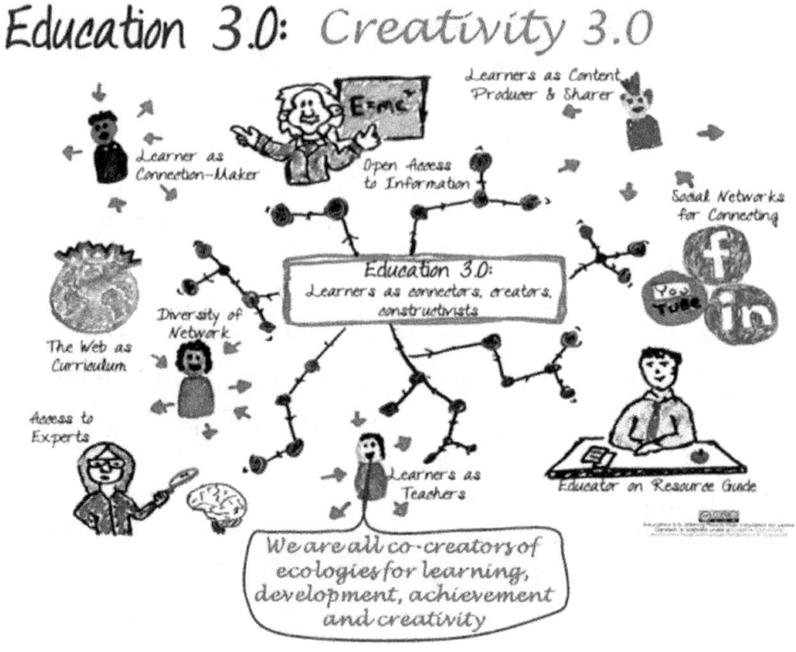

Figure 7.5 Education 3.0 [8].

With Education 3.0, the teacher becomes a coach or cheerleader as learners create their learning journey. Figure 7.5 depicts Education 3.0 [8]. Education 3.0 is a means of navigating the "C's" of education: Creativity, Critical thinking, Competency, Care, Cognition, Content, Classes, Calculation, Communication, Compelling Questions, Challenge, Computer literacy, Context, Culture, and much more are all top-of-mind issues for academia. These Cs are similar to the seven Cs of 21st-century lifelong skills: Critical thinking-and-doing, Creativity, Collaboration, Cross-cultural Understanding, Communication, Computing/ICT Literacy, and Career & Learning Self-reliance [9,10].

Schools are working on Education 1.0; talking about doing Education 2.0; when they should be implementing and addressing Education 3.0/4.0. Education 4.0 is the next big thing after Education 3.0.

7.4 EMERGENCE OF INDUSTRY 4.0

The innovations in fields such as artificial intelligence, the Internet of things, cloud computing, big data, mobile supercomputing, intelligent robots, self-driving vehicles, biotechnology, nanotechnology, 3-D Printing, and quantum computing have made the fourth industrial revolution evolve at a rapid pace and disrupt almost every industry. These innovations have created an opportunity to build a learning ecosystem that allows personalized learning independent of time and location.

In the last 250 years, society has experienced four Industrial Revolutions, which have entirely changed the face of the industry as we know it. These revolutions are shown in Figure 7.6 [11] and explained below.

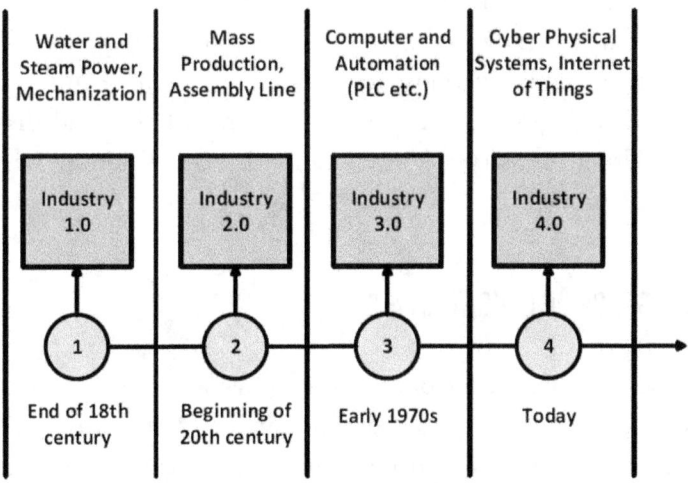

Figure 7.6 The industrial revolutions [11].

Industry 1.0: (1784): Based on mechanical production equipment driven by water and steam power. The invention of the steam engine by James Watts in 1780 changed the workforce forever.

Industry 2.0: (1870): Based on mass production enabled by the division of labor and the use of electricity.

Industry 3.0 (1969): Based on the use of electronics and IT to further automate production. Just 70 years later, the computer brought a third industrial revolution.

Industry 4.0 (today): Based on the use of cyber-physical systems, Internet of things, and smart technologies. In 2000, the ubiquitous nature of the Internet ushered in the fourth industrial revolution.

Industry 4.0 is the current and gradual industrial transformation with automation, cloud computing, cyber-physical systems, robots, and industrial IoT to realize smart industry and manufacturing [12]. The 4th industrial revolution will require a shift in approaches and models. It utilizes cyber-physical systems in which machines communicate efficiently with each other. Industry 4.0 has brought disruptive change, which takes place in the manufacturing industry through the pervasive application of ICT. There are basically six different design principles to perform Industry 4.0 [13]: interoperability, transparency of information, technical support, real-time data acquisition and processing, modularity, and distributed decision. Using Industry 4.0 in education is very important of training qualified personnel.

7.5 EMERGENCE OF EDUCATION 4.0

The global education technology market is growing rapidly with the growing need for skills and changing workforce in the 21st century. Emerging technologies such as the Internet of things, social media, mobile, and cloud computing are impacting all areas of education. These new resources can empower individuals to develop competencies, skills, and knowledge [14]. The emergence of Industry 4.0 requires that Education 4.0 also leapfrogs from the current Education 2.0 framework to Education 3.0/4.0.

Education 1.0: Limited to a few privileged people and governed by informal teaching methods.

Education 2.0: With the invention of the printing press, knowledge dissemination could be done to the masses through printed books.

Education 3.0: The Internet has provided a platform that has greatly expanded access to education and changed the ways of learning.

Education 4.0: Empowering education to produce innovation through personalization of the learning experience.

Most of the world's education is at the 1.0 level, and only a fraction of world education is moving toward Education 2.0 [7]. While education delivery has evolved over the years from Education 1.0 to Education 3.0, the main process of teaching has not changed, and the main learning methods have remained unchanged. E-Learning may be regarded as the third education revolution, and the subject of E-Learning has been Massive Open Online Courses (MOOC). Artificial Intelligence will play a major role in the fourth revolution in education. Education 4.0 responds to the need of Industry 4.0, where man and machine work together to enable new possibilities. Education 4.0 puts the learner at the center of the ecosystem and enables him to go through experiential learning. Innovations and digital technology are driving the "personalization" of learning. The requirement for life-long learning has become a given.

In 2000, the ubiquitous nature of the Internet ushered in the fourth industrial revolution. The innovations in fields such as artificial intelligence, the Internet of things, cloud computing, big data, mobile supercomputing, intelligent robots, self-driving vehicles, biotechnology, nanotechnology, 3-D Printing, and cloud computing have made the fourth industrial revolution evolve at a rapid pace and disrupt almost every industry. These innovations have created an opportunity to build a learning ecosystem that allows personalized learning independent of time and location, since every individual learns differently. Education 4.0 is a learning approach aligning with the emerging fourth industrial revolution [12]. Figure 7.7 shows the movement toward the fourth era [15].

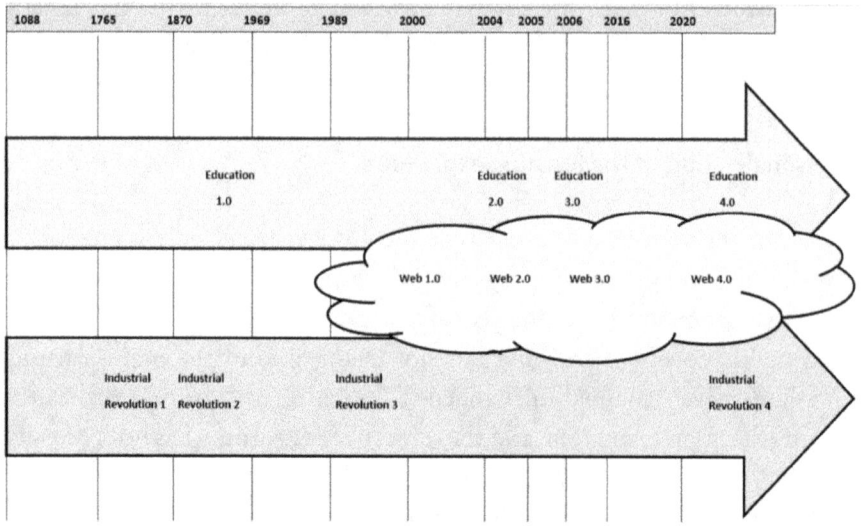

Figure 7.7 Moving towards the 4th Era [15].

Education 4.0 requires a new way of thinking for teachers and students. Being a good teacher requires acquiring a large set of interdisciplinary skills. Today's student is a digital native comfortable with mobile and computing devices. New skills, new curricula, new teaching, new learning, new training, and new flexibility in education are necessary. Due to rapid economic and technological changes, students need to be prepared for jobs that have not yet been created. Education 4.0 also needs a strong partnership between industry and academia in developing human resources for Industry 4.0 [14]. Some of the characteristics of Education 4.0 are displayed in Figure 7.8 [16].

Education 4.0 is tipped as the future of education and is poised to change information consumption. It is deemed a disruptive system that focuses on what is taught and how it is taught. Education 4.0 includes online assessments, robotics, artificial intelligence, big data, virtual reality, and augmented reality as tools set to replace the clumsy old procedures of obsolete conventional education through creativity and student centricity, where personalization is key.

EDUCATION 4.0

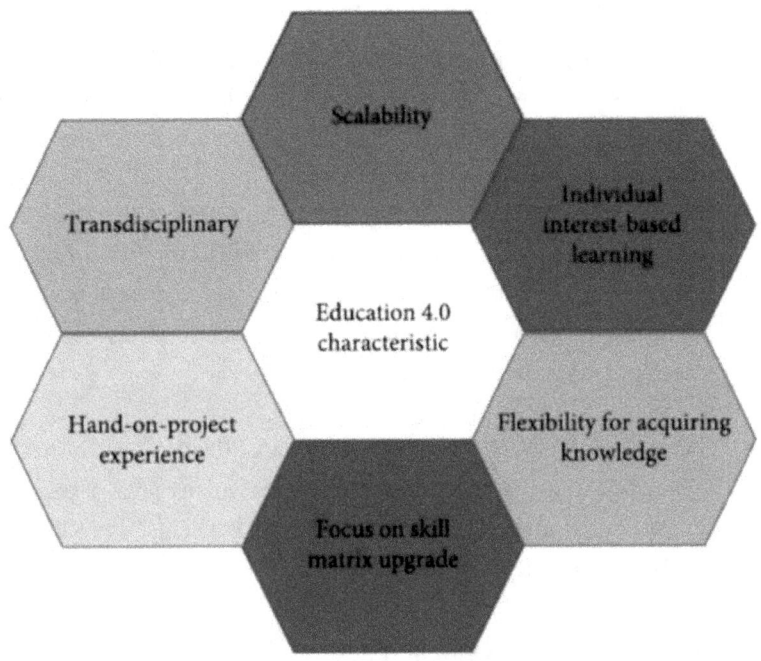

Figure 7.8 Some of the characteristics of Education 4.0 [16].

7.6 BENEFITS

Education 4.0's most essential goal for all educational institutions is to motivate students and improve their learning outcomes. Students are treated as beneficiaries in Education 4.0. Education 4.0 aims to equip students with cognitive, social, interpersonal, and technical skills It helps learners understand the learning contexts more effectively than the traditional approach. Education 4.0 is beneficial not only to students but also to teachers at any level of education. Every educator needs to change. Higher learning educators have started using open learning platforms such as Massive Open Online Courses (MOOCs), which can be accessed from anywhere on the Internet and offer thousands of courses. The major benefits of Education 4.0 include the following [17]:

- *Practical-Based Learning:* Education 4.0 benefits students by creating an opportunity to experience more practical-based learning instead of theocratical base knowledge. Most institutions have taken the initiative to make this successful and provide the students with a more meaningful learning experience through internships, mentor-mentee programs, and collaborative projects.

- *Deeper Connectivity:* Education 4.0 also connects a learner to gain deeper connectivity compared to the traditional ways of learning. Implementing Education 4.0 allows learners to experience a visual element that effectively improves the connection between learning concepts and information.

- *Becoming the 21st Century Instructor:* Education 4.0 is not only beneficial to students but also the teachers at any level of education. Every educator needs to relearn and prepare themselves with digital tools to meet the demand of the future learner.

- *Creates an Opportunity for Educators:* Education 4.0 creates an opportunity for educators to engage in new technology tools to make them relevant in the industry. This prospect requires designing tasks or activities that engage learners to become involved in the thinking and learning process.

- *Enhances the Knowledge & Usage of Technology:* Education 4.0 enhances knowledge and usage for both educators and students. It is crucial for every educator to learn and know how to operate and integrate technology tools effectively. Technology-based teaching and learning stimulate many interesting ways, such as brainstorming, educational videos, mind-mapping, guided discovery, and others, creating more meaningful experiences in learning and teaching contexts.

- *Development of the 21st Century Skills*: Education 4.0 creates a platform for every educator to promote the development of technology classrooms into 21st-century skills. All educators should be more responsible in better preparing today's graduates for a 21st-century world that requires exposing them to technology.

- *Shift in Exam & Assessment Patterns:* In a typical practice, a student's common habit of passing an exam is blindly memorizing the key information given by the teachers. However, this will no longer be a trend to follow as the government recognizes that this traditional practice may not serve the needs of future talent requirements.

- *Personalized Learning:* Students are not all the same. They are individuals with different interests, abilities, capabilities, timing, and preferred learning methods. They should not be taught in the same way and submitted to the same assessment scale. Education 4. offers a personalized learning experience through the use of artificial intelligence. Smart refers to Education 4.0 technologies that personalize learning and teaching in smart environments.

7.7 CHALLENGES

Technology in education has its benefits and challenges, but proper implementation might help keep the drawbacks to a minimum. Some challenges facing Education 4.0 include the following [17]:

- *Falling Behind:* Individuals are falling behind and not keeping pace with the rapidly evolving technology. The leaders of today are not digital natives. It is important to work toward the capability development of the teachers, educators, and leaders for the Education 4.0 ecosystem. Teachers are the key element to change when teaching with technology. Changing curriculum and teaching practices is a challenging and time-consuming process.

- *Resistance to Change*: One weakness of Education 4.0 is resistance to change factors occurs at a greater level. The teachers will resist change or stay in their comfort zone. Many educators feel unprepared to use technology to support student learning. Most of them are comfortable teaching the traditional ways. Sometimes staff and other personnel do not want to change. They prefer to replicate the status quo.

- *Digitally Connected, Socially Disconnected:* Our society is rapidly evolving in technology, with no doubts. Literally, every information is available at our convenience anytime and anywhere. With the amazing advancements of technology, we all get connected all across the globe in a second. However, technological advancements have limited the engagement or involvement of an educator toward its learner.

- *Regulatory Compliance:* Institutions face increasing regulatory compliance challenges to prevent hacking, block inappropriate content, safeguard personal information, and educate students about the risks associated with the Internet. To be an accredited institution requires complying with a lot of regulations.

7.8 GLOBAL ADOPTION OF EDUCATION 4.0

Education is strongly correlated with the advancement in technology. The worldwide explosion of digital technologies puts us in the midst of a revolution in education across K-12 and college environments. With the rapid growth in technology, institutions are moving toward a new age in education, known as Education 4.0. Educational institutions worldwide are realizing the potential of an Education 4.0 to increase personalization and improve outcomes. During lockdowns in 2020, the Fourth Education Revolution, or Education 4.0, began to bloom. We now consider how Education 4.0 is adopted in some nations.

- *United States:* Educational systems must adapt to give students the skills necessary to build a more just and productive world for society. Schools must provide the learning of hard skills (such as technology design and resource management) and soft skills (such as communication, empathy, and social awareness). Such skills are needed to enable people to progress in a more complex, interconnected, and rapidly changing world. Education 4.0 must address today's most pressing challenges, such as global climate change, ecosystem degradation, and depletion of natural resources [18]. Education 4.0 involves the use of tablets and smartphones as supportive tools in the classroom and focuses on smart and innovative technology. These technologies will dominate the life of students in the future.

- *United Kingdom:* From 2019 on, tectonic forces continue to reshape life, economies, industries, and jobs around the globe. Current generations will engage with state-of-the-art technology and Industry 4.0 advancements. They should receive an equally advanced Education 4.0. The University of Buckingham in the United Kingdom is creating a new two-year program in world History where Education 4.0 advanced technologies are going to provide a more expansive, engaging, and personalized educational experience. The ambitious History course will be taught with a blend of traditional methods and innovative solutions including flipped classrooms and online teaching, augmented reality, virtual reality, mixed reality, and artificial intelligence to create an engaging and effective learning experience [19].

- *China:* Education 4.0 describes how we need to prepare students for the fourth industrial revolution, or the advent of the 22nd century. China is leading in the application of new digital technologies in education. In China, the Ministry of Education encouraged schools and universities to promote online delivery to replace face-to-face teaching. In Education 4.0, educators' roles must shift from teacher-centered to student-centered learning. It is necessary that students have collaborative skills and an interest in lifelong learning. Education 4.0 is personalized, online-based, accessible 24/7 from anywhere, flexible delivery, peer, and mentor-led learning [20].

- *India:* India has a dynamic education technology landscape, though it faces some significant challenges. To spread digital literacy and support the creation of a knowledge-based society, the Indian government has launched several technology-enabled programs, such as Digital India and Education 4.0 India. Digital India seeks to make government services available to citizens electronically through improved online infrastructure. The Education 4.0 India initiative aims to use Fourth Industrial Revolution technologies to enhance learning and reduce inequalities in India and globally. The initiative suggests action in four focus areas: foundational literacy and numeracy, teachers' professional development, school-to-work transition, and connecting the unconnected. India can build on digital solutions to prepare Indian school students for success in the 21st century [21]. To fully capitalize on the technology transformation and make a difference in society, Education 4.0 has taken center stage, making education more interactive, networkable, and personalized.

- *Philippines:* Education must reflect the world it is training students for. Education 4.0 ensures that teaching-learning experiences will take advantage of the limitless opportunities created by advanced technology. Administrators and faculty members in the Philippines are ready in terms of their skills in selecting and integrating digital resources for teaching and learning, as they are also given capacity buildings through seminars and conferences related to technological literacy. However, they are neither skillful in using the learning management system and other online class modalities; nor in the utilization of augmented reality, robotics, and digital enablers like 3D printing. This lack may be attributed to the unavailability and inaccessibility of digital infrastructure and virtual laboratories in most teacher education institutions. There is a need for teacher education institutions to rethink infrastructure planning, redesign research initiatives, and strengthen teacher-training capabilities to be Education 4.0 ready [22].

- *Malaysia:* This nation needs to enhance and develop its education system to be one of the most competitive countries in the world. The Malaysian Ministry of Education plans to revamp the process of teaching and learning students. In 2016, the Malaysian government introduced a flexible mode of education, namely the Massive Open Online Course (MOOC). This application has been one of the initiatives taken in implementing online learning in Malaysia, which creates a more globalized online learner globally. The online course aims to encourage online and permanent learning pursuits among Malaysians through diversifying classroom experience and unlimited online access participation [17].

7.9 CONCLUSION

Education was a one-shot game, but it is now a lifelong game. Without a doubt, digital technologies have shaped the way of sharing knowledge. Education 4.0 is tipped as the future of education and is poised to change information consumption. It is deemed a disruptive system that focuses on what is taught and how it is taught. Human skills need constant upgrading to handle the key enabling technologies, including machines as cyber-physical systems, augmented reality, human-robot collaboration, and smart devices. The skill set necessary for the "jobs- of –the- future" would change drastically. Students across disciplines will, therefore, need to gain digital skills and data literacy during their studies. When looking for jobs, engineering students should be prepared to meet the demands of Society 4.0 and Industry 4.0 – resulting from a fourth industrial revolution.

Education 5.0 is the latest trend in the education field. It is the use of new technologies to provide more humanized teaching. It is a chain that links digital and technological knowledge to human social and emotional skills to promote well-being [23]. Figure 7.9 shows the components of Education 5.0 [24].

With the pace of change accelerating in the 21st century, lifelong learning and the ability to acquire new skills quickly is a key requirement to thrive. Education 4.0 enhances 21st-century skills for learners. More information about Industry 4.0 can be found in the books in [25-36] and the following journals related to Education 4.0:

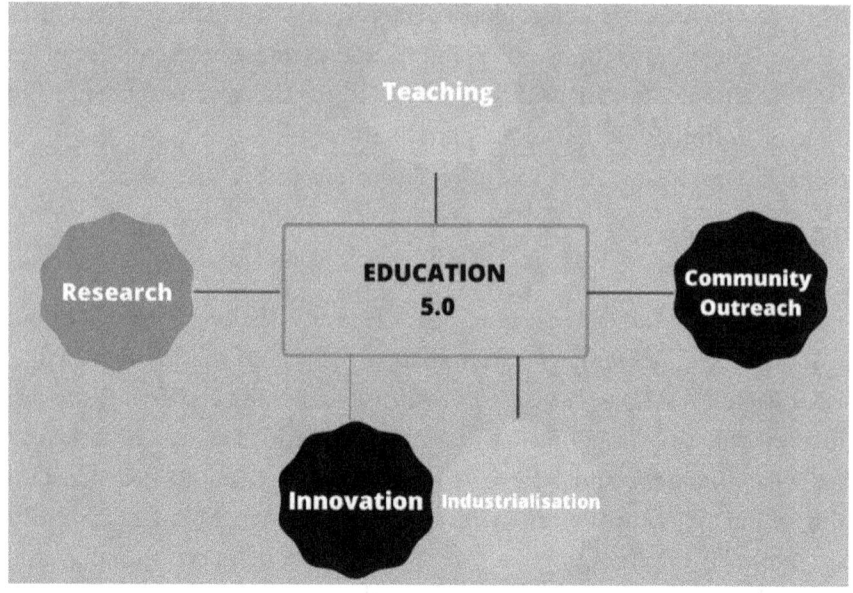

Figure 7.9 The components of Education 5.0 [24].

- *Informatics in Education*
- *IEEE Transactions on Education*
- *International Journal of Learning, Teaching and Educational Research*
- *International Journal of Educational Technology in Higher Education*

REFERENCES

[1] M. Church, "The evolution of education," https://www.mattchurch.com/talkingpoint/education-evolution

[2] R. A. Ramirez-Mendoza et al., " Engineering Education 4.0 - Proposal for a new curricula," *Proceedings of IEEE Global Engineering Education Conference*, Canary Islands, Spain, April 2018, pp. 1273-1282.

[3] M. Ciolacu et al.," Education 4.0 – Fostering student's performance with machine learning methods," *Proceeding of IEEE 23rd International Symposium for Design and Technology in Electronic Packaging*, 2017, pp. 438-443.

[4] M. Ciolacu et al.,"Education 4.0 for tall thin engineer in a data driven society," *Proceeding of IEEE 23rd International Symposium for Design and Technology in Electronic Packaging*, 2017, pp. 432-437.

[5] R. A. Abdullah, O. K. Rahmat, and K. Osman, "From traditional to self-regulated learners: UKM journey towards Education 3.0," *Procedia - Social and Behavioral Sciences*, vol. 59, 2012, pp. 2–8.

[6] D. Keats and J. P. Schmidt, "The genesis and emergence of Education 3.0 in higher education and its potential for Africa," *First Monday*, vol. 12, no. 3, March 2007.

[7] L. M. Blaschke, C. Kenyon, and S. Hase, "Experiences in self-determined learning: Moving from Education 1.0 through Education 2.0 towards Education 3.0," https://usergeneratededucation.wordpress.com/2014/12/01/experiences-in-self-determined-learning-moving-from-education-1-0-through-education-2-0-towards-education-3-0/

[8] N. Jackson, "Towards education 3.0: Narrative for the evolution of education, creativity & learning ecologies in HE," http://www.normanjackson.co.uk/uploads/1/0/8/4/10842717/towards education 3.0.pdf

[9] C. J. Bonk, "Education 3.0: My, our learning world is changing! https://facet.iu.edu/programs-events/falcon/past-falcon/2014/presentations/learning-world-changing.pdf

[10] M. N. O. Sadiku, P. O. Adebo, O. A. Okhria, and S. M. Musa, "Introduction to Education 3.0," *International Journal of Trend in Research and Development*, vol. 8, no. 2, March-April, 2022, pp. 182-186.

[11] M. Baygin et al., "An effect analysis of Industry 4.0 to higher education," *Proceedings of the 15th International Conference on Information Technology Based Higher Education and Training*, 2016

[12] M. N. O. Sadiku, S. M. Musa, and O. M. Musa, "The essence of Industry 4.0," *Invention Journal of Research Technology in Engineering and Management*, vol. 2, no. 9, September 2018, pp. 64-67.

[13] A. M. Harkins, " Leapfrog principles and practices: Core components of Education 3.0 and 4.0," *Futures Research Quarterly*, March 2008.

[14] M. N. O. Sadiku, A. Omotoso, and S. M. Musa, "Essence of Education 4.0," *International Journal of Trend in Scientific Research and Development*, vol. 4, no. 4, June 2020, pp. 1110-1112.

[15] G. Salmon, "May the fourth be with you: Creating Education 4.0," *Journal of Learning for Development*, vol. 6, no. 2, 2019, pp. 95-115.

[16] A. Gupta et al., "Transforming learning to online Education 4.0 during COVID-19: stakeholder perception, attitude, and experiences in higher education institutions at a tier-III city in India," *Education Research International*, 2023.

[17] J. Mutch "Are you ready for Education 3.0?" May 2016, https://www.itproportal.com/2016/05/04/are-you-ready-for-education-3-0/

[18] K. K. S. Oliveira and R. A. C. Souza, "Digital transformation towards education 4.0," *Informatics in Education*, vol. 21, no. 2, 2022, pp. 283–309.

[19] S. Fourtane, "Education 4.0: University launches world's first degree driven by 4.0 technologies," July 2021, https://www.fierceeducation.com/administration/education-4-0-university-launches-world-s-first-degree-driven-by-4-0-technologies

[20] D. Mourtzis, N. Panopoulosand, and J. Angelopoulo, "A hybrid teaching factory model towards personalized education 4.0," *International Journal of Computer Integrated Manufacturing*, October 2022, https://www.tandfonline.com/doi/epdf/10.1080/0951192X.2022.2145025?needAccess=true&role=button

[21] "Education 4.0 India," October 2022, https://www3.weforum.org/docs/WEF_Education_4.0_India_Report_2022.pdf

[22] R. Alda, H. Boholano, and F. Dayagbil, "Teacher education institutions in the Philippines towards Education 4.0," *International Journal of Learning, Teaching and Educational Research*, vol. 19, no. 8, 2020.

[23] "Education 5.0: What does it mean? How does it work?" May 2023, https://www.sydle.com/blog/education-5-0-61e71a99edf3b9259714e25a

[24] "University of Zimbabwe strategic plan 2019-2025," August 2020, https://www.uz.ac.zw/index.php/news/uz-main-news/49-about-uz

[25] J. G. Lengel, *Education 3.0: Seven Steps to Better Schools*. Teachers College Press, 2013.

[26] D. Barrett, *Education 3.0: How to Get Your Kids What They Need to Succeed*. Amazon.com Services LLC, 2017.

[27] D. Frau-Meigs, *Taking The Digital Social Turn for Online Freedoms and Education 3.0*. The Routledge Companion to Media and Human, 2017.

[28] J. E. Lane and D. B. Johnstone, *Higher Education Systems 3.0: Harnessing Systemness, Delivering Performance*. SUNY Press, 2013.

[29] C. Hong and W. W. K. Ma (eds.), *Applied Degree Education and the Future of Work: Education 4.0*. Springer, 2020.

[30] A. E. Tekkaya et al. (eds.), *Engineering Education 4.0: Excellent Teaching and Learning in Engineering Sciences*. Springer, 2017.

[31] A. Plutino and K. Borthwick (eds.), *Education 4.0 Revolution: Transformative Approaches to Language Teaching and Learning, Assessment and Campus Design*. Research-publishing.net, 2020.

[32] K. A. Jones and S. Ravishankar, *Higher Education 4.0: The Digital Transformation of Classroom Lectures to Blended Learning*. Springer, 2021.

[33] M. M. Echeverria, *Education 4.0: Addressing the Challenges and Opportunities of the Digital Era*. Amazon Digital Services LLC, 2023.

[34] P. Chew, *Education 4.0 Knowledge. Peter Chew Rule for Solution of Triangle [2nd Edition]*. PCET Ventures, 2023.

[35] T. Wilen-Daugenti, *Society 3.0: How Technology is Reshaping Education, Work and Society*. International Academic Publishers, 2017.

[36] S. Frerich et al. (eds.), *Engineering Education 4.0: Excellent Teaching and Learning in Engineering Sciences*. Springer, 2016.

CHAPTER 8

DIGITAL EDUCATION

"Education is a companion which no misfortune can depress, no crime can destroy, no enemy can alienate, no despotism can enslave..."
—Joseph Addison

8.1 INTRODUCTION

Education is a source of human capital and a valuable way of encouraging social and economic development. It is insurance against poverty. Before the digital age, distance learning took the form of correspondence courses emphasizing individual self-paced lessons. Education providers are moving from traditional face-to-face environments to completely electronic ones. The movement to online education requires applying new strategies to suit the new medium. With the modernization of distance education and training, online education uses computer networks and satellite communication networks to deliver education. It provides university equivalent courses for millions of students across the globe.

Computer networks such as the Internet and digital technologies have transformed education at all levels to meet the demand of the 21st century. Digital technologies (phone, computer, tablet, e-book, social networking, online videos, mobile devices, etc.) offer great hope for learners and teachers today. They play a crucial role in the administration of education. Digital technologies govern the work of policymakers, educators, parents, and learners. For example, the Internet provides easy access to unlimited information. It allows students and teachers to learn different ways of learning. The use of digital technologies to improve learning keeps climbing. The number of digital devices in K-12 classrooms continues to increase. Some school systems have so embraced technology that they provide every student with a laptop since they believe computers will improve student learning. This condition has significantly raised standardized test scores. It has also prepared the students for technology-heavy workplaces [1,2].

Digital education is training that applies digital technologies in various areas of human activity. It helps to develop students› digital literacy and prepare them for the global, digital labor market and social life. Digital education can be done well or poorly, like any other form of education. Computer-based learning requires well-trained teachers to make it effective [3].

This chapter provides an introduction to digital education. It begins by explaining what digital education is all about. It provides some applications of digital education. It covers digital textbooks. It discusses global digital education. It highlights some benefits and challenges of digital education. The last section concludes with comments.

8.2 WHAT IS DIGITAL EDUCATION?

Digital education is the process of using digital technology in teaching and learning. It is also known as online education, technology-enhanced learning (TEL), digital learning, or e-learning. Digital education uses digital tools and technologies during teaching and learning. Digital education prepares students for becoming digital citizens by acquiring skills for navigating and existing in the digital world. Education is no longer limited to textbooks and classrooms. It has become an amalgamation of technology, innovative teaching, and personalized learning. It is a field in which digital content has become incredibly popular.

The education sector was surprised by its forced transition to digital education. Furthermore, traditional classrooms have quickly made way for virtual classrooms. Digital or online education involves teaching and learning. Although remote education can take various forms, it now relies on digital technology. Digital technology has changed the way we teach and learn.

- *Teaching:* Teachers are pressured to use digital technologies to teach students and prepare them for work in a globalized digital economy. Online education offers exciting opportunities to expand the learning environment for diverse student populations. Digital education requires teachers to acquire new skills to handle digital natives. Digital education's benefits for teachers and learners provide significant impetus for teachers to develop new skills. As the demand for online teaching increases, educators may be asked to consider teaching their classes online. Online teaching shares much with face-to-face teaching but has unique skills and requirements. Both approaches are similar in content, except in pace and delivery. Rather than developing the courses from scratch, a company has emerged to take care of the courses. As the digital world requires educators to find new ways to incorporate and integrate technology into teaching practices, the schools that manage this the best will naturally rise above the others. Figure 8.1 shows digital teaching and learning [4].

Figure 8.1 Digital teaching and learning [4].

- *Learning:* Humans continuously learn through three learning systems—formal, non-formal, and informal education. The learning process involves the auditory, visual, and tactile senses.

The traditional way of learning at a campus university is not for everyone. Digital learning is learning facilitated by technology that offers students some factors of command over the place, time, pace, and path. It is gradually replacing traditional educational procedures [5]. The features of digital classrooms are illustrated in Figure 8.2. Online learning is for those who wish to study for a degree alongside work or other commitments. It allows the student to pursue an internationally recognized degree without attending campus classes. It is convenient since it will enable one to study anywhere with Internet access. They can learn whatever they want anywhere, anytime when they want it. The learning is self-paced and offered at a lower cost. Online courses are available 24/7. The digital era allows course materials to be created, shared with others, and developed together in the cloud. Digital learning means more than just digitizing traditional instruction materials. Using digital media in education will create new communication, cooperation, and networking areas. Learners need to be equipped to function effectively in the digitized 21st century.

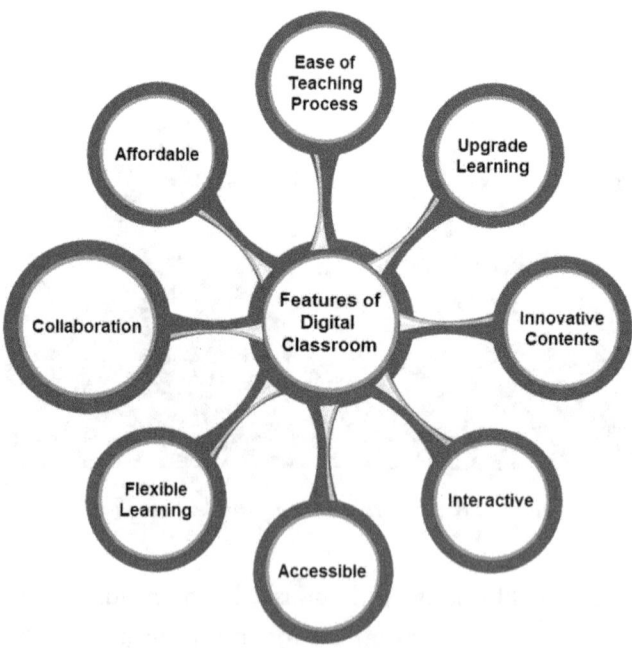

Figure 8.2 Features of digital classroom.

8.3 APPLICATIONS

Digital technology can enhance teaching, learning, and professional productivity in every educational setting. Digital education is essentially an innovation of the last few decades, although it already existed in various forms slightly earlier. We must harness the power of the digital revolution to ensure quality education is provided as a public good and a human right. To be successful in the workplace of the future, people will need to have the proper digital education. Some areas of application of digital education are provided.

- *Online Education:* Online education, often called distance education or web-based education, is currently the latest and most popular form of distance education. It applies the Internet and communication technologies and makes education open, dynamic, and affordable to those who want to learn, regardless of age or location. More and more universities and publishers worldwide have opted to use online education. For example, for-profit institutions such as the University of Phoenix, Kaplan University, National University, Nova Southeastern University, Walden University, and Athabasca University (in Canada) have dominated the online market. Many colleges in the US and abroad are moving from traditional face-to-face classes into fully online, web-based courses. They are joining the ranks of institutions offering online education. There are evening classes, weekend classes, satellite campuses, and cyberclasses. Online education is an equal opportunity phenomenon, giving all students, colleges, and universities the same opportunities. It should be regarded as a win-win because it achieves good and simultaneously opens new markets. Online courses refer to those in which at least 80 percent of the content is delivered online. Massive Online Open Courses (MOOCs) are a subset of online courses. Since the introduction of the first MOOCs in 2003 in the United Kingdom, millions of students worldwide have grabbed the opportunity to take courses online. MOOCs help students acquire knowledge in a self-paced manner and choose what they learn and when to learn. They have proved helpful for students, especially from underdeveloped countries. They enable them to access standard courses for little or no cost [6]. The rapid growth of the education sector in recent years and the growing proliferation of digital technology have led to an era where e-learning is becoming a norm in almost all institutions. As illustrated in Figure 8.3, e-learning platforms allow students to progress based on their intellectual capacities and levels of comprehension [7].

- *Education of Digital Natives:* The phenomenon of digital technologies has produced a distinctively new generation defined by digital media: the digital natives. Digital natives live and navigate the digital world with their digital skills. Digital natives were born into the digital age or after 1980. This generation of students is growing up in a digital world, and educators must employ new approaches to make learning real and relevant to them. Educational systems should be adapted to meet their education needs, which are different from those of the previous generations.

Figure 8.3 E-learning platforms allow students to progress based on their intellectual capacities [7].

It has become evident that our educational institutions need to change to meet the learning needs of digital natives. It is widely accepted that an effective way to facilitate learning is to allow students to actively engage in activities and processes that make them feel at home. To facilitate learning by digital natives, educators should embed digital technologies in their teaching, learning, and assessment. Our educational systems need to listen to the voices of the digital natives or face a future with disgruntled, disconnected learners. Research on digital natives is essential for developing 21st-century education [8,9]. Figure 8.4 shows some examples of digital natives [10].

- *Healthcare*: Healthcare is a complex system that covers disease diagnosis, treatment, and prevention. It constitutes a fundamental pillar of modern society. The healthcare industry is one of the largest industries in developed nations regarding job creation, number of employees, and expenditure. Health technologies comprise all the devices, medications, vaccines, processes, procedures, and systems designed to streamline healthcare operations, lower costs, and enhance the quality of care. Technology is drastically changing and improving healthcare, from anesthetics and antibiotics to MRI scanners and radiotherapy. Although emerging healthcare technologies will not fix all healthcare problems, they can improve the practice, decision-making, and management of healthcare.

Figure 8.4 Examples of digital natives [10

Some of these technologies will change the healthcare practice and transform our whole approach to disease management. It is well known that hospitals adopt new technologies that enhance their service capabilities and enable them to attract and retain physicians who use the technologies [11].

- *Leadership:* Leadership is one of the most extensively studied topics in social sciences because it is the heart of every organization, particularly education. It may be regarded as a process of leading followers. Leaders are needed in many social contexts, including workplaces, religious and secular communities, schools, colleges, classrooms, businesses, healthcare, government, politics, law enforcement, the military, organizations, and families. Leadership in these areas often influences how we work and live [12]. Leaders need to be the catalysts for change. Digital Education Leadership (DEL) program prepares one to meet the needs of today's learners. As new technologies enter the learning environment, digital education leadership program is the additional support educators often need.

8.4 DIGITAL TEXTBOOKS

For many years, textbooks were seen as an essential foundation for instruction and learning. They were regarded as a fundamental part of the educational infrastructure for acquiring knowledge. Traditional textbooks are also known as legacy or print textbooks. Print textbooks are often employed as textbooks in most universities. You do not need to worry about having a functioning electronic device to read print textbooks.

Digital textbook (also e-textbook, virtual textbook, or online textbook) is electronic versions of traditional, print textbook used in schools and colleges. It refers to an interactive set of learning content and tools accessed via a laptop, tablet, or other digital device. It is intended to serve as the text for a class or course. Digital textbooks can provide multimedia information that print textbooks cannot. Some digital textbooks are simply digitized versions of printed books, while others include additional features such as interactive features, multimedia content, and built-in study tools. These added elements increase engagement and comprehension and improve the overall learning experience of the students. Digital textbooks are often cheaper and more portable than traditional textbooks. Educators can find open-source digital textbooks online that are free to use [13].

Due to the recent COVID-19 virus, many schools choose to take online lessons at home. This condition made electronic textbooks essential for many students. Forward-looking publishers now commonly offer digital versions of their textbooks, while some publishers have even switched entirely to digital. Figure 8.5 shows reading electronic books with tablets [14].

Figure 8.5 Reading electronic book with tablet [14].

Modern classrooms are often equipped with several pieces of technology, including computers, televisions, whiteboards, and portable electronic devices, such as smartphones, tablet computers, and e-book readers. These devices aid learning and can accommodate digital textbooks [15]. A typical example of students using e-books in class is shown in Figure 8.6 [16]. Textbooks should be made available as digital licenses procured and managed by libraries. A digital textbook can be fabricated relatively easily by using Epub or DAISY. There are so many ways to download free textbooks. You can use the OpenStax, Open Textbook Library, and ScholarWorks websites as a college student. Sites that provide digital textbooks include Amazon Kindle, Barnes & Noble Nook, iBooks, Cengage Brain, Cengage Brain, eCampus, VitalSource, Chegg,Textbooks.com, and McGraw-Hill eBookstore.

Figure 8.6 A typical example of students using e-book in class [16].

Digital textbooks are the future of education, making learning more affordable and accessible for all. High textbook prices have long been a bane for students, but students now have the choice to purchase e-books. Today, college students can choose to buy either print or digital textbooks. Online textbooks are generally less expensive than physical textbooks because publishing books online eliminates paper, printing, and shipping costs. The digital textbook is the way to go for publishers who are still doubting about making the switch.

8.5 GLOBAL DIGITAL EDUCATION

Digital education is the innovative incorporation of modern technology and digital tools to assist teaching and learning progress. It has been reshaping classrooms all over the world. All nations can now adopt remote learning technologies utilizing a combination of TV, radio, online, and mobile platforms. These provide easy access to information and make education more interactive. It is time for governments and educators worldwide to realize the remarkable contribution of 24/7/365 digital education. Governments around the world are critical to the sustainability of digital education. We now consider how some nations are practicing digital education.

- *United States:* Technology is omnipresent in our rapidly changing digital world. Technologies are paramount for education systems to support a modern workforce. The surest way of guaranteeing a peaceful and prosperous future is to educate the next generation. Education in the classroom is no longer restricted to reading books, writing on the blackboard to explain concepts, and taking notes. Technology has continued to play an essential role in delivering education to children outside the classroom environment. Stimulating growth from the ground up is a strategy that benefits service providers as much as it helps the students. The Google for Digital Education Fund is designed to foster the development of a high-performing digital education ecosystem, including providing infrastructure, connectivity, and digital equipment, enabling digitally competent and confident teachers and training staff.

- *United Kingdom:* It goes without saying that the COVID-19 pandemic has had a remarkable effect on education worldwide. In the UK alone, it led to nationwide school closures in March 2020, with most children receiving remote education until the start of the new school year in September 2020. Concerns that the move to remote education has led to a digital divide. Cambridge Assessment and Cambridge University Press have developed a set of outline principles that will help all interested students continue the debate around teaching, learning, and assessment. The increased use of digital remote education practices such as videoconferencing may have led to increased digital exclusion. Should digital education practices become more commonplace, efforts will be required to ensure both teachers and parents gain adequate digital skills. Digital education practices are predicted to become more widespread. The digital divide will remain challenging for educators and governments to address to ensure that disadvantaged students do not fall further behind [17].

- *Europe:* The EU is promoting the development of a high-performing European digital education ecosystem and is seeking to enhance citizens› competencies and skills for the digital transition. The Digital Education Action Plan (2021-2027) is a renewed European Union (EU) policy initiative that sets out a shared vision of high-quality, inclusive, and accessible digital education in Europe. The Action Plan, adopted on September 30, 2020, calls for greater cooperation at the European level on digital education. The Plan is a critical enabler in fulfilling the vision of achieving a European Education Area by 2025. It sets out two strategic priorities and fourteen actions to support them. Priority 1 is fostering the development of a high-performing digital education ecosystem. In addition, Priority 2 enhances digital skills and competencies for digital transformation [18].

- *India:* Today, India is one of the world›s top destinations for education. India has the world›s second-largest school system after China. Gone are the days when classroom training was restricted to textbook learning, with teachers using the blackboard to write notes for the students to copy. Digital education is making its way into the education system in India, fixing the Indian education system, and overtaking traditional classroom training. Students use technology to take remote classes from home or enroll in full-time, public, or private online schools. Although technology is not the magic wand to fix all problems, it allows for more flexibility in the learning process [19]. About 320 million learners in India have been adversely affected by the COVID-19 pandemic and have transitioned to e-learning.

- *China:* China is escalating a crackdown on its online education sector. President Xi Jinping suggested in March 2022 that the surge in after-school tutoring was putting immense pressure on China's kids, signaling a personal interest in curbing excesses. Just months ago, edtech outfits were one of the hottest investments in China's post-COVID internet industry. Xi's administration is taking unusually straightforward steps to influence the industry's evolution in China. Beijing is zeroing in on tutoring startups that thrived when schools sent students home. Their main concern centers on reckless pricing or advertising and the widening divide between the haves and have-nots. To that end, officials laid out many restrictions, including limiting the after-school tuition fees companies can charge [20].

8.6 BENEFITS

In the wake of the pandemic, people have begun to realize the far-reaching power of education-driven technology. Institutions have realized that digitalization is paramount to providing positive learning experiences and student choice. Digital technology is becoming increasingly commonplace in K-12 education. The advantages society has gained from digital learning or digital education have been unprecedented. Digital adoption by educational organizations can help institutions become more competitive. Other benefits of digital education include the following [21]:

1. *Full-Time Access:* Materials are always available to students 24/7. This access gives students complete flexibility over when and where they study.

2. *Facilitates Collaboration:* Education can benefit from digital learning as a collaboration tool by bringing people together through video conferencing, enabling students and teachers to

use shared documents. Figure 8.7 shows collaboration among children [22].

3. *More Resources:* Resources such as recorded lectures or additional reading can be easily shared. Digital technologies allow students to experience the globe and go to faraway places from the comfort of their computers.

4. *Better Engagement*: Educational institutions can quickly notice when a student is becoming disengaged, struggling with the course, or is ill and have the tools to remedy the situation more efficiently.

5. *Personalized Learning*: Digital learning can help enable personalized learning because everybody has specific techniques and learning methods that suit them.

6. *Facilitates New Learning Strategies*: There is increasing evidence that learning strategies such as microlearning, gamification, and virtual/augmented reality are very effective teaching methods.

Figure 8.7 Collaboration among children [22].

7. *Preparation for Work:* Digital learning and teaching can be a great way to prepare students for working life and life-long learning.

8. *Develop Accountability:* Digital learning can help to enhance student accountability and help them have a degree of ownership over their education.

9. *Student Progress Tracking:* Technology allows educational institutions to track student progress closely. This tracking can include examination results, assessments, and attendance records.

10. *Students' Employability:* Digital learning equips students with all the necessary skills to become gainfully employed and have careers in the future.

11. *Breadth of Information:* The Internet provides information overload. It makes knowledge accessible, ready, and up to date. Technology helps break down many global barriers, allowing students to interact with each other regardless of location or attend schools on an entirely different continent.

12. *More Affordable:* A significant advantage of online classes is the tremendous savings for students and the learning institution, which no longer has to reserve a physical location to teach courses. In addition to saving on the basics like books and supplies when you take classes online, you also save money on lunch and travel costs.

13. *Improve Teaching Productivity:* Teaching productivity may be improved by using technological aids, which facilitate better planning, easy and practical learning, quick assessment, better resources, new skills, etc.

14. *Develop Online Libraries:* Technological advancements have helped create and develop online libraries, which have facilitated interaction among students, teachers, and researchers from across the globe.

15. *People with Disability:* The move to online teaching dramatically benefits people with some types of disability, such as students with mobility or respiratory problems. Computer-based games play an essential role in the education of students with disabilities.

8.7 CHALLENGES

Although digital education has imparted all education levels, some challenges must be overcome. These are challenges that online and digital educators must not ignore. The dominance of standardized testing means digital technologies must raise students' test scores to levels administrators and policymakers deem significant. Other challenges of digital education include the following [23-25]:

1. *People prefer the status quo:*
   Both teachers and students are not willing to change. The majority of teachers are apprehensive of new technologies. They are not motivated to attend educational technology conferences or read books dealing with creative applications of digital technologies.

2. *Take teacher time to prepare:* It takes more time for a professor to design and teach online courses than regular, traditional face-to-face courses. Long after he goes to bed, students send emails and post messages.

3. *Assessment is a problem:* The activity of measuring learning is a major problem in digital education. Course developers often use simple multiple-choice items in their exams. This approach is inadequate for future leaders, managers, engineers, and scientists.

4. *Accreditation is problematic:* There has been a proliferation of colleges and universities offering online programs. Some of these are unwilling to obtain accreditation for their programs. Accreditation agencies never deal with the issues of quality.

5. *Digital divide:* There are concerns that the move to remote education has led to inequalities in access to learning. There are concerns about a digital divide resulting in digital imbalance, with disadvantaged children most affected.

6. *Isolation:* Digital education causes social isolation. Everyone student is in their manner and must work independently.

7. *Lack of student feedback:* Teachers can immediately comment directly to students in traditional classrooms. Online learning still struggles with student feedback.

8. *Lack of communication:* Developing students› communication skills is an area that needs to be addressed in online education. Face-to-face interaction and communication are missing.

9. *Allows Cheating:* A major drawback of online education is constant cheating during exams using various methods. Without video testing, seeing students directly during exams is impossible.

10. *Limited Professions:* Online education is more suitable to social sciences and humanities than scientific fields such as medical sciences and engineering that require specific practical and lab experience.

11. *Social Trust:* A challenge of teaching online is social trust, but tele-proximity could be the road ahead to resolve transactional distance implications.

12. *Damaging Health:* Online education is particularly damaging to health. Long hours of screen time are exhausting and negatively affect teachers› and students› vision and productivity.

13. *Lack of a clear strategy:* There is an apparent lack of direction for digital adoption. The schools must have a clear goal for using digital education. They must have a proper policy on digital education, infrastructure, content, interaction, and multiple languages.

14. *Incomplete knowledge:* The skills needed to achieve meaningful digital adoption are lacking.

15. *Unclear data pictures for the institution*: A vital part of any digital transformation needs to include breaking down these data silos to understand how students interact with the school.

16. *The capability of existing systems:* Many educational institutions already have various tools and systems to employ some limited forms of technology.

8.8 CONCLUSION

Technology has changed the way we teach and learn. Digital technologies are increasingly becoming part of education at all levels. Moreover, online K-12 schools are spreading across the United States. Schooling that combines computerized learning seems to be the emerging model. It is believed that the digital revolution will change the way students learn. Digital education has tended to produce nomadic digital citizens who practice some utopian politics. The key priorities in digital education should be developing online undergraduate and graduate courses [26].

Learning can continue for a lifetime, but it must start now. Digital Learning Day (February 27) was started in 2012 by the Alliance for Excellent Education to embrace learning in classrooms worldwide and share breakthroughs with learners everywhere. Digital education is here to stay. If we are serious about taking advantage of its potential benefits, we must appropriately fund our institutions and educators. More information about digital education can be found in the books in [6, 27-41] and the following related journals:

- *Journal of Education*
- *International Journal of Technology in Education and Science*
- *International Journal of Educational Technology in Higher Education*
- *IEEE Transactions on Education*
- *Australasian Journal of Educational Technology*

- *Frontiers in Education*
- *Digital Education Review*
- *Journal of Digital Educational Technology*
- *Journal of Digital Learning in*
- *Journal of Digital Learning and Education*
- *Digital Education Journals*
- *British Journal of Educational Technology*
- *Cambridge Journal of Education*
- *Distance Education*
- *Journal of Computer-Assisted Learning*
- *Journal of Educational Technology and Society*
- *The Journal of Higher Education*
- *The Journal of Interactive Technology and Pedagogy*
- *Journal of Online Learning and Teaching*
- *Online Learning*

REFERENCES

[1] M. N. O. Sadiku, A. E. Shadare, and S.M. Musa, "Digital education," *International Journal of Advanced Engineering, Management and Science*, vol. 3, no.1, Jan. 2017, pp. 64-65.

[2] M. N. O. Sadiku, M. Tembely, and S.M. Musa, "Online education," *Journal of Multidisciplinary Engineering Science and Technology*, vol. 4, no. 1, Jan. 2017, pp. 6479-8481.

[3] I. Jellnek, "Digital education strategy for the Czech Republic," *IT Pro*, September/October 2015, pp. 8-11.

[4] K. Massin, "Supporting digital education in Europe," December 2009, https://blog.google/outreach-initiatives/education/supporting-digital-education-in-europe/

[5] A. Haleem et al., "Understanding the role of digital technologies in education: A review," *Sustainable Operations and Computers*, vol. 3, 2022, pp. 275-285.

[6] M. N. O. Sadiku, *Emerging Internet-Based Technologies.* Boca Raton, FL: CRC Press, 2019, pp.109-123.

[7] N. Channan, "How to make digital education more accessible," October 2017, https://www.deccanherald.com/content/639382/how-make-digital-education-more.html

[8] M. N. O. Sadiku, U. C. Chukwu, A. Ajayi-Majebi, and S. M. Musa, "Education for digital natives," *International Journal of Trend in Scientific Research and Development,* vol. 6, no. 3, March-April 2022, pp.751-757.

[9] M. N. O. Sadiku, U. C. Chukwu, A. Ajayi-Majebi, and S. M. Musa, "Educating digital natives," *Proceedings of Frontiers in Education: Computer Science & Computer E+STEM+Online,* Las Vegas, July 2022.

[10] B. Mesko et al, "Digital health is a cultural transformation of traditional healthcare," *Mhealth,* vol. 3, September 2017.

[11] M. N. O. Sadiku, R. A. K. Jaiyesimi, J. B. Idehen, and S.M. Musa, *Emerging Technologies in Healthcare.* Bloomington, IN: AuthorHouse, 2021, p. 1

[12] M. N. O. Sadiku and O. D. Olaleye, *Emotional Intelligence and Its Applications. Bloomington,* IN: Author House, 2020, p. 43.

[13] M. N. O. Sadiku, J. O. Sadiku, and U. C. Chukwu, "Digital textbooks," *International Journal on Integrated Education,* vol. 6, no. 3, March 2023.

[14] H. Soffar, "What are eBooks?, Electronic books review, features, advantages & disadvantages," January 2020, https://www.online-sciences.com/technology/what-are-ebooks-electronic-books-review-features-advantages-disadvantages/

[15] D. Wright, "Digital textbooks in K-12 Schools," October 2013, https://comptroller.tn.gov/office-functions/research-and-education-accountability/publications/prek-12/digital-textbooks-in-k-12-schools.html

[16] Korea Bizwire, "Majority of students say it's okay to use digital textbooks during class," August 2020, http://koreabizwire.com/majority-of-students-say-its-okay-to-use-digital-textbooks-during-class/167363

[17] "Has COVID-19 highlighted a digital divide in UK education?" July 2021, https://www.cambridge.org/news-and-insights/insights/Has-COVID19-highlighted-a-digital-divide-in-UK-education

[18] "Digital Education Action Plan: 2021-2027?" https://education.ec.europa.eu/focus-topics/digital-education/action-plan

[19] "This is how digital education is fixing education system in India," January 2020, https://www.indiatoday.in/education-today/featurephilia/story/digital-education-education-system-in-india-divd-1594399-2019-09-02

[20] "As China cracks down on online education, it wrecks IPO prospects," https://www.aljazeera.com/economy/2021/5/31/bb-as-china-cracks-down-on-ed-tech-it-wrecks-ipo-prospects

[21] H. Walters, "The top 10 benefits of digital learning," January 2022, https://elearningindustry.com/the-top-benefits-of-digital-learning

[22] A. Singh, " What is the digital education system and its advantages for students," September 2020, https://www.theasianschool.net/blog/what-is-the-digital-education-system-and-its-advantages-for-students/

[23] T. C. Reeves, "Storms clouds on digital education horizon," *Journal of Computing in Higher Education*, vol. 15, no. 1, Fall 2003, pp. 3-26.

[24] A. Bhattacharya, " Digital transformation challenges in education institutions," https://hospitalityinsights.ehl.edu/digital-transformation-challenges

[25] "Online education does more good than harm," October 2021, https://www.smarther.co/blog/online-education-does-more-good-than-harm/

[26] A. Emejulu and C. McGregor, "Towards a radical citizenship in digital education," *Critical Studies in Education*, 2016, pp. 1-17.

[27] S. Bayne et al., *The Manifesto of Teaching Online*. The MIT Press, 2020.

[28] M. Thomas, *Digital Education: Opportunities for Social Collaboration*. Springer, 2011.

[29] J. Conrads, et al., *Digital Education Policies in Europe and Beyond: Key Design Principles for More Effective Policies*. Publications Office of the European Union, 2017.

[30] P. Burch and A. G. Good. *Equal Scrutiny: Privatization and Accountability in Digital Education*. Cambridge, MA: Harvard Education Press, 208.

[31] A. Juarez and K. Goyette, *The Complete EdTech Coach: An Organic Approach to Supporting Digital Learning*. Dave Burgess Consulting Inc., 2020.

[32] S. Pal, T. Q. Cuong, and R. S. S. Nehru (eds.), *Digital Education for the 21st Century Technologies and Protocols*. Apple Academic Press, 2021.

[33] O. Zawacki-Richter and I. Jung (eds.), *Handbook of Open, Distance and Digital Education*. Springer, 2020.

[34] J. Traxler and M. Smith, *Digital Learning in Higher Education: COVID-19 and Beyond*. Edward Elgar Publishing, 2022.

[35] F. Rennie and K. Smyth, *Digital Learning: The Key Concepts*. Taylor & Francis, 2018.

[36] A. Marcus-Quinn and T. Hourigan (eds.), *Handbook on Digital Learning for K-12 Schools*. Springer, 2016.

[37] R. S. S. Nehru, S. Pal, T. Q. Cuong (eds.), *Digital Education Pedagogy: Principles and Paradigms*. Apple Academic Press, 2020.

[38] J. P. Costa, *Digital Learning for All, Now: A School Leader's Guide for 1:1 On a Budget*. SAGE Publications, 2012.

[39] A. Ochsner, W. G. Tierney, and Z. B. Corwin (eds.), *Diversifying Digital Learning: Online Literacy and Educational Opportunity*. Johns Hopkins University Press, 2018.

[40] D. Kergel, *Digital Learning in Motion: From Book Culture to the Digital Age*. Taylor & Francis, 2020.

[41] C. J. Heinrich, J. Darling-Aduana, A. G. Good, *Equity and Quality in Digital Learning: Realizing the Promise in K-12 Education*. Harvard Education Press, 2020.

CHAPTER 9

ONLINE EDUCATION

"It's a fact that online learning is the future and will undoubtedly replace land-based learning in the future."
—Forbes

9.1 INTRODUCTION

Education is the process of transferring knowledge, values, methods, skills, and beliefs from one individual to another. Distance education originated in the United States in the 1800s when teachers and learners at the University of Chicago were at different locations and tried to connect through correspondence courses. In the mid-1980s, several universities and schools initiated the first online college courses. The advent of the Internet was a catalyst for moving distance online education to the next level [1].

Before the digital age, distance learning took the form of correspondence courses emphasizing individual self-paced lessons. Education providers are moving from traditional face-to-face environments to those that are completely electronic. Online education is an emerging field that is situated at the junction of distance education and instructional technology. It is becoming a new paradigm in education. The movement to online education requires applying new strategies to suit the new medium. With the modernization of distance education and training, online education uses computer networks and satellite communication networks to deliver education. It provides University equivalent courses for millions of students globally [2]. It is unlike traditional learning, where students can directly share their views and clarify their queries with the teacher, thus getting their questions answered right away. Figure 9.1 compares online learning with traditional learning [3].

Online education, often called distance education or web-based education, is currently the latest, most popular form of distance education. It is a form of open and distance education widely used in higher education. It applies the Internet and communication technologies and makes education open, dynamic, and affordable to those who want to learn, regardless of their age or location. More and more universities and publishers worldwide have opted to use online education. For example, for-profit institutions such as University of Phoenix, Kaplan University, Walden University, and Athabasca University (in Canada) have dominated the online market. Now, there are evening classes, weekend classes, satellite campuses, and cyberclasses. Online education provides university equivalent courses for millions of students across the globe.

Online courses refer to those courses in which at least 80% of the content is delivered online. Massive Online Open Courses (MOOCs) are a subset of online courses. Since the introduction of the first MOOCs in 2003 in the United Kingdom, millions of students worldwide have grabbed the opportunity to take courses online. MOOCs help students acquire knowledge in a self-paced manner and choose what they learn and when to learn. They have proved useful for students, especially from underdeveloped countries. They enable them to access standard courses for little or no cost [4,5].

This chapter discusses the strengths, weaknesses, and potentiality of online education. It begins with providing the need for online education. It addresses online teaching, online learning, and online laboratory for courses that require developing hands-on skills. Then it covers MOOC, which is an open online course that allows anyone to register without time limitations. It discusses enabling technologies for online education, its quality and effectiveness, benefits, and challenges. It covers the global implementation of online education. The last section concludes with comments.

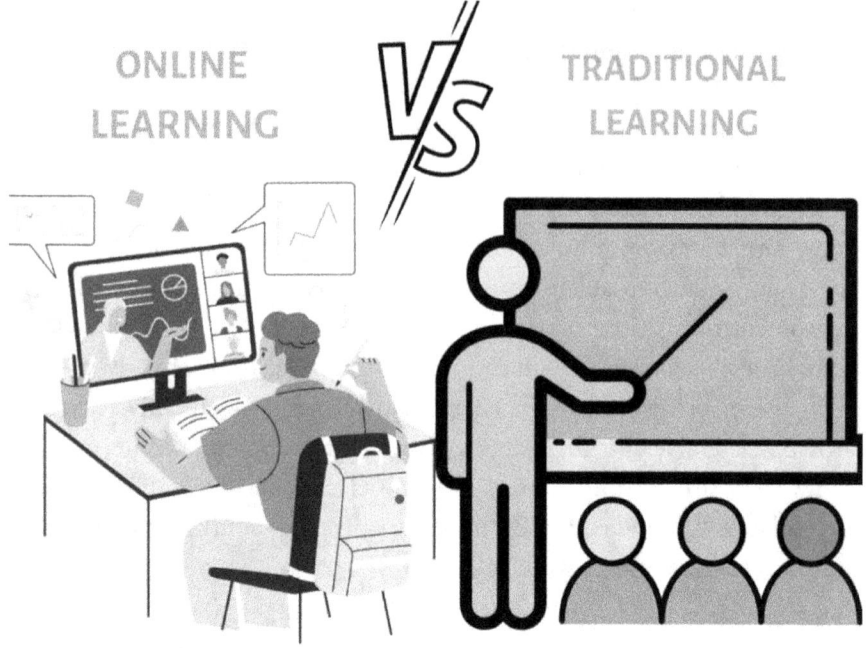

Figure 9.1 Comparing online learning with traditional learning [3].

9.2 NEED FOR ONLINE EDUCATION

The recent development in the Internet, coupled with low-cost communication, has caused a surge in online education. The use of animation, virtual reality, audio, video, chat, video conferencing, and social networking sites make online learning a rich experience. Online education is well known for its appeal to nontraditional students. Some factors are driving the need for online education. These include [6]:

- *Maintaining a competent workforce:* Due to the rapidly changing environment and competition, employees' knowledge and skills need constant updating. Using traditional methods is expensive. Online education reduces the cost of maintaining a competent workforce.

- *Lifelong learning:* Only a few people hold the same job throughout their lifetime. To remain relevant and employable, people need to acquire new skills. Online education provides a cheap, flexible, and convenient means for lifelong learning.

- *Cost:* The cost of traditional education has risen in recent years. Several cost-conscious students choose to take some of their courses online.

- *Convenience*: Online courses are available 24/7, and students can study them in their free, convenient time. They can keep their jobs and study at their own pace. Online education offers flexibility to both instructors and students. Online education is preferred by students who cannot participate in traditional classroom settings.

- *Decline in State Funding.* Traditional education is facing a lot of challenges—it is becoming more expensive, there is a shortage of professors, cuts in funding, busy classrooms, course shortages, limited infrastructures, etc. For more than two decades, state support for higher education has declined. Colleges and universities respond to this by raising tuition, cutting programs, increasing class sizes, and increasing their online course offerings to increase enrolment.

9.3 ONLINE TEACHING

Teachers are pressured to use digital technologies to teach students and prepare them for work in a globalized digital economy. Online teaching offers exciting opportunities to expand the learning environment for diverse student populations. As the demand for online teaching increases, college professors may be asked to consider teaching their classes online. Online teaching shares much with face-to-face teaching has a unique set of skills and requirements. Both approaches are similar in content, except in pace and delivery. Rather than developing the courses from scratch, companies have emerged to take care of the courses. Professors need to use course management system (CMS) software to prepare and deliver their courses. Using the software allows instructors to get it right from the beginning [7]. An example of online teaching is shown in Figure 9.2 [8].

Figure 9.2 An example of online teaching [8].

For online teaching to be successful, it is recommended that the instructor should follow the following seven principles [9]: (1) encourage student participation, (2) encourage student cooperation, (3) encourage active learning, (4) give prompt feedback, (5) emphasize time on task, (5) communicate high expectations, (7) Respect diverse talents and ways of learning. To these principles, one may add seven more [10]: (1) address individual differences, (2) motivate the student, (3) avoid information overload, (4) create a real-life context, (5) encourage social interaction, (6) provide hands-on activities, and (7) encourage student reflection.

Issues facing an online instructor include being effective in delivering the course, responding to student emails, getting used to the online tools and infrastructure. Critics of online teaching and learning question its value, effectiveness, and quality. Since online teaching and learning systems have not been able to convey interactions between the instructor and students, their educational effectiveness is lower than the traditional face-to-face lecture. Responding to student email messages in a timely manner can be challenging since it requires a significant amount of the instructor's time. It takes a lot of time to prepare and teach an online course. The challenge of online education largely depends on online instructors. There is also the issue of intellectual property and ownership of materials on the web [11].

9.4 ONLINE LEARNING

Online learning refers to a form of distance learning that takes place partially or entirely over the web. It is learning that is supported by information and communication technologies (ICTs). The "brick and mortar" classroom has started losing its monopoly as the sole place of learning.

The learning process is complex and it involves the auditory, visual, and tactile senses. The traditional way of learning at a campus university is not for everyone. Online learning is for those who wish to study for a degree alongside work or other commitments. It allows students to pursue an internationally recognized degree without the need to attend classes on campus. It is convenient since it allows one to study anywhere with Internet access. They can learn whatever they want when they want it. The learning is self-paced and offered at a lower cost. Online courses are available 24/7.

Online learning started in 1989 when the University of Phoenix started began to offer courses through the Internet. Online learning has been referred to as a form of distance education and as web-based learning, e-learning, and digital learning. It is offered over the Internet and uses web-based materials and activities.

Online courses may be delivered in two ways: asynchronous learning or synchronous learning format. Asynchronous learning takes place when online participants are not required to be online at the same time. It is flexible because it allows instructors and learners to communicate anytime, anywhere. Although students communicate through emails and phone calls, asynchronous learning is regarded as less social in nature and can cause learners to feel isolated. Distance education is customarily asynchronous. Synchronous learning takes place when the online class meets at the same specified meeting time, and the learners utilize the online media at the same time. It serves four functions: instruction, collaboration, support, and information exchange. In a synchronous environment, instructors and students can interact with real-time responses. This is close to face-to-face learning [12]. Figure 9.3 shows an example of online learning using Zoom [13].

Figure 9.3 Online learning using zoom [13].

Students need to be technologically savvy to use technology tools that may be required. Students of the digital age appear to be independent, more technology-disciplined, and technology savvy, and well suited for an online environment. Online learning at your own pace can allow introverts to thrive in ways that traditional settings cannot.

Online learning is under the broader scope of electronic learning (or e-learning). An e-learning process involves technological infrastructure, an e-learning software platform, e-learning content, and participants. Popular e-learning platforms include Moodle, Claroline, and EdX. Moodle is a free online learning management system (LMS) used for blended learning, distance education, and flipped classrooms. Claroline is a collaborative online learning and working open-source platform. It is easy to use and available in several countries and languages. EdX is an open-source and free online LMS. Its goal was to act as the WordPress for MOOC [14].

Whether offered on campus or delivered online, each course must meet the same rigorous criteria and strict academic standards. The only difference is in the way the course is delivered. Generally, students are required to have access to a computer system with high-speed Internet connections. They may also expect electronic academic support services such as registration, financial aid, libraries, tutoring, and advisement.

Issues facing online students include the requirement of self-directed learning and self-discipline, which may influence the success or failure of online learners. They may be tempted to procrastinate in working on their assignments. The issue of quality in online learning has been raised, and it is as complex as the reality of online learning itself. The Quality Matters Program based in the US (www.qmprogram.org) has established national benchmarks for online courses and has become internationally recognized [15].

9.5 ONLINE LABORATORY

The online laboratory (OL) offers a convenient, less expensive, and more efficient means of providing laboratory experiments to students using the Internet. The experiments can be accessed anytime and anywhere with limited access to a traditional campus setting. Online laboratories are becoming important and common for two reasons. First, laboratories have become indispensable tools for teaching, training, and learning in science, engineering, and technology. Engineering, in particular, is all about hands-on learning of concepts and needs effective laboratory courseware to complement the theoretical courses. Second, online learning has become a part of the educational landscape. It is growing in scope and acceptance because of the flexibility for the learner and cost-effectiveness for the institution. Online education needs virtual laboratories that can meet the needs of modern science education for their students.

The online laboratory (or laboratory at a distance) allows students to conduct scientific experiments in a virtual environment. Internet-based experimentation permits the use of resources, knowledge, software, and data available on the web. It is bringing a laboratory into the home. This approach can cater to students at the undergraduate and graduate levels. The motivation for developing an online laboratory is to make the whole experience of a laboratory more accessible, more convenient, less expensive, and efficient. Also, providing the resources necessary in the traditional physical laboratory setting is challenged by increasing budgetary and space constraints. Delivery of an online laboratory is a potentially cost-effective solution to the problem. Compared to their offline (or onsite) equivalents, online experiments are more customizable and scalable [16].

Online laboratories are no longer just a science fiction dream. Many institutions of learning have started to implement them into their learning process. The online lab is offered in electric circuits, electronics, communication, control systems, computer science, electrical engineering, mechanical engineering, civil engineering, biomedical engineering, physical sciences, medicine, and psychology. A typical lab in a virtual learning environment is shown in Figure 9.4 [17].

There are two types of online laboratories: (1) Remote labs allow students to collect data from a real physical laboratory setup. It uses real plants and physical devices which are teleoperated in real-time. (2) Virtual lab simulates the real equipment. Simulations have evolved into interactive graphical user interfaces where students can manipulate the experiment parameters and do some exploration. The two types of labs can be combined to support specific learning activities.

Motivating Internet users to participate in a web-based experiment can be a resource-intensive and difficult task. Online experiments require a great deal of technical expertise to create and maintain [16,18].

Figure 9.4 A typical lab in a virtual learning environment [17].

An online lab will generally consist of hardware-based remote experiments. Since there are many ways to offer online laboratories, it is difficult to provide a general outline. The following tips are helpful in understanding what an OL consists of. A sound OL should have [19,20]:

- Clearly stated learning objectives
- List of equipment
- Key theoretical concepts needed to perform the experiment
- Clear and precise step-by-step instructions on how to perform experiments
- Use Graphical User Interface design approaches

An online laboratory includes web-based multimedia and interactive resources. While there are many possibilities to format transmitted data, the data exchange formats most widely used by web developers are XML (eXtensible Markup Language) and JSON (JavaScript Object Notation). JSON has the advantage of being easier to read and map to variables, not only in JavaScript.

The mass adoption of smart devices automatically means that their users may need to have access to online laboratories from them. Today mobile laboratories constitute the most appropriate way to implement Massive Open Online Laboratories (MOOLs). A mobile laboratory is possible using a mobile smart device. Educators across the globe can contribute to the laboratory and access the lab courseware created by other fellow educators.

9.6 MASSIVE OPEN ONLINE COURSES

MOOC is an open online course that allows anyone to register without time limitations, geographic restrictions, or prerequisites. MOOCs are essentially a new type of online education that allows anyone, anywhere, to participate via video lectures, peer-to-peer activities, computer-graded tests, and discussion forums.

They invite unlimited participation over the Internet. MOOCs aim to provide online education for busy people for the careers of tomorrow and extend knowledge and skills to the world. MOOC providers aim at offering the best courses over the Internet, from the best professors and the best schools, covering several disciplines.

MOOC is a form of distance education that was introduced in 2006. The term "Massive Open Online Course" was coined in 2008 by George Siemens and Stephen Downes after completing an online course at the University of Manitoba, Canada [21]. New York Times declared 2012 as the Year of MOOC because that was when MOOCs hit the mainstream, with private companies including Coursera and Udacity established and set out to partner with top-tier US universities. MOOCs are a collective effort to bring higher education into the digital age. The main characteristics of a MOOC include the following [22]:

- It is massive. There is no limit to the number of learners.
- It is flexible. Learners can participate at various levels.
- It is a web-based education that facilitates learners' empowerment.
- It is easily accessible. Participants have access to additional resources.
- It offers lower costs of education.
- It cuts down the costs of labor and infrastructure.

The major non-profits MOOC providers include Khan Academy and edX, while for-profit MOOC providers include Udacity, and Coursera. Other non-academic MOOC providers include Saylor, Udemy, Skillfeed, UoPeople, and Academic Earth. University MOOC pioneers include Massachusetts Institute of Technology, Stanford University, Harvard University, University of Pennsylvania, Georgina Institute of Technology, University of Texas at Austin, University of California at Berkeley, San Jose State University, and Kaplan University [23]. There are several other MOOC providers worldwide, in the United Kingdom, Canada, India, China, etc. They offer MOOCs in many areas, such as engineering, computer science, finance, business, education, health sciences, criminal justice, cyber-security, IT, psychology, archeology, legal studies, and nursing. It is claimed that MOOCs are based on sound pedagogical principles that are comparable with courses offered by colleges and universities in face-to-face mode.

MOOCs have some advantages: democratizing learning, free courses, and economy of scale. The MOOC phenomenon is recent, disruptive, and revolutionary in higher education. Although MOOCs represent a recent, huge step in open education, many issues and questions remain open and need to be addressed. They have come under increased scrutiny over their goals, uses, and effectiveness. Although MOOCs may not displace brick-and-mortar higher education, they are here to stay and provide innovative, lifelong education through professors at prestigious universities in partnership with MOOC providers [24].

9.7 ENABLING TECHNOLOGY

Online education needs effective tools to create and deliver content. More than 110-course management software packages have been introduced into the online education market [25]. Digital technologies govern the work of policymakers, educators, parents, and learners. For example, the Internet provides easy access to unlimited information. It allows students and teachers to learn different ways of learning. Online courses are best taught when they are engineered to take advantage of the learning opportunities the digital online technologies offer. Technology has been a boom for educators and learners. It has been the catalyst for online delivery of higher education. The application of technology and the proliferation of computers, the Internet, and smart devices have transformed the way education is delivered and received. Technology is used as a medium for online or virtual education. The main requirement is a computer system and Internet connectivity (cable, wireless, DSL, etc.). Modern technologies such as web-based applications, multimedia, video records, and search engines are used in online education. Using audio/video-based delivery is the closest to traditional face-to-face learning environments. The use of Facebook, Twitter, and Skype chat enhances student-to-student or student-to-professor interactions.

The minimum technological infrastructure required for online education include computers, computer networks, online student services, and a CMS [26]. The tools required for developing online education includes email servers, web servers, list servers, bulletin boards, chat rooms, audio/video servers, Internet conference servers, and web channel servers [27].

9.8 PRESENCE

In the face-to-face learning environment, we do not need to think much about being present because we are there physically. Creating a sense of presence is important for online education because it can enhance instructor-learner relationships. People are social beings by nature. Our sense of presence is experienced in different ways. Presence involves two things: telepresence and social presence. Telepresence occurs when learners feel that they are present at a remote location. Social presence implies that there are interactions with others online. There is feeling of being there with other learners and the instructor.

One cannot be pragmatic in designing instructor presence. Instructor presence includes the planning that goes into developing your course and what you do when interacting with the students. The sense of instructor presence is created through a combination of videos, photos, and narratives, depending on how comfortable the instructors are with the medium. By the middle of the courses, learners should have identified others they feel a kinship. It feels that the instructors and learners are accessible to each other. As technology evolves, we are no longer limited by physical interactions. We are interconnected, and our world becomes smaller [28].

9.9 QUALITY AND EFFECTIVENESS

Little is known about the effectiveness of online courses in engaging students in the learning process. We do not know whether the course offered is of the highest standard of education. Although most online courses, such as MOOCs, are well-packaged, their instructional quality is relatively poor. Both administrators and faculty have expressed concern regarding the quality and effectiveness of online education. Even prospective employees are skeptical and concerned about the quality of online education and the graduates it produces.

Since the primary goal of education is learning, learning effectiveness must be the first measure by which online education is assessed. Online education is not equivalent to traditional education, as student learning may not be the same quality. Instructional quality refers to concerns about the effectiveness of teaching or learning environments in light of educational standards. Advocates of online education need to demonstrate that online teaching and learning are at least as good as classroom education. While some observe worse performance in online courses compared with traditional courses, others find the opposite. Thus, quality depends on the beholder and the situation at hand. The traditional indicators for quality are changing [29]. Figure 9.5 shows some quality elements of online education [30].

Figure 9.5 Some quality elements in online education [30].

Some institutions use faculty effectiveness as a measure of quality. Technology cannot replace the role of a well-prepared teacher. Others see the student ultimately influencing an online course's effectiveness and performance. Effective learning stems from the active participation and involvement of the learner. Healthy participation is energetic, spontaneous, and helpful in motivating students. There is a high correlation between instructor-student and student-student interactions in online courses and student satisfaction.

9.10 BENEFITS

The impact of online education is obvious in many fields, such as lifelong learning, professional development, and business training. Online education is growing in popularity for several reasons and has attracted people from diverse groups. It is scalable and less expensive [31]. Courses that are not offered in many institutions can be offered online. Online education has been employed as a means of achieving a balance between the competing demands of family, work, and school. It provides numerous opportunities for both educators and learners. It opens classrooms to the world. Course contents may be translated into several languages. Although online education may not work for everyone, some less-developed countries see online education as cost-effective.

Other benefits of online education include the following [3]:

(1) *Convenience*: Perhaps the greatest initial appeal for online education is its convenience, accessibility, and availability to learners. A student can live in New York and take a class in London. The online student can take a French course from a teacher in France without having to leave home. Students can work -time and earn their degrees.

(2) *Accessibility:* Online education improves access to higher education and makes it possible for more people to attend college. It makes the best quality education and best educators available to the whole world. Access to the world's top professors is priceless. Since the courses are self-paced, the student can complete them whenever possible.

(3) *Learn from anywhere at any time*: It allows students to work on the course anywhere with an Internet connection. Since everything is available online, accessing class materials and submitting work is very convenient.

(4) *No discrimination:* There is no discrimination among students on the basis of race, sex, religion, and nationality. Students can study what they want. Cultures may be shared through online learning, and gender is not an issue.

(5) *Review lectures instantly:* It is easy for minds to be distracted during a lecture. In many online programs, students can review words from professors instantly, either by rewinding the audio or video or by reading the transcript.

(6) *Less intimidating*: Many students in traditional classroom environments are not comfortable speaking in public. Online education tends to foster better class participation.

(7) *More time to think before sharing:* In an online environment, students can spend as much time as they want thinking about and honing their ideas. This attribute can lead to greater confidence.

(8) *Group communication:* Distance learning programs foster virtual communication and allow students to work with team members via email, chat rooms, and other easy-to-use methods.

(9) *Flexible learning schedule*: There is flexible class time and the ability to attend class anywhere with an Internet connection. Because they are unscheduled, online courses increase student autonomy. A student can experience the first half of a lesson one day and the second half the next day.

(10) *Cost:* The cost of an online course may be comparable with a traditional course. Students can save money by avoiding many fees typical of traditional education, including lab fees, commuting

costs, parking, accommodation, etc. Time and money are saved by not driving to school.

(11) *Instructor availability:* Web-based technologies make conversing with several students at once much easier.

(12) *Diversity:* It eliminates a "one-size-fits-all" approach (which is ineffective) and can be customized to meet diverse learning needs.

Some of these benefits are shown in Figure 9.6.

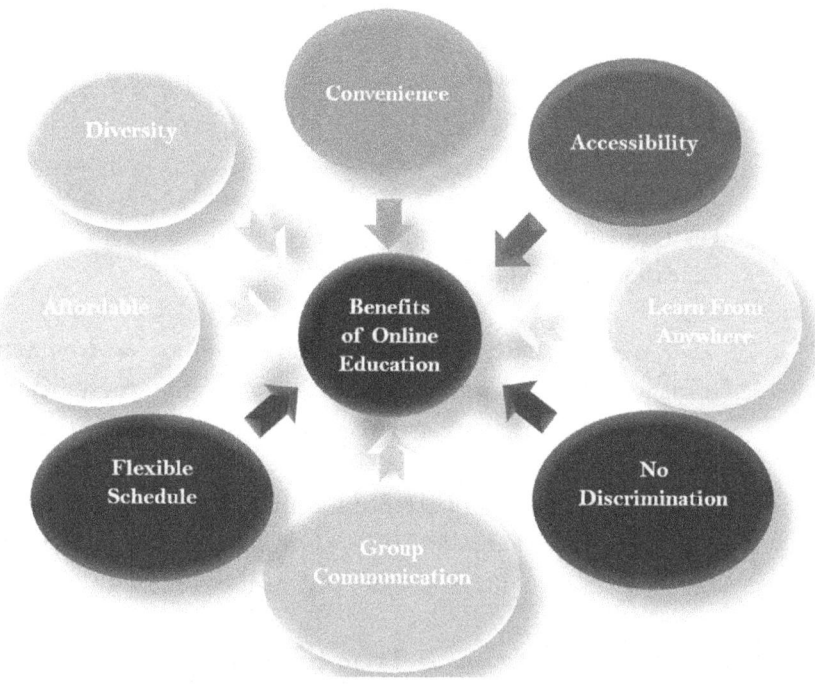

Figure 9.6 Some benefits of online education.

9.11 CHALLENGES

While online education solves some problems facing traditional education, it poses a different challenges. Despite the proliferation of online courses, some observers have expressed some concerns. First, faculty support is mixed. While some faculty members embrace online education, some resist the shift to online course delivery. They resist supporting and actively participating in online education. They see online education as a potential threat to current education models and a low-quality substitute for traditional ways of learning. It takes more time for a professor to prepare and teach online courses than regular, traditional face-to-face courses. Long after he goes to bed, students send emails and post messages.

Second, the majority of faculty members are apprehensive about new technologies. They express apprehension about online education because the associated technologies can be frustrating. They are not motivated to attend educational technology conferences or read books dealing with creative applications of digital technologies.

Third, assessment, the activity of measuring learning, is a major problem in online education. Course developers often use simple multiple-choice items in their exams. This approach is inadequate for future leaders, managers, engineers, and scientists.

Fourth, there is a problem with accreditation. There has been a proliferation of colleges and universities offering online programs. Some of these are unwilling to obtain accreditation for their programs. Accreditation agencies never deal with the issues of quality [32].

Fifth, a major disadvantage of online education is the absence of face-to-face or interpersonal interactions with instructors and fellow students. Most students are working full-time and have many distractions. There is the problem of assuring the identity of online students.

Sixth, online education has several direct and indirect costs, including hardware, software, website development and maintenance, and video recording. Developing a course for online education (for edX and Coursera, for example) may take a professor hundreds of hours and more time to revise. Students taking online courses complain that it is time-consuming navigating the web.

Seventh, some critics of online education complain that one cannot ensure the rigor of the offerings and the quality of the education. Many stakeholders are apprehensive over the lack of quality or richness of online courses. Some for-profit online education providers are more concerned about revenue and enrollment numbers than the quality of their programs. Verifying that students are not cheating in an online test-taking environment is harder. It lacks the moral and ethical engagement necessary for literal education. Instructors can use tools such as Turnitin to detect plagiarism.

Eighth, the focus of online education is geared toward the delivery of information, rather than student engagement. What is lacking is the ability to change from data to information, from information to knowledge, and from knowledge to wisdom within each learner [33].

Ninth, incorporating hands-on laboratory experiments in an online engineering course is a challenge. Also, there is the perception that online courses take more time and work; only self-disciplined and self-motivated students are likely to succeed. It is perceived as an extension of the university of capitalism, which is now digital and global.

Finally, there are also a set of legal and ethical issues which must be resolved. The legal problem particularly involves copyright and intellectual property. Students' online self-disclosure remains permanent and risks electronic breaches or hacking. In developing nations, online education barriers include prohibitive Internet connection costs and inadequate technical infrastructures.

These are challenges that online educators and institutions must not ignore.

9.12 GLOBAL ONLINE EDUCATION

Online education refers to courses taken at home with access to the Internet and with the help of an electronic device such as a mobile, tablet, laptop, or desktop computer. It opens classrooms to the world. It is now gaining popularity worldwide. Cultures may be shared through online learning, and gender is not an issue. Course contents may be translated into several languages. If you desire to specialize or improve your education and you cannot afford the tuition and leave your home, then online education is the solution. As students, parents, and educators begin to value online education worldwide, more and more schools are choosing to move online. Seeking online education has become common among students, working professionals, housewives, and senior citizens. A significant number of colleges in the US and abroad are moving om the traditional face-to-face classes into fully online, web-based courses. They are joining the ranks of institutions offering online education. We consider how online education is implemented in some nations.

- *United States:* Computer networks such as the Internet and digital technologies have transformed education at all levels to meet the demand of the 21st century. Online K-12 schools are spreading across the United States. Schooling that combines computerized learning seems to be the emerging model. With the advances in Internet technologies, online education has gained a lot of popularity in recent times and plays a formidable role in US higher education today. It will continue to become an increasingly mainstream mode of instruction. The COVID-19 pandemic accelerated a teacher shortage in schools across the nation. Millions of people want to earn their degrees but cannot because they cannot afford to go to school. Online education solves this problem by meeting paraprofessionals where they are. Education is not about where you learn but what you learn. All students can have equal access to education, no matter where they are. Several companies like Cisco and AT&T are helping to provide online education. For example, Cisco is committed to powering inclusive learning for all. Through AT&T Connected Learning, AT&T is investing in connectivity and technology, digital literacy, and digital learning solutions to help connect today's learners as part of its commitment to help bridge the digital divide and remove barriers to affordability, access, and adoption of tech. Online education is a great way to experience the US education system without leaving home. US institutions offer a variety of degree programs at undergraduate and graduate levels. Students usually pay a tuition fee to receive credit from a US institution for online education [34].

- *United Kingdom:* British education is known for its high quality, and many people worldwide dream about graduating from a UK university. The UK has the highest number of highly ranked universities in relation to the size of the nation. Critical thinking, creative methods of teaching, and quality-control mix successfully in British higher education. It is no surprise that many international students choose to study in the UK. The UK is a great provider of online education degrees. Several universities offer online degrees designed with input from top employers so you can learn the most in-demand skills for your future. The top ten UK Universities that offer online education are the following [35]:

    1. University College London
    2. The University of Edinburgh
    3. The University of Manchester
    4. King's College London
    5. University of Warwick
    6. University of Glasgow
    7. University of Sheffield
    8. University of Birmingham
    9. University of Leeds
    10. University of Nottingham

    The listed universities may provide all types of degrees, such as distance learning Bachelors, Masters, and PhDs, or just some degree levels. The University of London offers a range of free online courses and Massive Open Online Courses (MOOCs).

- *Europe:* Europe is a relatively small continent with astounding natural, historical, artistic, and cultural diversity. Most Europeans speak two or more languages, and studying a second foreign language for at least one year is compulsory in more than 20 European countries. Studying in a European class can greatly benefit students' ability to learn important international languages such as English, German, French, Spanish, Portuguese, Italian, and more. Finding the right online school can broaden a student's educational possibilities and help students who might have struggled with traditional schools shine [36]. The top ten European universities offering online education degrees [37]:

1. Wageningen University and Research, the Netherlands
2. Freie Universitat Berlin, Germany
3. Stockholm University, Sweden
4. Trinity College Dublin, Ireland
5. University of Oxford, the UK
6. European University Cyprus
7. EU Business School, Spain
8. Swiss School of Business and Management, Switzerland
9. International Telematic University UNINETTUNO, Italy
10. Université Catholique de Louvain (UCL), Belgium

These universities have an excellent reputation both nationally and internationally. Some of them participate in the MOOCs system teaching in English.

- *China:* China's compulsory education system is widely considered to be one of the world's most arduous. Online education in China, previously considered ineffective, has undergone significant infrastructural improvements as a result of the COVID-19 pandemic, which compelled students to take classes at home. Since then, online education for degree-seekers has become a more acceptable way to expand access to higher education in China. While there is a growing acceptance of online education, there remain key challenges online educators must overcome to gain true legitimacy in China's higher education sector. Unlike the considerable startup costs associated with building brick-and-mortar educational institutions, the creation of online degrees could be a more cost-effective means to afford large quantities of students the ability to receive post-secondary education provided they have access to the Internet [38].

- *India:* India is a diverse nation, and within these diversities come wide varieties of cultures and beliefs. India suffers a huge socioeconomic divide – the division of classes like high, low, and middle. Not even one-third of the population receives online education. Due to the COVID-19 pandemic and consecutive lockdowns, there has been a rising shift to online education. This shift seems to be becoming more permanent as eLearning is believed to be the future. Online education in India is growing tremendously and is spreading its roots in almost all sectors. Many university faculties are setting up accounts on online video conferencing platforms such as Zoom, Skype, Google Classroom, and Meet, among others, to engage with students. There are multiple advantages of pursuing online education in India that people can use to their fullest potential. The benefits of this unique and comfortable mode of attaining education have allured many [39]. Some factors affecting online education in India are depicted in Figure 9.7 [40].

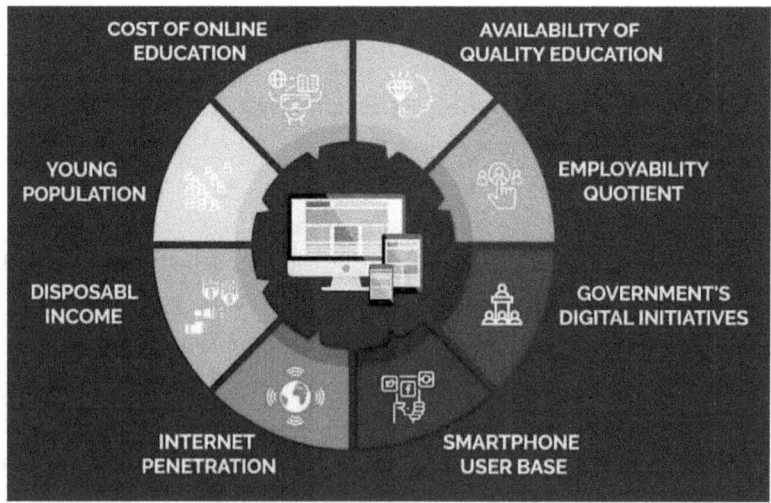

Figure 9.7 Some factors affecting online education in India [40].

9.13 CONCLUSION

Online education has a great potential to reach students with personalized education at a low cost. It also can potentially revolutionize global education and narrow the gap between developing and developed nations. It is gaining ground as an extension of traditional education. The emergence of social networking technologies is rapidly changing the delivery of online education. By taking advantage of these technologies, online education can provide quality education anywhere, anytime. Online education is growing, and traditional colleges and universities should begin leveraging it. Businesses and corporations are quick to accept online training. Online education is applied in all disciplines, such as engineering, computer science, medicine, nursing, business, music, and social sciences [41].

Online education is relatively new. It is here to stay and grow. It has been exploding in recent years as an option in colleges and universities both within the US and abroad. Most universities and colleges agree that online education is critical to their long-term strategy. It is the future of education. Transforming higher education will leave no stone of the institution untouched. It can be predicted that very soon, most college courses will use some form of online communication.

As the demand for online education by those who have jobs and require lifelong education increases, there are more and more expectations for implementing a teaching and learning system. More information about online education can be found in books [42-56] and the following journals exclusively devoted to it:

- *Distance Education,*
- *Journal of Distance Education*
- *Journal of Interactive Online Learning*
- *Journal of Educators Online.*

REFERENCES

[1] A. Sun and X. Chen, "Online education and its effective practice: A research review," *Journal of Information Technology Education: Research*, vol. 15, 2016, pp. 157-190.

[2] M. N. O. Sadiku, M. Tembely, and S. M. Musa, "Online education," *Journal of Multidisciplinary Engineering Science and Technology*, vol. 4, no. 1, January 2017, pp. 6479-8481.

[3] "10 benefits of online learning," https://indiaeducation.net/online-education/10-benefits-of-online-learning/

[4] I. Literat, "Implications of massive open online courses for higher education: mitigating or reifying educational inequalities?" *Higher Education Research & Development*, vol. 34. no. 6, 2015, pp. 1164-1177.

[5] S. K. Ch and S. Popuri, "Impact of online education: A study of online learning platforms and edX," *Proceedings of IEEE International Conference on MOOC, Innovation and Technology in Education*, 2013, pp. 366-370.

[6] A. H. Huang, "A supply-chain management perspective of online education," *Journal of Educational Technology Systems*, vol. 29, no. 2, 2000, pp. 93-106.

[7] M. N. O. Sadiku, P. O. Adebo, and S. M. Musa, "Online teaching and learning," *International Journal of Advanced Research in Computer Science and Software Engineering*, vol. 8, no. 2, February 2018, pp. 73-75.

[8] E. Dans, "Whether we like it or not, online teaching is the future, so let's start learning how to do it properly," https://www.forbes.com/sites/enriquedans/2020/11/30/whether-we-like-it-or-not-online-teaching-is-the-future-so-lets-start-learning-how-to-do-itproperly/?sh=715937f753ff

[9] J. Stern, "Introduction to online teaching and learning," www.wlac.edu/online/ documents/otl.pdf.

[10] H. Zsohar and J. A. Smith, "Transition from the classroom to the web: successful strategies Of teaching online," http://northeast.edu/CTC/Pdf/Successfulstrategies-for-teaching-online.pdf.

[11] S. Suryanarayanan and E. Kyriakides, "An online portal for collaborative learning and teaching for power engineering education," *IEEE Transactions on Power Systems;* vol. 19, no. 1, February 2004, pp. 73-80.

[12] " Online learning in higher education," *Wikipedia,* the free encyclopedia https://en.wikipedia.org/wiki/Online_learning_in_higher_education

[13] E. O. Wesch, "The ultimate zoom course 2022 - Beginner to expert fast," November 2021, https://www.udemy.com/course/zoom-course/

[14] N. Harrati, I. Bouchrika, and Z. Mahfouf, "e-Learning: On the uptake of modern technologies for online education," *Proceedings of the 6th International Conference on Information Communication and Management,* 2016, pp. 162—166.

[15] N. Butcher and M. Wilson-Strydom, *A Guide to Quality in Online Learning.* Dallas, TX: Academic Partnerships, 2013.

[16] M. N. O. Sadiku, M. Tembely, and S. M. Musa, "Online laboratory," *International Journal of Engineering Research,* vol. 6, no. 9, September 2017, pp. 425—426.

[17] E. Hodge, "Organizing workshops and lab in a virtual learning environment," February 2020, https://www.keg.com/news/organizing-workshops-and-lab-in-a-virtual-learning-environment

[18] A. Maiti and B. Tripathy, "Remote laboratories: design of experiments and their web implementation," *Educational Technology & Society,* vol. 16, no. 3, 2013, pp. 220-233.

[19] S. B. B Kanmani and M. Soni, "Online courseware for electronics laboratory courses: An example," *Proceedings of the IEEE International*

Conference on MOOC, Innovation and Technology in Education (MITE), 2014, pp. 372-376.

[20] A. Maiti and B. Tripathy, "Remote laboratories: design of experiments and their Web implementation," *Educational Technology & Society*, vol. 16, no. 3, 2013, pp. 220–233.

[21] T. R. Liyanagunawardena, "Massive open online courses," *Humanities*, vol. 4, no. I, 2015, pp. 35—41.

[22] W. Rubens, M. Kalz, and R. Koper, "Improving the learning design of massive open online courses," *The Turkish Online Journal of Educational Technology*, vol. 13, no. 4, October 2014, pp. 71—80.

[23] "Massive open online course," *Wikipedia*, the free encyclopedia https://en.wikipedia.org/wiki/Massive_open_online_course.

[24] M. N. O. Sadiku, S. M. Musa, and S. R. Nelatury, "Massive open online courses," *International Journal of Engineering Research and Allied Sciences*, vol. 2, no. 5, May 2017, pp. 1-3.

[25] Y. Kim, "Online education tools," *Public Performance & Management Review*, vol. 28, no. 2, 2004, pp. 275-280.

[26] R. L. G. Mitchell, "Online education and organizational change," *Community College Review*, vol. 37, no. I, July 2009, pp. 81—101.

[27] A. Bucur, "Components of online education in gerontology," *Gerontology & Geriatrics Education*, vol. 20, no. 4, 2000, pp. 31—45.

[28] R. M. Lehmand and S. C. O. Conceicao, *Creating a Sense of Presence in Online Teaching: How to "Be There" for Distance Learners*. San Francisco, CA: John Wiley & sons, 2010.

[29] K. Shelton, "A quality scorecard for the administration of online education programs: A Delphi study," *Doctoral Dissertation*, University of Nebraska, September 2010.

[30] S. Shakeeb, "Quality assurance matters: Time to tame the wild online education delivery," September 2021, https://mnu.edu.mv/quality-assurance-matters-time-to-tame-the-wild-online-education-delivery/

[31] J, Harish, "Online education: A revolution in the making," *CADMLIS*, vol. 2, no. 1, October 2013, pp. 26-39.

[32] T. C. Reeves, "Storms clouds on digital education horizon," *Journal of Computing in Higher Education*, vol. 15, no. I, Fall 2003, pp. 3—26.

[33] S. M. Natale and A. F. Libertella, "Online education: values dilemma in business and the search for emphatic engagement," *Journal of Business Ethics*, vol. 138, 2016, pp. 175-184.

[34] "Online learning," https://educationusa.state.gov/your-5-steps-us-study/research-your-options/online-learning

[35] "10 Top UK universities ideal for distance learning," January 2022, https://www.distancelearningportal.com/articles/294/10-top-uk-universities-ideal-for-distance-learning.html

[36] "Top online schools in Europe," https://world-schools.com/top-online-schools-in-europe/

[37] "10 Great European distance learning universities," January 2022, https://www.mastersportal.com/articles/1308/10-great-european-distance-learning-universities.html

[38] B. A. Swanson and A. Valdois, "Acceptance of online education in China: A reassessment in light of changed circumstances due to the COVID-19 pandemic," *International Journal of Educational Research Open*, vol. 3, October 2022.

[39] "Online education in India," January 2022, https://leverageedu.com/blog/online-education-in-india/

[40] "Online education," July 2020, https://www.drishtiias.com/daily-news-analysis/online-education

[41] M. N. O. Sadiku, A. E. Shadare, and S. M. Musa, "Digital education," *International Journal of Advanced Engineering, Management and Science*, vol. 3, no.1, January 2017, pp. 64-65.

[42] M. N. O. Sadiku, *Emerging Internet-Based Technologies*. Boca Raton, FL: CRC Press, chapter 7, 2019.

[43] K. C. Cook and K. Grant-Davie (eds.), *Online Education: Global Questions, Local Answers*. Amityville, NY: Baywood Publishing Company, 2005.

[44] K. Shattuck, *Assuring Quality in Online Education: Practices and Processes at the Teaching, Resource, and Program Levels*. Stylus Publishing, 2014.

[45] G. Veletsianos, *Learning Online: The Student Experience*. Johns Hopkins University Press, 2020

[46] M. Barbour and T. Clark (eds.), *Online, Blended, and Distance Education in Schools: Building Successful Programs*. Stylus Publishing, 2015

[47] J. C. Moore and J. R. Bourne (eds.), *Elements of Quality Online Education: Engaging Communities*. Sloan Consortium, 2005.

[48] C. N. Gunawardena and I. Jung (eds.), *Culture and Online Learning: Global Perspectives and Research*. Stylus Publishing, 2015.

[49] C. M. Hayes and K. E. Linder (eds.), *High-Impact Practices in Online Education: Research and Best Practices*. Stylus Publishing, 2019.

[50] G. Kearsley, *Online Education: Learning and Teaching in Cyberspace*. Wadsworth Thomson Learning, 2010.

[51] K. Grant-Davie and K. C. Cook (eds.), *Online Education 2.0: Evolving, Adapting, and Reinventing Online Technical Education*. Amityville, NY: Baywood Publishing Company, 2013.

[52] M. A. Maddix, J. R. Estep, and M. E. Lowe (eds.), *Best Practices of Online Education*. Charlotte, NV: Information Age Publishing, 2012.

[53] C. Haythornthwaite and M. M. Kazmer (eds.), *Learning, Culture and Community in Online Education: Research and Practice*. New York: Peter Lang Publishing, 2004.

[54] J. V. Boettcher and R. M. Conrad, *The Online Teaching Survival Guide*. San Francisco, CA: John Wiley & Sons, 2nd ed., 2016.

[55] T. Stavredes, *Effective Online Teaching*. San Francisco, CA: John Wiley & Sons, 2011.

[56] M. G. Moore and G. Kearsley, *Distance Education: A Systems View of Online Learning*. Belmont, CA: Wadsworth, 3rd ed., 2012.

CHAPTER 10

3D PRINTING IN EDUCATION

"3D printing turns digital files into physical objects by building them up layer-by-layer. It gives everyday consumers the power of manufacturing."
—Rudrabots

10.1 INTRODUCTION

Education is one of the most precious gifts we can offer our future generation. It continues to be a major concern for many Americans. This attribute is evident by the unparallel amount of money the US spends on education. Educators have a monumental task before them and face many challenges. Skills sought after in the job market evolve faster than their curriculums. Educators need to determine which technology is the best for their curriculum. Educational technology is the means of accelerating progress, delivering on the future of design potential, and making the earth a better learning environment. One of such emerging technologies in education is 3D printing. 3D printing is a cutting-edge technology that has been around for about 40 years. It is a technology that allows the creation of physical 3D objects through additive manufacturing techniques.

The 3D printer uses raw material combinations and builds an object one layer at a time. New material advances keep 3D printing at the forefront of innovation across many industries. Education is now being identified as a key target market within the 3D printing industry because 3D printing engages students more profoundly to learn lessons. It is currently in the process of revolutionizing the manufacturing industry worldwide. The concept of 3D printing is a simple, tried, and tested educational tool for teachers. Today the importance of including 3D printing in professional degrees and schools is a fact. 3D printing should be added to the curriculum in all academic institutions because it prepares the youths for the future. It presents opportunities to learn and use the same cutting-edge tools as professionals in the industry [1,2].

3D printing is bringing disruptive innovation in several sectors, including education.

The use of 3D printing as a support tool in education is increasing. 3D printers can be used in several areas of education. For example, history students can print out historical artifacts for investigation; graphic design students can print 3D versions of their artwork; geography students can print topography or demographic maps; chemistry students can print 3D models of molecules; biology students can print out cells, viruses, organs, and other biological artifacts; and math students can print out 3D models of problems to solve [3].

This chapter provides an overview of 3D printing in education. It begins by explaining what 3D printing is all about. It provides some applications of 3D printing in education. It highlights the benefits and challenges of using 3D printing in education. It covers the global use of 3D printing in education. The last section concludes with comments.

10.2 WHAT IS 3D PRINTING?

3D printing (also known as additive manufacturing (AM) or rapid prototyping (RP)) was invented in the early 1980s by Charles Hull, who is regarded as the father of 3D printing. Since then, it has been used in manufacturing, automotive, electronics, aviation, aerospace, aeronautics, engineering, architecture, pharmaceutics, consumer products, education, entertainment, medicine, space missions, the military, chemical industry, maritime industry, printing industry, and jewelry industry [4]

A 3D printer works by "printing" objects. Instead of using ink, it uses more substantive materials–plastics, metal, rubber, and the like. It scans an object—or takes an existing scan of an object—and slices it into layers, which can then convert it into a physical object. Layer by layer, the 3D printer can replicate images created in CAD programs. In other words, 3D printing instructs a computer to apply layer upon layer of a specific material (such as plastic or metal) until the final product is built. This feature is distinct from conventional manufacturing methods, which often rely on removal (cutting, drilling, chopping, grinding, forging, etc.) instead of adding. Models can be multi-colored to highlight important features, such as tumors, cavities, and vascular tracks. 3DP technology can build a 3D object in almost any shape imaginable as defined in a computer-aided design (CAD) file. It is additive technology distinct from traditional manufacturing techniques, which are subtractive processes in which material is removed by cutting or drilling [5].

3D printing has started breaking into the mainstream in recent years, with some models becoming affordable enough for home use. Many industries and professions around the world now use 3D printing. It plays a key role in making companies more competitive. The gap between industry and graduating students can be bridged by including the same cutting-edge tools, such as 3D printing, professionals use every day in the curriculum. There are 3D-printed homes, prosthetics, surgical devices, drones, hearing aids, and electric engine components. A typical 3D printer is shown in Figure 10.1 [6].

Figure 10.1 A typical 3D printer [6].

Before 3D printing was introduced in the classroom, teachers relied on pre-designed teaching aids to teach new material to students. Students and teachers were limited in expressing their ideas through writing and two-dimensional or three-dimensional drawings. Now 3D printing enables schools to make modeling part of the educational process cost-effectively. Educators from elementary school to university can use 3D printing in classrooms to show physical prototypes. 3D printing meets current educational requirements for STEM. It will make the dreams and creativity of students and teachers at all levels become reality. 3D printing will become an important driving force to encourage innovation among students and teachers [7].

3D printing is the means of producing three-dimensional solid objects from a digital model. It has been regarded as one of the pillars of the third industrial revolution. It could become an instrumental learning tool, helping to illustrate learning fundamentals, inspiring creativity in learning, and educating students to think outside the box. Today, if students can dream it, they can create it with 3D printing. As professionals across almost every industry continue to increase investment in 3D printing, the technology becomes an ever greater part of our daily lives.

3D printing technology can benefit educators in many ways. 3D printing is inspiring educators to develop creative ways of helping students. It provides teachers with three-dimensional visual aids in their classroom, particularly in illustrating a hard-to-grasp concept. Personalized educational aids can be 3D printed on demand. 3D printers can work as educational aids in classrooms. Educators are leveraging 3D printing to increase students' creativity and prepare the next generation of designers, artists, and scientists.

10.3 APPLICATIONS

3D printing has a variety of uses in numerous disciplines, such as healthcare, aerospace, engineering, printing, manufacturing, entertainment, education, chemistry, mathematics, biology, history, and architecture. 3D printing in education is applied in kindergarten, elementary, middle, and high schools, universities, libraries, technical colleges, and other educational settings.

From K-12 schools to post-graduate college programs, 3D printing is a way for educators to encourage more active participation in the learning process. However, the needs of educators vary widely; from elementary teachers to university professors, there is more than one job description. Thus, we cannot have one 3D printer that solves every problem. Every educator needs to incorporate 3D printing to provide the opportunity to learn more about the technology that is shaping the world. Figure 10.2 shows various uses of the 3D printer [8]. Some educational values of 3D printing are demonstrated in the following applications.

- *Elementary School Education:* Introducing K-12 students to engineering design practices as early as possible can prepare them better for future education and careers. Currently, 3D printers are in over 5,000 schools across the US. Schoolchildren live in a concrete world while trying to learn the abstract. 3D printing is an easy tactile medium for them to work with. Our students could learn so much from some things in this world if they had access to them. Those items could be recreated for any purpose with a good 3D artist in a CAD program. You can create appealing, accurate, and high-quality creations for the students with exciting student projects.

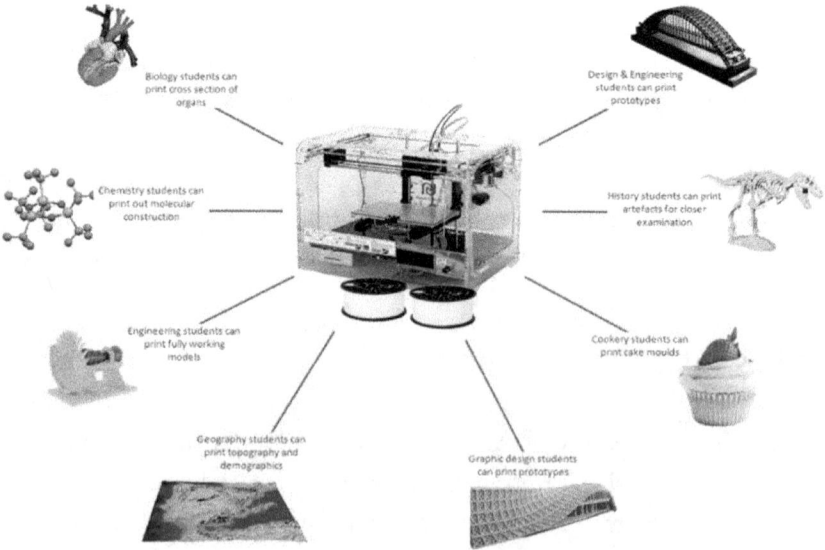

Figure 10.2 Various uses of the 3D printer [8].

3D PRINTING IN EDUCATION

Figure 10.3 An example of children using 3D printer [9].

The hands-on aspect of 3D printing in the classroom helps improve engagement and participation. Schools need robust, affordable, and user-friendly printers. XYZ Printing has been popular in education K-12 for years because it is cost-effective and easy to use. A Taiwanese 3D printer manufacturer manufactures this, providing a complete K–12 STEAM curriculum to accompany its hardware. Another 3D printer often found in classrooms is an FDM (Fused Deposition Modeling) machine. Figure 10.3 shows an example of children using a 3D printer [9]. Here are some examples of how schools and students can use a 3D printer in the classroom [10]:

➢ History students can print out historical artifacts to examine

➢ Graphic design students can print out 3D versions of their artwork

➢ Geography students can print out topography, demographic, or population maps

- Chemistry students can print out 3D models of molecules

- Biology students can print out cells, viruses, organs, and other biological artifacts

- Math students can print out 3D models of problems to solve

• *STEM Lesson:* The Science, Technology, Engineering, and Maths (STEM) program is an interdisciplinary approach to educating children from an early age with knowledge and skills in the four key disciplines of science, technology, engineering, and mathematics. STEAM (the A stands for Art) education builds on the foundations of STEM education and embeds the arts into its educational philosophy. STEM and STEAM naturally fit with project-based learning. Students integrate several disciplines, including science, math, and design, to understand concepts. Embedding 3D printing in STEM and STEAM learning encourages the critical thinking, problem-solving, and communication skills needed for future workforces. No technology enables STEM education better than 3D printing.

• *Higher Education:* 3D printing is widely applied in higher education. Universities play a major role in the diffusion of 3D printing. Some colleges have started to incorporate 3D printing in their curriculum, whereby students are challenged to create a variety of chemical models. This application motivates and engages students in learning chemistry while at the same time acquiring the skills of innovation, collaboration, and technological literacy necessary for 21st-century professionals [11]. For example, MIT offers courses at graduate and undergraduate levels that teach the basics of 3D printing. 3D printing is making the rapid distribution of up-to-the-minute anthropological discoveries to higher education a reality. Researchers around the US use Fusion3 3D printers in a wide variety of fields. The Fusion3 EDGE enables the printing of high-quality objects at high speeds.

Here are some of the ways 3D printing is used in higher education [12]:

➢ Engineering design students can print out prototypes

➢ Architecture students can print out 3D models of designs

➢ Cooking students can create molds for food products

➢ Automotive students can print out replacement parts or modified examples of existing parts for testing

➢ Math students can print out "problems" to solve in their own learning spaces, from scale models to city infrastructural design challenges

➢ Medical students can print human organs, develop prosthetics, and improve their understanding of a human body

- *Medical Education:* 3D printing is a technology perfectly tailored for the healthcare industry. It offers a range of precision healthcare solutions, including tissue and organ fabrication, creation of customized prosthetics, implants, and anatomical models, drug delivery, and testing, as well as in clinical practice. There are several reasons 3D printing works well for medical applications and education. An on-demand 3D printing service can be used to manufacture medical devices for patients in need quickly. With 3D technology, one can rapidly create prototype devices and anatomy-based models for testing and training. For example, viewing a model from different angles helps students understand the steps involved in surgery more clearly. 3DP models allow students to view a patient's anatomy. They enhance the student's ability to provide out-of-the-box solutions for unusual challenges that require patient personalization. 3D printing is the ultimate tool for education and training in oral surgery [13]. For years, 3D printing has been used in the medical field for splints and implants. 3D models are also used for clinical training and patient education. In short, 3D printing increases the quality of medical education. Figure 10.4 shows the use of 3D printing in medical training [14].

Figure 10.4 The use of 3D printing in medical education [14].

- *Engineering Education:* A 3D printer in the engineering classroom is akin to a toolkit for a carpenter. Students can experience design and creative engineering and see their projects come to life in front of them. With 3D printing as the foundation for STEM learning, students have the resources to re-engineer the world. As the use of 3D printing continues to grow, there will be a demand for skilled designers and engineers to meet industry demands. A single 3D printer can be useful for multiple disciplines in science, engineering, and technology, paving the way for students to explore STEM. Technology students can work on developing new products using 3D printing for rapid prototyping and, eventually, the production of real parts [15,16].

- *Mathematics Education:* Regardless of the academic discipline, a 3D printer will find its worth in any subject. 3D printing can be of great assistance when learning mathematics. 3D printing for mathematics offers a wide array of options for student learning.

It helps them to understand mathematics in a whole new way, visualizing everything from basic geometry to fractals. From kindergarten to graduate school, 3D printers are helping math students represent numbers and symbols with objects in the physical world. Any object represented by mathematical meaning can be printed and integrated into the curriculum. If designed properly, 3D printing can be used to teach fractions, decimals, algebra, and more. A typical 3D printer used in math education is shown in Figure 10.5 [17].

Figure 10.5 A 3D printer used in math education [17].

- *Architecture Education:* Interest in architecture is growing among students, partly due to 3D printers and digital modeling systems. From buildings to bridges, 3D printers provide a physical representation of the student's vision. 3D printing enhances a variety of educational experiences that architecture students are exposed to. Architecture and design students can print their models, making those tangible and having better ways of communicating their ideas. Learning basic CAD software and using 3D printers to create houses, landscapes, and objects provide a great way to generate interest in students. 3D printing helps students to fabricate their designs into 3D models for better display and visualization [18]. An example of 3D printing in architecture is shown in Figure 10.6 [19].

Figure 10.6 Examples of 3D printing in architecture [19].

10.4 BENEFITS

Businesses from various industries leverage 3D printing products and services to facilitate rapid prototyping, accelerate manufacturing, and simplify supply chain management. 3D printing has been incorporated into education for years. Academic institutions also leverage 3D technology to deliver a superior learning experience.

3D printing brings an object to life in real 3D. 3D printing has the major benefit of keeping interested for learners through a visual aid. The benefits of 3D printing for students are vast. The possibilities of educational purposes for 3D printers are endless. 3D printing and associated skills are transportable across disciplines. Since 3D printers have come down in price and size, one of the most exciting applications of the technology has been in the classroom.

Other benefits of 3D in education include the following:

- 3D printing is a technology that scientists and engineers are using to change the world and solve real-world problems.

- 3D printing is a way to accelerate a typical manufacturing process.

- 3D printing is the ultimate tool for building engagement.

- 3D printing is widely used to develop practical skills that can be used beyond the classroom

- 3D printing gives students the ability to physically implement a prototype.

- 3D printing has opened up another way of thinking about the curriculum.

- 3D printing is useful for validation research.

- With 3D printing, students can leverage their CAD skills to design a product idea.

- 3D printer transforms any class into an interactive learning experience.

- 3D printing can empower students to take their skills from the classroom into a new application.

- 3D printers can improve the learning experience in any situation.

- 3D printing makes it possible for every student to dream bigger and better.

- 3D printers are more affordable than ever and easier to use.

- 3D is used as classroom technology to teach coding and problem-solving skills.

- It boosts communication and collaboration skills between students.

- 3D printers can bring almost any educational concept to life.

- Improves student creativity and design skills

- Promotes problem-solving skills and opens new possibilities for learning.

- It enhances hands-on learning and learning by doing.

- It provides more room for interactive class activities.

10.5 CHALLENGES

The step towards digitalization in schools costs money, but not much more money is available to schools than their standard budget. Every nation should be aware of the future importance of 3D printing in many areas. There remain some challenges to the widespread adoption of 3D printing in schools and colleges. 3D printing is still a new technology not readily available to average consumer. The finish of their models is usually inferior to those produced with higher-end RP machines. Safety, security, accessibility, and ease of use are important concerns for using 3D printers in the classroom. Choosing a 3D printer with an automatic, lockable door ensures the printer cannot be opened while it works. Making your 3D printers easily accessible to students through a secure login addresses security concerns. Other challenges include the following:

- 3D printers are difficult to afford for most school budgets.

- It takes teachers some time to become familiar with the technology, find the right materials, overcome software issues, and fix technical faults.

- The choice of materials is often limited to just one or two colors.

- 3D printing is a process that takes some patience – not an asset that the average 12-year-old has in abundance.

- The level of engagement drops, and subjects become discouraged if the hardware involved is not fit-for-purpose.

- It is an intriguing new technology that is yet to find its place in the home.

These challenges can limit the value of having machines such as 3D printers in the classroom.

10.6 GLOBAL USE OF 3D PRINTING

3D printing is an increasingly popular technology, finding practical applications in many sectors, from manufacturing to medicine, construction to the food industry, to mention a few. Its educational benefits include greater student involvement, the ability to visualize and better understand theoretical concepts, and the integration of practical and theoretical skills. 3D printing is taught in schools and colleges to inspire young minds and enhance creative thinking. Students want to touch and feel 3D printing products and inventions and play around with them to unlock human ingenuity. The use of 3D printing in education is gaining popularity around the world. We consider how some nations implement 3D printing in their educational system.

- *United States*: Having a 3D printer in your maker space can be a great resource for students to use. These printers quickly create prototypes of historical artifacts, 3D versions of their artwork, topography, and so much more. Ohio is the place of many firsts in additive manufacturing technology innovation. Innovations in Ohio have been developed for a broad range of industries, including defense, education, aerospace, healthcare, and industrial tooling, due to partnerships with industry, academia, agencies, and the additive manufacturing workforce. Preparing students for their future careers and teaching them valuable skills using 3D printing is a highly viable path that many schools are utilizing today. 3D printing labs are a comprehensive solution for introducing students to the world of 3D printing and design [20]. NASA has been developing 3D printing technology, competing to design and build a 3-D printed habitat for deep space exploration.

- *United Kingdom:* 3D printing offers a wealth of opportunities to enhance science, technology, engineering, design, art, and maths skills. With Markforged's 3D printing solutions and Mark3D as an education partner, students develop hands-on skills supported by resources that inspire and help keep them running. Mark3D's 3D printing solutions allow students to prototype, test, and optimize their designs. Markforged's metal and composite 3D printing solutions provide students with hands-on learning with tools used by professional engineers daily. It can already be found in almost all areas of the education industry, including research institutes, universities and colleges, technical schools, high schools, and elementary schools. 3D printing can also enable discoveries for research and the laboratory. To present students with practical challenges, they are confronted with a hands-on problem-solving approach [21]. The RepRap project is a worldwide initiative started in the UK in 2005. It is an open design project aiming at developing a low-cost 3D printer that can print most of its components.

- *Europe:* In education, 3D printing creates excitement in students and prevents them from having a passive role in the learning process. Although 3D printing is a priority for the European Commission, teachers and trainers need to acquire specific competencies to introduce 3D printing in the training program. In Ukraine, a new primary school construction was based on 3D printing technology, as shown in Figure 10.7 [22]. The school is designed to provide access to education for children affected by the full-scale war in Ukraine. The construction of Europe's first

3D-printed school is seen as an example of the resilience and determination of the Ukrainian people.

Figure 10.7 First 3D printed school in Ukraine [22].

- *China:* From 2015 to 2017, the Chinese government set up 3D printers in each of its 400,000 elementary schools. The Chinese space program is building 3D-printed space suits. 3D printing would allow astronauts to print items with a 3D printer directly in space with no freight difficulties. People from all backgrounds are acquiring 3D printers, and large-scale utilizations will increase customer options. The democratization of 3D printing technology and knowledge is expected to change the nature of commerce [23]. Flashforge is a Chinese pioneer in manufacturing 3D printing devices and 3D printing materials. The company is actively collaborating with higher educational institutions, both domestically and abroad, to further the use of 3D printing in education. Figure 10.8 shows the 3D printing lab of the University of Nottingham Ningbo, China [24].

- *India:* Education holds the key to unlocking the true potential of human ingenuity. Today's Education should be multi-dimensional, giving equal importance to theoretical and a hands-on, practical approach. Due to their versatile nature, 3D printers can facilitate real-world applications and knowledge in various fields of Education.

Figure 10.8 3D printing lab of University of Nottingham Ningbo, China [24].

Figure 10.9 Some Indian women in the 3D printing society [25].

Indian doctors are now incorporating 3D-printed body parts in surgery and organ replacement, while a young startup is using the technology to reinvent education in Indian schools. The Indian Women in 3D Printing Society (IW3DP) was formally launched in Bengaluru on April 18, 2023. The Society is intended to bridge the gender gap in the Indian 3D printing and additive manufacturing industry. It provides exposure and training to secondary and college students in 3D printing through workshops and experiential learning labs. Figure 10.9 shows some women in the 3D printing society [25].

10.7 CONCLUSION

3D printing is a technology that allows users to turn any digital file into a three-dimensional physical object. 3D printing in education is the most exciting application. In education, 3D printing technologies facilitate improved learning, skills development and increased student and teacher engagement with the subject matter. It has been a wonderful new way to teach and motivate students. With the decreasing cost of 3D printers, they have become an essential and valuable educational tool.

It is important to have the right tools in place to use 3D to teach STEM subjects. The choice of the right 3D printing technology depends on the projected size and number of models. Other major factors to consider in purchasing a 3D printer include ease of use, reliability, safety, cost-effectiveness, and print speed. It may be expedient to start with do-it-yourself 3D printer kits before purchasing. The use of 3D printers in education is growing rapidly at all levels. Education is probably one of the sectors that will benefit the most from 3D printers in the long run. The future of 3D printing in the education industry is unlimited. For more information about 3D printing in education, one should consult the book in [26-33] and the following related journals:

- *American Society for Engineering Education*
- *IEEE Transactions on Education*
- *International Journal of Progressive Education*
- *EURASIA Journal of Mathematics, Science and Technology Education*

REFERENCES

[1] M. N. O. Sadiku, U. C. Chukwu. A. Ajayi-Majebi, and S. M. Musa, "3D Printing: An introduction, " *International Journal of Trend in Scientific Research and Development*, vol. 6, no. 7, November-December 2022, pp. 573-577

[2] M. N. O. Sadiku, U. C. Chukwu. A. Ajayi-Majebi, and S. M. Musa, "3D printing in Education, " *International Journal of Trend in Scientific Research and Development*, vol. 6, no. 7, November-December 2022, pp. 661-668.

[3] D. Assante, G. M. Cennamo, and L. Placidi, "3D printing in education: An European perspective," *Proceedings of 2020 IEEE Global Engineering Education Conference (EDUCON)*, April 2020.

[4] F. R. Ishengoma and T. A. B. Mtaho, "3D printing: Developing countries perspectives computer engineering and applications," *International Journal of Computer Applications*, vol. 104, no. 11, October 2014, pp. 30-34.

[5] M. N. O. Sadiku, S. M. Musa, and O. S. Musa, "3D Printing in the chemical industry," *Invention Journal of Research Technology in Engineering and Management*, vol. 2, no. 2, February 2018, pp. 24-26.

[6] "The benefits of 3D Printing in children's education," February 2021, https://www.kidsinthehouse.com/blogs/kidsinthehouse2/the-benefits-of-3d-printing-in-childrens-education

[7] "3D printing creates a whirlwind of innovation in the field of education," July 2021, https://www.raise3d.com/case/3d-printing-creates-a-whirlwind-of-innovation-in-the-field-of-education/

[8] "3D printing solution," Unknown Source.

[9] "3D printing in education," https://www.learnbylayers.com/3d-printing-education-2/

[10] "The top 5 benefits of 3D printing in education," https://www.makerbot.com/stories/3d-printing-education/5-benefits-of-3d-printing/

[11] O. A. H. Jones and M. J. S. Spencer, "A simplified method for the 3D printing of molecular models for chemical education," *Journal of Chemical Education*, October 2017.

[12] "10 Ways 3D printing can be used in education," https://www.teachthought.com/technology/3d-printing-education/

[13] M. N. O. Sadiku, J. Foreman, and S. M. Musa, "3D Printing in healthcare," *International Journal of Scientific Engineering and Technology*, vol. 7, no. 7, July 2018, pp. 65-67.

[14] "3D printed anatomy series offers alternative to cadavers for medical training," July 2015, https://www.embodi3d.com/blogs/entry/200-3d-printed-anatomy-series-offers-alternative-to-cadavers-for-medical-training/

[15] "3D printers for science & engineering education," https://3dsupplyguys.com/education-center/3d-printers-in-education/3d-printers-for-science-engineering-education/

[16] Y. AbouHashem et al., "The application of 3D printing in anatomy education," *Medical Education Online*, vol. 20, no.1, 2015.

[17] "3D printers for mathematics education," https://3dsupplyguys.com/education-center/3d-printers-in-education/3d-printers-for-mathematics-education/

[18] "3D printers for architecture education," https://3dsupplyguys.com/education-center/3d-printers-in-education/3d-printers-for-architecture-education/

[19] "3D printing education & training," http://my3dconcepts.com/education/

[20] "Additive manufacturing," https://www.jobsohio.com/industries/additive-manufacturing?gad=1&gclid=EAIaIQobChMIibHwnai0_wIVem1vBB0GZw66EAAYAiAAEgJXpvD_BwE

[21] "3D printing from Markforged in education," https://www.mark3d.com/en/3d-printing-in-education/

[22] A. Shaikhnag, "First 3D printed school in Europe under construction in Ukraine," June 2023, https://3dprintingindustry.com/news/first-3d-printed-school-in-europe-under-construction-in-ukraine-222486/

[23] "Future applications of 3D printing in China," July 2020, https://daxueconsulting.com/3d-printing-in-china/#:~:text=In%20addition%2C%20according%20to%20Simon,technology%20from%20a%20young%20age.

[24] "Flashforge boosts Chinese colleges in cultivating 3D intelligent manufacturing talents," January 2023, https://www.flashforge.com/news-detail/3d-printer-being-used-in-education-Chinese-school-cases

[25] "Indian women in 3D Printing Society launched," April 2023, https://www.educationworld.in/karnataka-3d-printing-technology-to-be-introduced-from-school-level-onwards/

[26] I. M. R. Santos, N. Ali, and S. Areepattamannil (eds), *Interdisciplinary and International Perspectives on 3D Printing in Education*. IGI Global, 2019

[27] D. D. Thornburg. N. Thornburg, and S. Armstrong, *The Invent to Learn Guide to 3D Printing in the Classroom: Recipes for Success (Invent to Learn Guides)*. Constructing Modern Knowledge Press, 2014.

[28] C. K. Chua et al., *3D Printing and Additive Manufacturing of Electronics: Principles and Applications*. World Scientific, 2021.

[29] S. Torta and J. Torta, *3D Printing: An Introduction*. Mercury Learning and Information, 2019.

[30] K. A. Boozarjomehri, *3D Printing at School and Makerspaces*. Cavendish Square Publishing, 2017.

[31] M. S. Khine and N. Ali (eds), *Integrating 3D Printing Into Teaching and Learning: Practitioners' Perspectives*. Brill, 2020.

[32] B. Bobbitt, *3D Printing Made Simple for Education*. Independently Published, 2016.

[33] Information Resources Management Association (ed.), *Research Anthology on Makerspaces and 3D Printing in Education*. IGI Global, 2022.

CHAPTER 11

VIRTUAL REALITY IN EDUCATION

> *"The impact of VR and AR on education cannot be understated. Humans learn best spatially, and we're seeing this play out in tremendously exciting ways.... I defer to Buckminster Fuller here: 'If you want to teach people a new way of thinking, don't bother trying to teach them. Instead, give them a tool, the use of which will lead to new ways of thinking.'"*
> —Jesse Damiani

11.1 INTRODUCTION

Education is the foundation for a thriving society, and knowledge transfer has been a top priority for civilizations since the beginning. Over the years, educators have constantly searched for ways to make knowledge transfer more easily and more effectively. Gone are the days when a simple chalkboard would suffice for instruction in the classroom. Today, various methods and tools are used in the educational system as educators use all sorts of breakthrough technologies as primary mediums of instruction. Virtual reality has emerged as a tool that helps improve the learning process. It helps the students study their content and increases student engagement in their studies.

Human beings are visual creatures. Both hearing and seeing are central to our sense of space. As we have been spending an increasing amount of time in front of computers, the need to explore more of the role of virtual environments also needs to be increased. Virtual reality is the key technology for experiencing sensations of sight, hearing, and touch of the past, present, and future. VR is a fully immersive technology where users wear a head-mounted display and experience a simulated world of imagery and sounds. VR enables active learning [1].

Virtual reality is a human-designed system with the help of computers and electronic devices such as cameras and sensors to interact with 3-D environments. Many challenges that educators face in online teaching can be addressed by using VR. VR can provide learners with an immersed environment that students otherwise cannot access. VR is an exciting way to turn ordinary classrooms into places of wonder, inquiry, and adventure. VR increases students' engagement and interest in learning. It makes many hard topics easy with a 360-degree realistic view. Among the various emerging technologies, virtual reality is of particular interest in education as it has many features that make it desirable for distance learning.

This chapter provides an introduction to virtual reality. It begins by explaining the concept of virtual reality. It presents some applications of virtual reality in education. It highlights the benefits and challenges of virtual reality in education. It covers the global implementation of virtual reality in education. The last section concludes with comments.

11.2 CONCEPT OF VIRTUAL REALITY

The term "virtual reality" essentially means "near-reality." Virtual reality has been known by different names, such as synthetic environment, cyberspace, artificial reality, virtual environments, and simulator technology. The terms, "virtual reality" and "cyberspace" are often used interchangeably. A cyberspace may be regarded as a networked virtual reality. Virtual reality is a simulated experience that can be similar to or different from the real world. It is a computer-generated, 3D environment that completely immerses the senses of sight, sound, and touch. The complete immersion of the senses overwhelms users engrossing them in the action [2]. As shown in Figure 11.1, the mixed reality (MR) continuum captures all possible combinations of the real and virtual worlds [3].

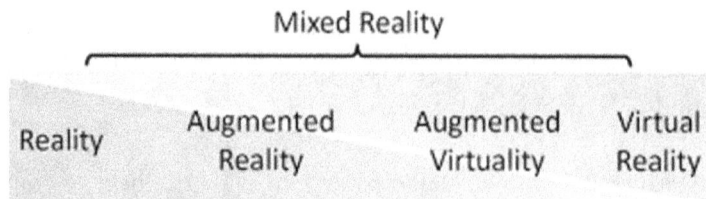

Figure 11.1 The mixed reality continuum captures all possible combinations of the real and virtual worlds [3].

Virtual reality (VR) describes a three-dimensional (3D), computer-generated environment that can be explored and interacted with by a person. Once entered, it becomes a reality to the person. Instead of viewing a screen in front of them as when using traditional interfaces, users are immersed and able to interact with 3D worlds.

Based on data entered by programmers, computers create virtual environments by generating 3D images. Users can view these images by using a head-mounted device, which can be a helmet or goggles. Mobile VR glasses enable users to be present in any environment they want at any time and place. Users may use a joystick or trackball to move through the virtual environment. A person using virtual reality equipment can dive into a fully immersive 3D environment, look around the artificial world, move around in it, and interact with virtual objects. The virtual environment can be viewed using a cell phone screen, monitor, projector, or head-mounted display (HMD). As the person is immersed in the computer-generated environment, the brain is deluded into thinking the virtual world is reality.

VR has three main characteristics [4]: interaction, immersion, and imagination. Interaction refers to the natural interaction between the user and the virtual scene. Immersion means that the user feels that they are part of the virtual world as if they are immersed. Imagination refers to the use of multi-dimensional perception information provided by the VR scenes. A type of VR known as 360VR is most commonly used in education. There are two major ways in which VR is implemented in the classroom: VR headsets and immersive classrooms.

Virtual reality technology includes multiple components divided into two main groups: hardware and software components [5].

- *Hardware Components:* The hardware components include a computer workstation, sensory displays, a tracking system, wearable devices, and input devices. Sensory displays are used to display the simulated virtual worlds to the user. The most common type is the head-mounted displays (HMDs), which is used in combination with tracking systems. Head-mounted displays are shown in Figure 11.2 [6]. Users interact with the simulated environment through some wearable devices. VR depends on special responses such as raising hands, turning the head, or swinging the body. A wearable device is important in making these effects realistic. Special input devices are required to interact with the virtual world. These include the 3D mouse, the wired glove, motion controllers, and optical tracking sensors. These devices are used to stimulate our senses together to create the illusion of reality.

Figure 11.2 Head-mounted displays [6].

- *Software Components:* Besides the hardware, the underlying software plays an important role. It is responsible for the managing of I/O devices and time-critical applications. The software components are 3D modeling software, 2D graphics software, digital sound editing software, and VR simulation software. VR technology has been designed to ensure visual comfort and ergonomic usage.

11.3 APPLICATIONS

VR technologies are being applied in various disciplines, including healthcare, law, engineering, business, social sciences, education and training, simulation, marketing, commerce, architecture, arts, sport, fashion, engineering, construction, environmental navigation, factory, tourism, archaeology, military, media, music, cinema, scientific visualization, telecommunication, and programming languages. We consider the applications of VR in various disciplines of education.

- *Elementary Schools:* There are possibilities for bringing the curriculum to life using virtual reality experiences. Students in elementary schools participate in immersive education with the help of virtual reality applications. Educators are taking students on virtual field trips to give them exposure to the real world without going outside the campus. Assistive technology can be used for students with special needs. Parents can take their children anywhere around or inside the world [8]. VR enables students to simply grasp what they struggle to know when being taught by their teachers. Figure 11.3 shows how VR is used in teaching children [9]. VR is also useful for high school, college, and university students.

VIRTUAL REALITY IN EDUCATION

Figure 11.3 VR is used in teaching children [9].

- *Medical Education:* Schools of medicine in different parts of the world are among the most ardent VR technology supporters. VR technologies have been used to treat several mental disorders, such as anxiety disorders. Dental healthcare issues are becoming increasingly important due to the crisis of aging populations. VR can be used as an effective treatment for patients with dental phobia, a common problem in our society. Concerning medical education, several requests have been made to eliminate outdated, inefficient, and passive learning approaches and embrace newer learning methodologies, such as VR. The use of VR devices allows learning to occur through hands-on, immersive experiences. They are ideal for training in hands-on procedures without harming actual patients. VR is becoming useful for training physicians through visual simulation technology. It can be used to train medical students and resident physicians for surgeries in a risk-free environment without physically being in an operating room. VR trainers are available for various medical procedures. VR technologies will play an increasing role in teaching, surgery, learning anatomy, anesthesia, and dentistry. Physicians can produce a three-dimensional model of a particular patient's anatomy and map out the surgery ahead of time. Figure 11.4 shows virtual reality in surgery [9].

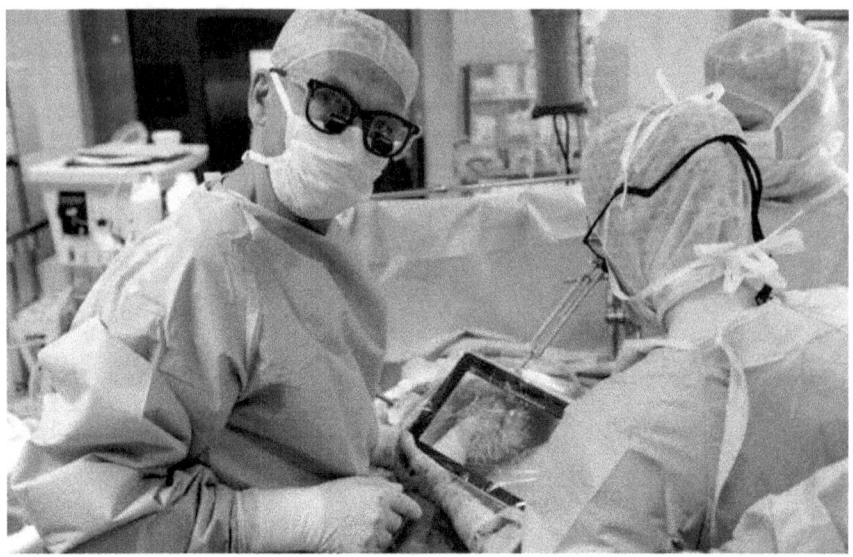

Figure 11.4 Virtual reality in surgery [9].

- *Distance Education:* Schools are leveraging VR technology to help facilitate distance learning. Some educational applications can be accessed from anywhere using a smartphone and an Internet connection. Such applications keep the learners connected, and they do not need to be physically present in the institution. This feature removes the barrier of location and time as they can learn by using the application anytime, anywhere. Students can rewatch such pre-recorded virtual graphics as often as they want and at their own pace using the appropriate devices. Distant educators can share their ideas and communicate virtually [10].

- *Special Education:* Having other special educational needs and disabilities (SEND) can affect a student's learning ability in various ways. Virtual reality technology makes it possible for teachers to create personalized educational content that can tailor to these students' unique needs. For SEND students, simply moving around and participating in some activities can be stressful. Immersive VR experiences can be calming for students [11].

- *Virtual Field Trips*: Field trips are a time-honored tradition for educational institutions. They are becoming a vital part of a child's education. They provide exposure and practicality to the students. However, in certain cases, the field trips do not possibly take place due to COVID-19. In other cases, certain trips are too expensive for all the students to participate in. Virtual field trips have become one of the most popular applications of VR technology for education. They offer a cost-effective option for schools. VR has become one of the best applications for learning as students can travel to any place in the world without moving a step aside from their seats. It can be a great opportunity to take the travel and tour experience without actually visiting the place. They can see realistic graphic-based images and have views of the place. VR technology makes all this possible without leaving the classroom [10].

- *Virtual Campus Visits:* Many schools have started using virtual reality campus tours as a way to connect applicants to university campuses. These campus visits allow students to see what it would be like to attend universities in other cities and countries even if they cannot visit in person. The virtual reality tours use photos and videos of campuses and their surroundings, enabling students to explore the campuses at 360-degree angles [12].

11.4 BENEFITS

A key benefit of using VR in education is learning through experience. VR enables students to experience real scenarios or fabricated experiences over and over and learn in an immersive way. Both students and teachers are embracing the rapid developments in virtual reality. Virtual reality presents endless opportunities in the field of education. Virtual reality makes the educational impact and learning roots deeper than the traditional methods. With all the advantages of virtual reality, it will soon become a standard educational tool Some of its advantages include the following [13]:

- Increase memory power and knowledge retention
- Boost excitement and engagement in the classroom
- Improve learning outcomes
- Focus student attention on the lesson
- Open up new opportunities and create accessibility for every student
- Improve understanding of complex, conceptual subjects
- Build emotional intelligence, awareness, and understanding
- Improve communication and collaboration skills
- Make learning more interesting
- Add a new level of learning to lessons
- VR makes the demonstration of practical skills easier.

Figure 11.5 shows some benefits of using VR in the classroom [14].

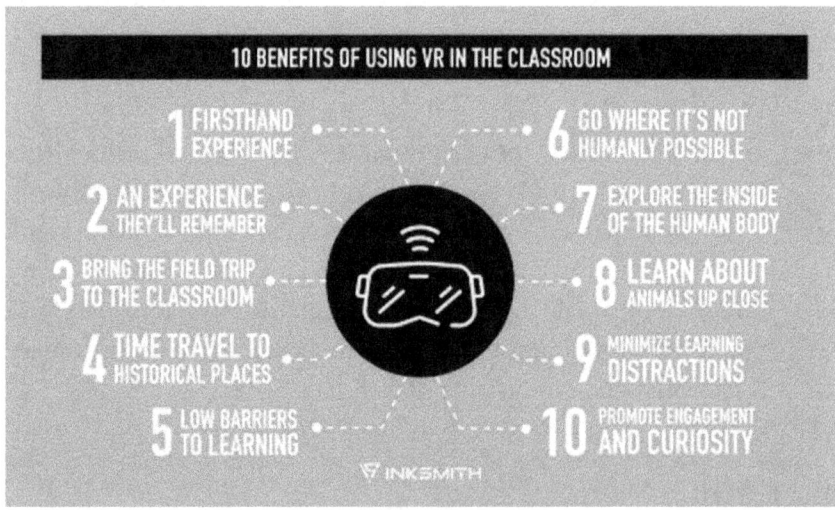

Figure 11.5 Ten benefits of using VR in the classroom [14].

11.5 CHALLENGES

Many educators embrace the benefits of virtual reality in education, but some are still reluctant to use it in their classrooms. VR critics argue that it is too expensive, too challenging to implement, and too distracting for students. Figure 11.6 shows some of the disadvantages of using VR in the classroom [15]. Other challenges include [16]:

- Bad-quality headsets can cause discomfort in the form of motion sickness and headaches.

- Avoid limiting the number of headsets per class to reduce cost; this can result in poor educational experiences

- Poor Internet connectivity will result in visual lag

- High cost is a major barrier to its adoption in education

- There is a lack of content, and developing more content can be very expensive

- Some students do not have the money to buy a VR headset.

- Cyber-sickness can prevent students from learning

Despite these challenges, the demand for VR in education will grow in the coming years.

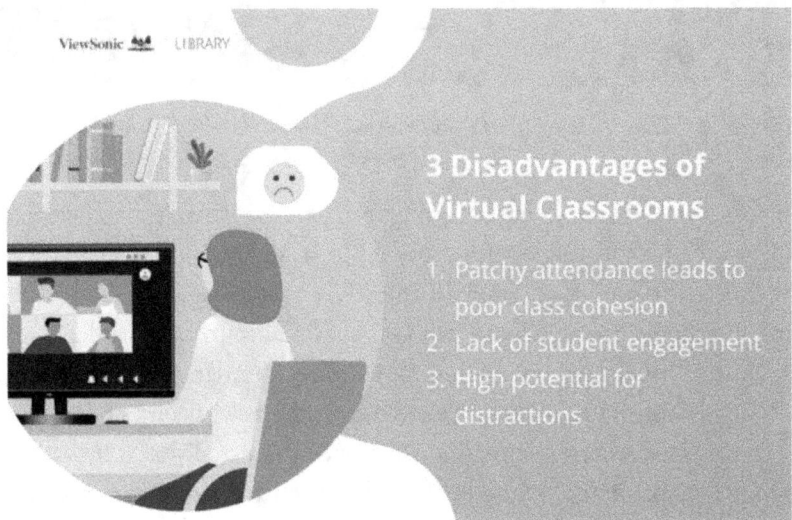

Figure 11.6 Some of disadvantages of using VR in the classroom [15].

11.6 GLOBAL USE OF VIRTUAL REALITY

Virtual reality is fully immersive, accessed through a headset, creating a computer-generated world that users can manipulate. Schools worldwide are also leveraging virtual reality technology to help facilitate distance learning. VR can create an immersive learning environment that allows teachers and students to be present within the same "room" virtually. Virtual reality is creating a buzz in the education world. Around the world, it is estimated that some 19 million people were using VR in 2019. Figure 11.7 shows how Google expeditions enable virtual field trips worldwide [17]. We consider how VR is being used in the educational systems of some nations.

Figure 11.7 Google expeditions enable virtual field trips all over the world [17].

- *United States:* Virtual reality technology is creating new means of education by opening doors for students to learn and teachers to instruct in a more immersive, technological environment. Schools in the US are using virtual reality to help students learn technical and vocational skills. The simulated scenarios made possible by virtual reality provide students with a much better and more immersive learning experience than traditional instruction. For example, virtual reality allows chemistry students to learn and practice chemistry principles safely by eliminating the risks associated with conducting potentially dangerous experiments. Medical school students can engage in experimental surgeries in virtual reality environments. Biology students can engage with plants, mammals, birds, insects, and amphibians via technological simulations [18].

- *United Kingdom:* Virtual reality is taking off in education, with an increasing number of UK schools adopting the technology. It allows students to experience destinations worldwide without leaving the classroom. VR can be effectively used in primary education and is becoming increasingly common in the UK. VR has been found to be helpful for students with autism and students with learning difficulties. Schools can save time and money by providing travel experiences without having to leave the classroom [19]. The Unimersiv app allows schools in the UK to use virtual reality to explore Ancient Rome as it was in its brightest days. The technology gives schools in the UK access to multiple virtual reality educational experiences.

- *Europe:* From medical schools to engineering designs, VR is used in a variety of academic and professional settings to provide immersive, hands-on learning experiences. With its immersive and interactive capabilities, virtual reality is allowing students and professionals to gain valuable knowledge and skills in a variety of fields. In Europe, many universities and schools are already taking advantage of the educational potential of virtual reality. For example, students at the University of Malta can use virtual reality to explore the human body in an interactive way. At the Technical University of Madrid, students can use virtual reality to simulate complex engineering tasks [20].

- *China:* VR virtual reality technology uses computer simulation to generate a three-dimensional virtual world, providing users with simulations of visual, auditory, tactile, and other senses. Today in China, VR is concentrated almost exclusively on education. Both on a national and local level, Chinese educators are investing heavily in VR technology. In 2020, the People's Republic of China's Ministry of Education launched a laboratory to provide VR to Chinese universities, colleges, and vocational schools. VR brings EdTech in China to a new level. Academics have called for new design guidelines, an assessment of the effective use of VR in everyday teaching and learning, and a greater awareness of how VR can address cultural sensitivities. Whether game-based learning, virtual field trips, campus visits, language immersion, architecture, and design, enhancing educational experience through visualization is a powerful tool to bring learning into the 21st century [21].

- *India:* Virtual Reality technologies have great potential to revolutionize education by creating immersive and engaging learning experiences. They make learning more interactive, allowing students to visualize complex concepts and understand them better. They also provide a more personalized learning experience, as students can choose to focus on the content that interests them the most. The education industry in India has witnessed a huge shift towards eLearning. It is no longer restricted to just traditional classroom setups or the old ways of the passive learning environment. VR technology can be used to take students on virtual field trips to places that are difficult or impossible to visit in real life. Researchers at the Indian Institute of Technology, Madras, are developing teaching and learning models using digital technologies. They have developed an AR / VR-based enabled learning [22].

11.5 CONCLUSION

Virtual reality is produced by a combination of technologies that are used to visualize and provide interaction with a virtual environment. It allows users to interact with a computer-generated 3D model or virtual environment. In 3D virtual reality, the interaction with computers is expanded from purely visual interaction to diverse interaction.

VR has opened several opportunities in the education sector for students and teachers. It is transforming education in smart classrooms around the world. Although virtual reality has existed in education for over half a century, its widespread adoption is still yet to occur. This observation is due to some limitations of the VR technology and the costs and logistics required to deploy it. Virtual reality applications in education have emerged as rapidly developing technologies that can potentially change education. Many teachers and students believe VR deserves a place in today's classrooms. For more information on the applications of virtual reality in education, one should consult the books in [23-42].

REFERENCES

[1] M. N. O. Sadiku, J. O. Sadiku, and U. C. Chukwu, "Virtual reality in education," *International Journal on Integrated Education,* vol. 27, vol. 6, no. 3, March 2023.

[2] M. N. O. Sadiku, K. G. Eze, and S. M. Musa, "Virtual reality: A primer," *International Journal of Trend in Research and Development,* vol. 7, no. 2, March-April 2020, pp. 160-162.

[3] "Introduction to augmented reality," June 2016, https://www.informit.com/articles/article.aspx?p=2516729&seqNum=4

[4] Y. Li et al., "Gesture interaction in virtual reality," *Virtual Reality & Intelligent Hardware,* vol.1, no.1, February 2019, pp. 84-112.

[5] M. O. Onyesolu and F. U. Eze, "Understanding virtual reality technology: Advances and applications," *Advances in Computer Science and Engineering,* March 2011, pp. 53-70.

[6] "VR rundown: What you need to know before buying a VR System for your school," https://vreddo.com.au/vr-rundown-what-you-need-to-know-before-buying-a-vr-system-for-your-school/

[7] "How virtual reality is used in education," July 2022, Unknown Source

[8] K. Larson, "Teach your students with virtual reality," https://ideas.demco.com/blog/teach-with-virtual-reality/?sfw=pass1679014760

[9] "In a first, British hospital livestreams surgery in virtual reality," April 2016, https://www.indiatoday.in/world/story/in-a-first-british-hospital-livestreams-surgery-in-virtual-reality-318214-2016-04-15

[10] "5 Applications of virtual reality in education," July 2021, https://www.analyticssteps.com/blogs/5-applications-virtual-reality-education

[11] P. Ip, 'Virtual reality in education: how schools are using VR," December 2022, https://www.adorama.com/alc/virtual-reality-in-education/

[12] M. Stenger, "10 Ways virtual reality is already being used in education," October 2017, https://www.opencolleges.edu.au/informed/edtech-integration/10-ways-virtual-reality-already-used-education/

[13] "Advantages of virtual reality in education," August 2022, https://www.classvr.com/blog/advantages-of-virtual-reality-in-education/#:~:text=So%2C%20in%20summary%20virtual%20reality,skills%20needed%20for%20the%20future.

[14] "Technology virtual reality 10 benefits of using VR in the classroom," https://www.inksmith.ca/blogs/news/technology-virtual-reality-10-benefits-of-using-vr-in-the-classroom

[15] "3 Disadvantages of virtual classrooms (and how to overcome them)," November 2021, https://www.viewsonic.com/library/education/3-disadvantages-of-virtual-classrooms-how-to-overcome/

[16] A. Hassan, "Virtual reality in education: Achievements and challenges," February 2021, https://www.emergingedtech.com/2021/02/virtual-reality-in-education-achievements-challenges/

[17] N. Babich, " How VR in education will change how we learn and teach," September 2019, https://xd.adobe.com/ideas/principles/emerging-technology/virtual-reality-will-change-learn-teach/

[18] "How schools are using virtual reality," https://www.adorama.com/alc/virtual-reality-in-education/#:~:text=Schools%20are%20also%20leveraging%20virtual,can%20provide%20a%20viable%20alternative.

[19] "What is virtual reality learning?" https://immersionvr.co.uk/about-360vr/vr-for-education/

[20] R. C. Mendes, "Virtual reality: Transforming education and training in Europe," May 2023, https://www.linkedin.com/pulse/virtual-reality-transforming-education-training-rui-castelo-mendes#:~:text=From%20medical%20schools%20to%20engineering,educational%20potential%20of%20virtual%20reality.

[21] O. Halsall, "The good, the bad and the ugly: VR in China's classrooms," June 2020, https://pandaily.com/the-good-the-bad-and-the-ugly-vr-in-chinas-classrooms/#:~:text=Today%20in%20China%2C%20VR%20is,Industry%20of%20Virtual%20Reality%20Alliance.

[22] "Learning beyond the classroom with AR/VR technology," https://www.devdensolutions.com/ar-and-vr-in-education/

[23] C. M. Moran (ed.), *Virtual and Augmented Reality in English Language Arts Education.* Lexington Books, 2023.

[24] Information Resources Management Association (ed.), *Virtual Reality in Education: Breakthroughs in Research and Practice.* IGI Global, 2019.

[25] A. Dailey-Hebert, D. H. Choi, and J. S. Estes (eds.), *Emerging Tools and Applications of Virtual Reality in Education.* IGI Global, 2016.

[26] L. Daniela (ed.), *New Perspectives on Virtual and Augmented Reality: Finding New Ways to Teach in a Transformed Learning Environment.* Taylor & Francis, 2020.

[27] Z. Tacgin, *Virtual and Augmented Reality: An Educational Handbook.* Cambridge Scholars Publishing, 2020.

[28] A. Dailey-Hebert, D. H. Choi, and J. S. Estes (eds.), *Current and Prospective Applications of Virtual Reality in Higher Education*. IGI Global, 2020.

[29] C. Dede et al. (eds.), *Virtual, Augmented, and Mixed Realities in Education*. Springer, 2017.

[30] C. D. Epp and G. Akcayir (eds.), *Designing, Deploying, and Evaluating Virtual and Augmented Reality in Education*. IGI Global, 2020.

[31] C. Frehlich, *Immersive Learning: A Practical Guide to Virtual Reality's Superpowers in Education*. Rowman & Littlefield Publishers, 2020.

[32] A. S. Pillai and G. Guazzaroni (eds.), *Virtual and Augmented Reality in Education, Art, and Museums*. IGI Global, 2019.

[33] D. Cvetković, *Virtual Reality and Its Application in Education*. IntechOpen, 2021.

[34] Information Resources Management Association (ed.), *Virtual Reality in Education: Breakthroughs in Research and Practice*. IGI Global, 2019.

[35] E. Southgate, *Virtual Reality in Curriculum and Pedagogy: Evidence from Secondary Classrooms (Digital Games, Simulations, and Learning)*. Routledge, 2020.

[36] A. Anderson, *Virtual Reality, Augmented Reality and Artificial Intelligence in Special Education: A Practical Guide to Supporting Students with Learning Differences*. Routledge, 2019.

[37] P. M. Parker, *The 2023-2028 Outlook for Virtual Reality in Education in Japan*. ICON Group International, Inc., 2022.

[38] R. Swift and A. Allatt, *Virtual Reality in Education: Oculearning: Our Path to Reality*. Kindle Edition, 2016.

[39] B. Patterson, *Profiles of Use of Virtual Reality in Medical Education*. Primary Research Group Inc., 2020.

[40] M. Zaralli, *Virtual Reality in Education: How to Use Technology to Enhance Learning (Virtual Reality: Instruction for Use Book 2)*. Kindle Edition, 2023.

[41] D. W. Staat (ed.), *Virtual Reality in Higher Education: Instruction for the Digital Age*. Rowman & Littlefield Publishers, 2021.

[42] D. Kaser, K. Grijalva, and M. Thompson, *Envisioning Virtual Reality: A Toolkit for Implementing VR In Education*. Lulu.com, 2019.

CHAPTER 12

AUGMENTED REALITY IN EDUCATION

> *"Simply put, we believe augmented reality is going to change the way we use technology forever. We're already seeing things that will transform the way you work, play, connect and learn."*
> —Tim Cook

12.1 INTRODUCTION

The education industry is constantly being disrupted by technology. Traditional education methods are disappearing and are becoming increasingly digitized. Today, school and university students prefer incorporating the power of technology into their classrooms. Adapting technological solutions to education is becoming increasingly popular. You can find chatbots, gamification, and virtual and augmented reality in the curricula of both elementary schools and universities. Augmented reality is an emerging technology that interactively combines virtually generated computer graphics to the live scenario in real-time.

Augmented reality is one of the cloud technologies that bridge the gap between what you see and what you imagine. It allows the students to see 3D objects in the classroom. Digital natives perceive AR technology as more of a part of routine rather than an exception [1]. They do not know a world without technology. Schools should do their best to integrate technological tools into classroom settings so that digital natives can learn well.

There are four types of digital realities [2,3]:

- *Augmented reality* (AR)— designed to add digital elements over real-world views with limited interaction.

- *Virtual reality* (VR)— immersive experiences helping to isolate users from the real world, usually via a headset device and headphones designed for such activities.

- *Mixed reality* (MR)— combining AR and VR elements so that digital objects can interact with the real world means businesses can design elements anchored within a real environment.

- *Extended reality* (XR)— covering all types of technologies that enhance our senses, including the three types previously mentioned.

These four types are illustrated in Figure 12.1 [4]. AR effectively "augments" or "enhances" our experience of the world around us.

Augmented reality is a significant emerging trend that is digitally enhancing our world. It superimposes sounds, videos, and graphics onto an existing environment. It is an interactive experience that brings digital content to the real world. AR technology is useful in numerous fields, including education, because it enables an interactive experience with the real world. Augmented reality offers various benefits in education. It is gradually becoming the future of education [5].

This chapter introduces the readers to the use of augmented reality in education. It begins by describing the concept of augmented reality. It provides some applications of AR in education. It highlights the challenges and benefits of AR in education. It covers the global use of AR in education. The last section concludes with comments.

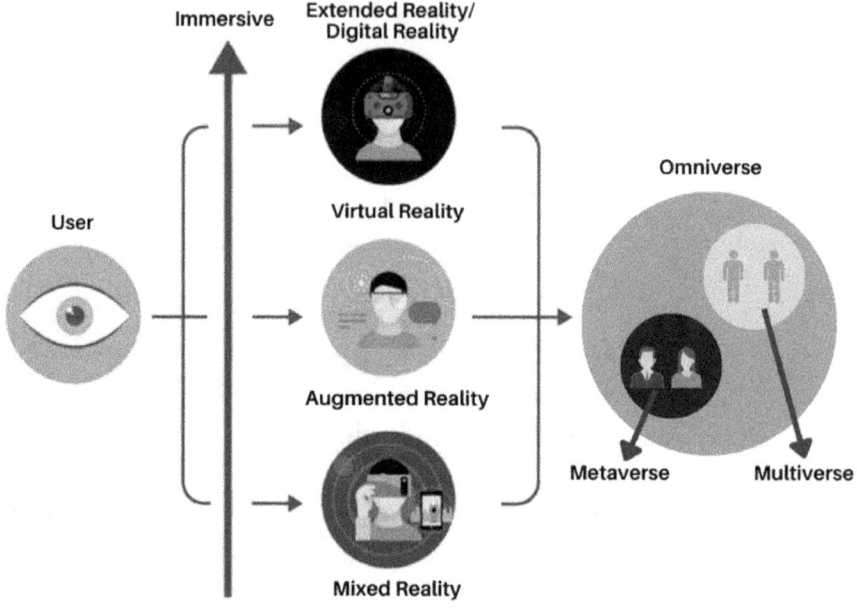

Figure 12.1 These four types of digital realities [4].

12.2 CONCEPT OF AUGMENTED REALITY

The term "augmented reality" was coined in 1990 by Tom Caudell, a former Boeing researcher. Since then, the technology has vastly improved. The rise in AR use stems from four main developments [6]: (1) the pervasiveness of low-cost visual sensors, such as phone cameras, (2) progress in environmental perception algorithms, such as visual simultaneous localization and mapping, (3) advances in optics, and (4) the maturity of multimedia techniques.

Augmented reality (AR) is a technology that combines real-world environments with computer-generated generated information such as images, text, videos, animations, and sound. It can record and analyze the environment in real-time. The technology is accessible to the ordinary user. It is becoming more attractive as a mainstream technology due to the proliferation of modern mobile computing devices like smartphones and tablet computers with location-based services. For example, AR allows consumers to visualize a product in more detail before they purchase it. This feature enhances consumer interaction and helps them never to repurchase the wrong item.

The key objective of AR is to bring computer-generated objects into the real world and allows the user only to see them. In other words, we use AR to track the position and orientation of the user's head to enhance/augment their perception of the world. Projected images are overlaid on top of a pair of goggles or glasses, which allow the images and interactive virtual objects to lay on top of the user's view of the real world. Thus, augmented/enhanced reality involves extending the real-time environment with a digital overlay, in which computer-generated images and sound enhance real life. The digital overlay scene appears on the actual scene the user is experiencing.

Augmented reality falls into two categories: 2D information overlays and 3D presentations, like those used with games. It combines multiple technologies allowing users to interact with virtual entities in real-time. Various technologies used for augmented reality include a processor, monitors, handheld devices, display systems, sensors, and input devices. Modern mobile computing devices like smartphones and tablet computers contain these elements also, making them suitable AR platforms.

To obtain a sufficiently accurate representation of reality, AR needs the following five components [7]:

- *Sensors:* AR needs suitable sensors in the environment and possibly on a user, including fine-grained geolocation and image recognition. These are activating elements that trigger the display of virtual information.

- *Image augmentation:* This requires techniques such as image processing and face recognition.

- *Head-mounted Display*: HMDs are used to view the augmented world where the virtual computer-generated information is properly aligned with the real world. Display technologies are of two types: video display and optical see-through display.

- *User Interface:* This includes technologies for input modalities that include gaze tracking, touch, and gesture. AR is a user interface technology in which a camera-recorded view of the real world is augmented with computer-generated content such as graphics, animations, and 2D or 3D models.

- *Information infrastructure:* AR requires significant computing and communications infrastructure undergirding all these technologies. The infrastructure determines what real-world components to augment, with what, and when.

The AR systems, based on these technologies, should be more accurate, smaller, lighter, faster, simpler, cheaper, and convenient for the users. Google Glass was the first AR platform to get broad public exposure. Figure 12.2 shows the evolution of AR [8].

AR technology has been used in many fields, such as education, healthcare, military, business, engineering, architecture, robotics, manufacturing, entertainment, space industry, maintenance, coding, consumer design, psychology, etc. When incorporating AR in the classroom, it is important to keep the following best practices in mind to ensure a smooth and effective integration [9].

Setting clear goals and objectives for using AR;

- Creating a plan for how AR will be used in the classroom;

- Providing training for educators and students on how to use AR tools;

- Incorporating AR into existing curriculum and lesson plans;

- Assessing and evaluating the effectiveness of AR in achieving educational goals.

12.3 APPLICATIONS OF AR IN EDUCATION

Most AR applications run on smartphones or tablets, needing no special equipment since young people use smartphones for almost anything. Modern AR apps are used for various purposes, from entertainment to enterprise applications to military training. One can get an AR app for almost any subject, including chemistry, geometry, zoology, grammar, healthcare, military, and programming. Augmented Reality is revolutionizing education. It is applied in many areas, such as the following:

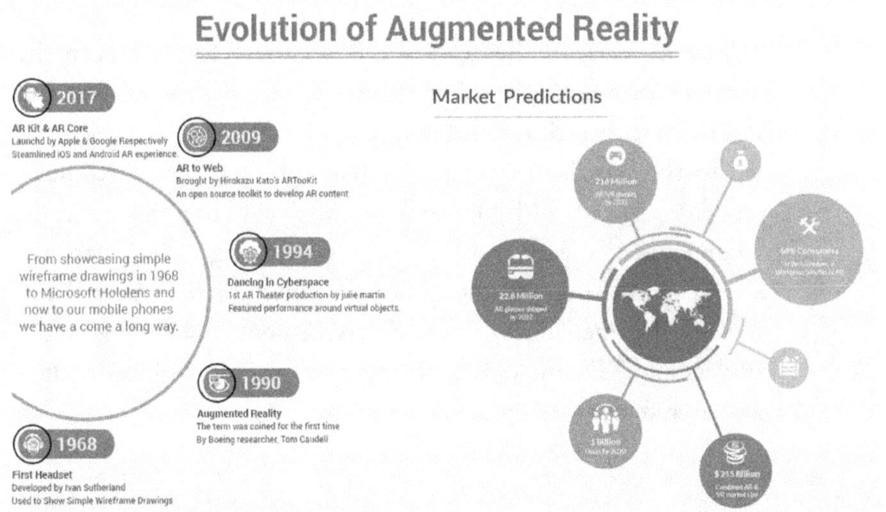

Figure 12.2 The evolution of AR [8].

- *Classroom*: The most popular application for augmented reality in education is the use of AR apps directly in the classroom. Augmented reality is becoming popular in schools worldwide because it makes learning fun and interactive. It turns classrooms into learning environments where students can enter unknown worlds. Using AR in the classroom can turn an ordinary class into an engaging experience. AR technology provides virtual examples and adds gaming elements to support textbook materials. As a result, classes become more interactive. AR helps students better remember the information they learn. It is replacing traditional methods and introducing creative ways to learn. It helps students to deepen their knowledge in various areas such as reading, content creation, playing, and spatial concepts. Figure 12.3 shows different types of AR learning [10].

- *Elementary Education:* Although children's needs have not changed, the world around them has. Augmented reality for elementary education focuses on helping children familiarize and associate themselves with real-life situations. AR puts children in the driver's seat as the creators, while technology is just an enabler.

- *Higher Education:* The academic community has not been shy about experimenting with emerging technologies such as VR and AR to increase efficacy and outcomes. Drastic cost reduction has led to the broader use of AR systems in education. AR allows students virtually visit locations that they cannot visit physically. Many students learn more effectively by doing rather than just seeing or hearing. As the famous Chinese proverb says: "Tell me and I forget. Show me and I remember. Involve me and I understand." Examples of learning by doing are engineering labs and architectural designs.

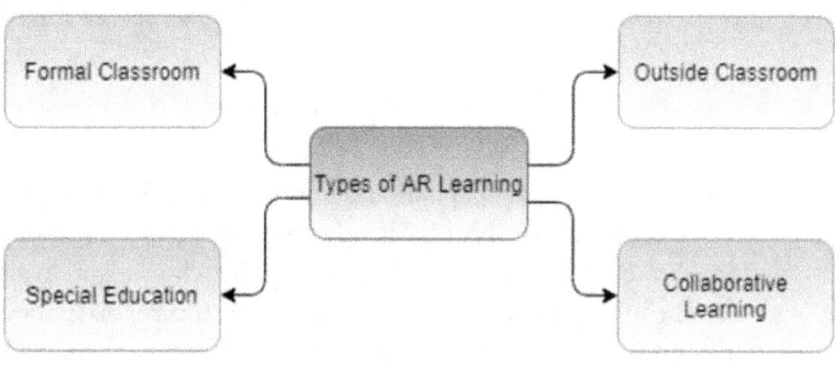

Figure 12.3 Different types of AR learning [10].

AUGMENTED REALITY IN EDUCATION

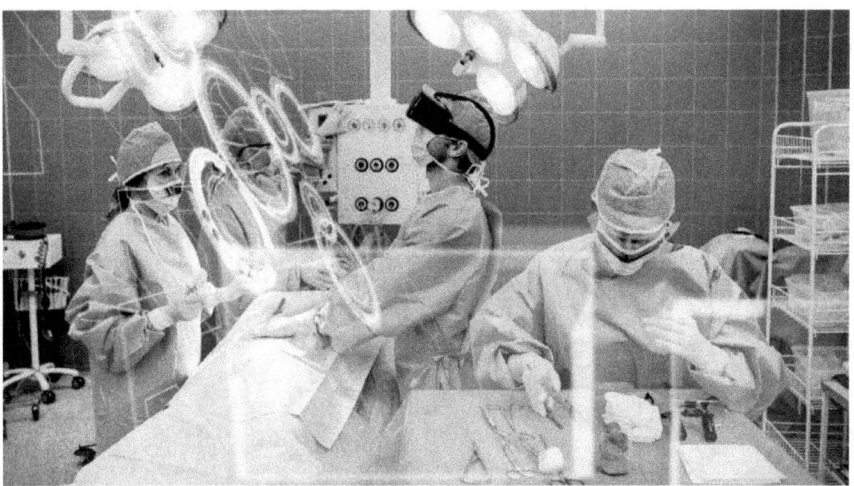

Figure 12.4 AR can assist surgeons [11].

- *Healthcare Education:* Healthcare professions require high proficiency and accuracy since any possible mistakes can be costly. AR application can be used for studying the human body and observing the functioning of the internal organs. From patient education and physician training to surgical visualization and disease prevention simulations, AR's benefits for healthcare are many. In anatomy lessons, students no longer need to dissect real animals; this can be accurately simulated using AR. Human Anatomy Atlas is an app that lets students explore the human body to understand how it works. An example of how AR can assist surgeons is displayed in Figure 12.4 [11].

- *Chemistry:* AR-based apps allow students to study chemical reactions, properties, atomic weight, and other relevant information. AR technology allows for conducting experiments without harming students and university property. Elements 4D uses AR to make chemistry more fun, exciting, and engaging. Augmented reality gives students the ability to see a molecule from all its angles and visualize how atoms are arranged in an element. A typical use of AR in chemistry is shown in Figure 12.5 [12].

EMERGING TECHNOLOGIES IN EDUCATION

Figure 12.5 A typical use of AR in chemistry [12].

- *Military Training:* Nothing can substitute for the intense and grueling physical aspects of training soldiers for combat. Soldiers often need to relocate to a particular setting for military training, which may involve time and expenses. AR is used to create a virtual environment required to train the soldiers better, enhance their skills, and let them train more often.

- *Space Education:* This can get outstanding development using AR. The space industry has been exploring the use of augmented reality. Technologies like AR and MR can help astronauts with tasks like maintaining a space station. Using goggles, workers can receive visual work instructions without turning to manuals. Lockheed Martin engineers use AR headsets to assemble the NASA space capsule faster. An example of using AR in space is shown in Figure 12.6 [13].

- *Manufacturing Workforce Education:* Workforce education in manufacturing has traditionally been very low-tech, one-on-one apprenticeship and written manuals. With increasing technological advancements, some manufacturers now turn to AR to teach their workers new skills. An example of the use of AR in the manufacturing workforce is shown in Figure 12.7 [14].

Other applications of AR in education include museums, mathematics, biology, history, coding, and learning languages.

Figure 12.6 Use of augmented reality in space [13].

Figure 12.7 An example of the use of AR in manufacturing workforce [14].

12.4 BENEFITS

Augmented reality in education offers many benefits that make learning more interesting, interactive, and practical. With a mobile device, educators and students can use AR apps to access projection-based or location-based experiences so that objects or media appear to be in the classroom. AR technology can be integrated into the classroom in all grades. Unlike traditional classrooms, augmented reality does not have any boundaries of time. AR can improve student engagement and motivation. Other benefits include the following [15]:

- *Accessibility:* The learning materials are accessible anytime, anywhere. Augmented reality has the potential to replace paper textbooks and offer portable and less expensive learning materials. In an AR application, you can download and display the latest data in an interactive format. Mobile technologies can promote access to materials from anywhere. With AR, you can access an endless number of resources, all at the click of a button.

- *Interactivity:* AR is an interactive technology that overlays digital features in the real world. It is increasingly used to enhance the learning experience for today's audience that craves interactivity. It makes learning an interactive and immersive experience. Interactivity gives a higher degree of autonomy to students. With AR, teachers can recreate 3D models of almost any object, and students can manipulate the 3D models as if they were real.

- *Faster learning:* Many students find it hard to perceive theoretical information without visuals or relatable examples. AR can change how children apprehend learning material. A new way of presenting information reduces the overall learning time. Learning apps based on augmented reality are finding ways into schools and universities. AR-based learning makes the learning experience more prosperous, engaging, fun, and inviting.

- *Retention of Information:* Human memory does not easily forget visuals. AR can enhance the retention of information. By using AR to supplement traditional teaching methods, students can better remember the information long-term.

- *Professional Training:* AR can help in professional training. Industries like aerospace, aviation, hospitality, military, and others have to invest a huge amount of money and equipment in training. With AR, expenses can be reduced drastically and can make the training interactive and enjoyable. Companies can now hire and train employees on the go using AR instructions. AR can play a vital role in training warehouses, factories, and manufacturing workers. For example, police departments are now using VR to train officers to deal with riots or arrest people in specific situations.

- *Collaboration:* Collaboration is one of the most important AR applications. AR has the potential to enable collaboration. The collaboration element of AR technology stems from online games and chats. In collaborating, you may need to implement strong security controls to protect data.

- *Cost Efficiency:* Integrating AR in education allows cheaper and easier creation than the traditional approach. AR-enabled content and all its visuals can be viewed on a reader's device, allowing a BYOD scenario.

Seven of these and other benefits of AR in education are displayed in Figure 12.8 [16].

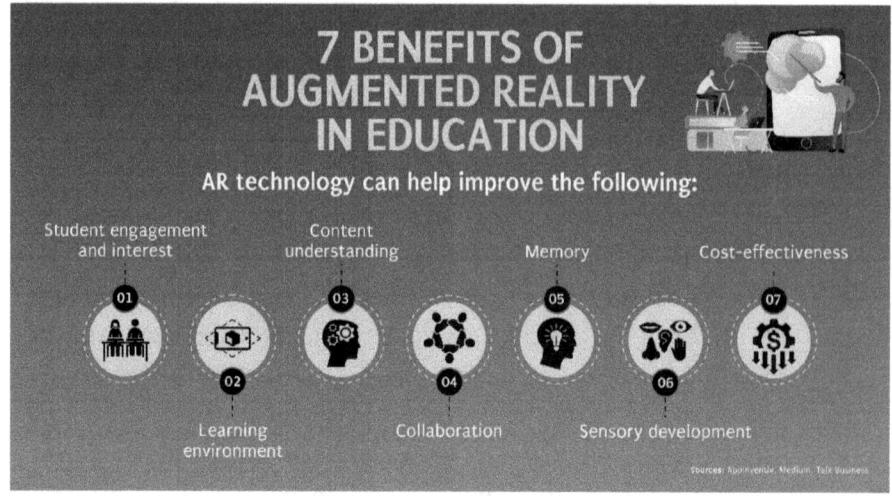

Figure 12.8 Some benefits of AR in education [16].

12.5 CHALLENGES

Implementing augmented reality in the classroom can initially seem daunting. There is no consistent and standardized curriculum for educators to follow. An AR application cannot be installed on old phones that do not support immersion. Other challenges of augmented reality in education include the following [17]:

- *Cost:* Cost is usually people's concern about any new technology or process. AR headsets have bulky hardware that may be too expensive for the masses.

- *Specialized hardware:* Using augmented reality in the classroom requires certain hardware, which may not be readily available.

- *A lack of necessary training*: A major challenge to implementing AR in education is the lack of teacher comfort and familiarity with the technology. Some teachers might struggle to put these new technologies into practice as their background training does not provide the necessary skills.

- *Content portability issues:* It is practically impossible to provide the same quality of AR content on all platforms and devices.

- *Lack of regulation:* Currently, there are no regulations to govern the use of AR.

- *Ethical concern:* A major challenge of using AR in education is the ethical implications and risks of the technology. AR raises questions about the privacy and security of personal data and information collected, stored, and shared by devices and software.

- *Battery life:* This is a major challenge. We doubt the public will ever embrace a separate battery and processor pack.

12.6 GLOBAL USE OF AUGMENTED REALITY IN EDUCATION

Regarding education, augmented reality is one technology that is shaking things up. Traditional methods of schooling are becoming irrelevant in the new century.

Simple blackboards are now replaced with interactive whiteboards where online shared content can be projected and explained simultaneously. Adding VR to the traditional way of schooling enhances and extends how students can learn. AR is an interactive experience that brings digital content to the real world. With augmented reality in education, teachers can develop new, hands-on examples and experiences that students can easily understand. Augmented reality is used worldwide in educational institutions. The top market players in augmented reality and virtual reality companies include the following [18] :

- Google (US), Microsoft (US),
- Sony Corporation (Japan),
- Samsung Electronics (South Korea),
- HTC (Taiwan),
- Apple Inc. (US),
- PTC Inc., (US),

- Seiko Epson (Japan),
- Oculus VR (by Facebook (US)),
- Lenovo (China).

We consider how some nations adopt AR in their educational systems.

- *United States*: Augmented reality has quickly become one of the most popular trends among software and hardware developers. It has the power to transform the classroom. It is increasingly adopted in educational fields to help students with complicated subjects. AR creates opportunities for teachers to help students grasp abstract concepts. Using AR in the classroom can improve learning by assisting educators in creating interactive classrooms that increase student engagement. For example, students struggling with geometry can use AR to see and manipulate 3D geometric forms [19]. We are aware of augmented reality being used in mobile games like Pokémon Go and social media platforms like Snapchat. An example of AR/VR in education is Google Expeditions, which enables users to see 3D objects in the classroom.

- *United Kingdom:* Augmented reality adds computer-generated objects (CGI) to the real world we see around us. Augmented reality is changing the education industry, one of the UK's most lucrative and important industries. It allows everyone to customize their experiences and adjust their AR sets to specs matching their strategies. This feature gives learning a new degree of flexibility [21]. AR helps educators create an environment suitable for students' focus and concentration on the subject. Teachers can instruct students either on an individual basis with a personalized experience or as a group.

- *Europe:* ARETE (Augmented Reality Interactive Educational Ecosystem) was funded by the EU in 2020 to support the dissemination of augmented reality and mixed reality content in education. The Augmented Reality in Formal European University Education (AR-FOR-EU) project will establish and deepen a strategic partnership for teaching Augmented Reality in Higher Education at scale on undergraduate and graduate levels. AR-FOR-EU brings together five internationally renowned institutions to reflect their research, development, and teaching expertise into a validated course offer of excellence, extended with rich and professionally produced open course materials. AR-FOR-EU will help improve the quality of educational programs by creating a new offer in an area conducive to Europe's global competitiveness. While the augmented reality R&D community is growing stronger in Europe, the teaching competence and exchange of good practices in this field are still fragmented. Most countries in Europe struggle when it comes to deciding on the best way to help those with less purchasing power [21].

- *China:* China is one of the fastest-growing economies in the world. The Chinese industrial sector has started investing in R&D activities pertaining to rapidly evolving technologies such as AR, VR, and MR. It has started using AR and VR technologies for employee training, simulation projects, etc. As a means to display abstract concepts and provide an interactive experience, AR has shown unparalleled superiority in the educational domain [18]. The challenges were insufficient Chinese learning content on the market, time-consuming course preparation, technical issues, and a lack of pre-training guidelines.

- *India:* Emerging technologies are currently being welcomed in Indian schools to enrich the quality of teaching and learning. AR is one such technology that can be introduced in the classrooms. Learning through AR is the closest to real-life experience. Genions, a National Education Policy-based interactive learning program designed to improve abstract concepts and spatial intelligence, was launched in September 2022. This experience is India's first augmented reality-based integrated learning program for kids. It has been developed by a skilled team of four co-founders – Sajid Shamim, Jayanta Pal, Siddhartha Saha, and Vijay Gupta. Genions are based on the assumption that "what you learn you might forget, but what you experience you will remember" [22].

12.7 CONCLUSION

The education system is evolving, and technology is at the forefront of this evolution. AR technology can bring about a wealth of benefits for students, educators, and academic institutions. It is cool and amazing how much educators can add to their experience of the world with modern technology such as AR. With giants like Apple and Google pushing AR technologies forward, this may be the best time to join the trend.

Using AR in the classroom is relatively new, and educators are still finding new ways to use it effectively. By using AR to create interactive and engaging learning experiences, students are more likely to work together and share ideas. AR can help improve their problem-solving and critical thinking skills that are essential for success in today's job market. More information about AR in education can be found in the books in [23-35].

REFERENCES

[1] S. Mack, "Augmented reality in education: Looking forward," April 2021, https://www.emergingedtech.com/2021/04/augmented-reality-in-education-looking-forward/

[2] M. N. O. Sadiku, C. M. M. Kotteti, and S. M. Musa, "Augmented reality: A primer," *International Journal of Trend in Research and Development,* vol. 7, no. 3, 2020.

[3] "What is augmented reality or AR?" https://dynamics.microsoft.com/en-us/mixed-reality/guides/what-is-augmented-reality-ar/

[4] "Metaverse and multiverse: The real sense of AR, VR, MR, XR and IR," https://yp.ieee.org/metaverse-and-multiverse-the-real-sense-of-ar-vr-mr-xr-and-ir/

[5] M. N. O. Sadiku, U. C. Chukwu, and J. O. Sadiku, "Augmented reality in education," *International Journal on Integrated Education,* 2023, pp. 252-260.

[6] H. Ling, "Augmented reality in reality," *IEEE MultiMedia*, July–September 2017, pp. 10-15.

[7] M. Singh and M. P. Singh, "Augmented reality interfaces," *IEEE Internet Computing*, November/December 2013, pp. 66-70.

[8] D. Miller, "The potential of augmented reality in business," December 2018, https://www.epikso.com/blog/the-potential-of-augmented-reality-in-business/

[9] N. Sahota, "Augmented reality in Education: The future of learning is here," February 2023, https://www.neilsahota.com/augmented-reality-in-education-the-future-of-learning-is-here/

[10] M. Z. Iqbal, E. Mangina, and A.G. Campbell, "Current challenges and future research directions in augmented reality for education," *Multimodal Technologies and Interaction*, vol. 6, no. 9, 2022.

[11] " 7 Uses of augmented reality in healthcare education," https://www.cognihab.com/blog/augmented-reality-in-healthcare-education/

[12] "Augmented reality for learning chemistry," March 2021, https://observatory.tec.mx/edu-bits-2/augmented-reality-for-learning-chemistry/

[13] "Use cases of augmented reality in education and training," January 2019, https://rubygarage.org/blog/augmented-reality-in-education-and-training

[14] "Augmented reality to provide new skills for manufacturing workforce education," October 2020, https://www.purdue.edu/newsroom/releases/2020/Q4/augmented-reality-to-provide-new-skills-for-manufacturing-workforce-education.html

[15] S. Mack, "Augmented reality in education: A staggering insight into the future," https://www.robotlab.com/blog/augmented-reality-in-education-a-staggering-insight-into-the-future

[16] "Augmented reality in education: Interactive classrooms," https://online.maryville.edu/blog/augmented-reality-in-education/

[17] A. Shalimov, "Augmented reality in education: How to apply it to your edtech business," April 2023, https://easternpeak.com/blog/augmented-reality-in-education/

[18] "China augmented reality and virtual reality industry to grow at a CAGR 32.0% [2022-2027]," May 2023, https://www.globenewswire.com/en/news-release/2023/05/29/2677519/0/en/China-Augmented-Reality-and-Virtual-Reality-Industry-to-Grow-at-a-CAGR-32-0-2022-2027.html

[19] "Augmented reality in education: Interactive classrooms," https://online.maryville.edu/blog/augmented-reality-in-education/#:~:text=Why%20use%20augmented%20reality%20in,solve%20problems%20and%20improve%20inefficiencies.

[20] "Ways augmented reality is changing education industry in the UK: the future of learning is now," https://eureta.org/ways-augmented-reality-is-changing-education-industry-in-the-uk-the-future-of-learning-is-now/

[21] "About the AR-FOR-EU project," https://codereality.net/project/

[22] "Genions, India's first AR (Augmented Reality) based integrated learning program for kids, launches," https://indiaeducationdiary.in/genions-indias-first-ar-augmented-reality-based-integrated-learning-program-for-kids-launches/

[23] V. Geroimenko (ed.), *Augmented Reality in Education: A New Technology for Teaching and Learning.* Springer, 2020.

[24] C. Dede et al. (eds.), *Virtual, Augmented, and Mixed Realities in Education.* Springer, 2017.

[25] A. S. Pillai and G. Guazzaroni (eds.), *Virtual and Augmented Reality in Education, Art, and Museums*. IGI Global, 2019.

[26] A. Anderson, *Virtual Reality, Augmented Reality and Artificial Intelligence in Special Education: A Practical Guide to Supporting Students with Learning Differences*. Routledge, 2019.

[27] T. Prodromou (ed.), *Augmented Reality in Educational Settings*. Brill/Sense, 2020.

[28] V. Geroimenko (ed.), *Augmented Reality Games II: The Gamification of Education, Medicine and Art*. Springer, 2019

[29] Z. Tacgin, *Virtual and Augmented Reality: An Educational Handbook*. Cambridge Scholars Publishing, 2020.

[30] C. D. Epp and G. Akcayir (eds.), *Designing, Deploying, and Evaluating Virtual and Augmented Reality in Education*. IGI Global, 2020.

[31] G. R. Ruiz and M. H. Hernandez (eds.), *Augmented Reality for Enhanced Learning Environments*. IGI Global, 2018.

[32] C. M. Moran (ed.), *Virtual and Augmented Reality in English Language Arts Education*. Lexington Books, 2023.

[33] L. Daniela (ed.), *New Perspectives on Virtual and Augmented Reality: Finding New Ways to Teach in a Transformed Learning Environment*. Taylor & Francis, 2020.

[34] S. Zagoranski and S. Divjak, *Use of Augmented Reality in Education*. Vol. 2. IEEE, 2003.

[35] G. Guazzaroni and A. S. Pillai (eds.), *Virtual and Augmented Reality in Education, Art, and Museums*. IGI Global, 2019

CHAPTER 13

GAMIFICATION IN EDUCATION

"Gamification is the craft of deriving fun and engaging elements found typically in games and thoughtfully applying them to real-world or productive activities."
—Yu-kai Chou,

13.1 INTRODUCTION

Technology permeates a lot of our day-to-day lives. It has changed the way we live, shop, work, play, eat, connect, meet people, and socialize. Rapid advances in digital technologies are constantly unveiling new ways to interact with the world. Due to these technologies, the education industry has undergone a major transformation. One of the trends sweeping the industry is gamification.

Games are widely popular and entertaining. The games industry is one of the most lucrative industries due to the billion-dollar sales of digital games. The global game marketplace includes video game console hardware and software and online, mobile, and PC games. Games are designed systematically, thoughtfully, and artistically to create fun and enjoyment. Although games and gamification have a lot in common, they are not exactly the same [1,2]. Gamification is the process of applying the science and psychology of digital gaming (such as video game elements) in a non-game environment. It is the craft of deriving all the fun in games and applying them to productive activities. It involves taking something that already exists and integrating game mechanics into it to motivate participation and increase engagement [3]. For example, it is being employed to enhance user engagement by adding playfulness and fun to existing information systems.

Gamification is the use of game-based elements (such as point scoring, implementation of goals, and competition) and game principles in non-game contexts. It is the application of elements of video games, game-thinking, and game mechanics to help solve everyday real-life problems. It has emerged as a promising area for imparting education. It transforms students from passive participants to active ones. It assumes that students learn best when they are also having fun. Gamification aims to maximize teaching and engagement by capturing student interest and inspiring them to continue learning [4].

This chapter provides an overview of gamification in education and its applications.

It begins by explaining what gamification is all about. It describes the various components of gamification. It provides some applications of gamification in education. It highlights the challenges and benefits of gamification in education. It covers the global use of gamification in education. The last section concludes with comments.

13.2 WHAT IS GAMIFICATION?

The word "gamification" was coined in 2002 by Nick Pelling, a British inventor, but it did not gain popularity until 2010. The idea of gamification came from the fact that the gaming industry was the first to master human-focused design, and we are now learning from games. Gamification is not a new concept; but is deeply rooted in marketing endeavors, such as points cards, grades, degrees, and workplace productivity [5]. Researchers became interested in gamification because the concept could be implemented in different ways to motivate people. Gamification has become hugely popular in all walks of life, including education. The concept of gamification is illustrated in Figure 13.1 [6].

Figure 13.1 The concept of gamification [6].

Everyone loves games. Gamification in education is the process of transforming typical academic components into gaming themes. Education is perhaps the most successful and well-known area of application for gamification. Traditional education has been found to be ineffective in motivating and engaging many students. Gamification in education is a viable alternative to some of the existing educational delivery methods. It is fast emerging as an effective technique to motivate and engage learners. It facilitates a better learning experience and environment, increases recall and retention, provides instant feedback, engages and entertains learners, and drives strong behavioral change [7]. Education gamification aims not to replace regular lectures but to be a supplemental tool for students in learning concepts. Gamification simply means improving the learning that occurs in an experience. It unifies educators and engages learners through an effective, systematic approach [8].-It inherently promises to provide students with learning at a comparably low cost. It has the positive effect of making difficult subjects (such as engineering) more manageable and increases intrinsic motivation, scientific knowledge, and collaboration [9].

Games have some distinctive features which play a key role in gamification [10]:

- *users* are all participants – employees or clients (for companies), students (for educational institutions);
- *challenges/tasks* that users perform and progress towards defined objectives;
- *points* that are accumulated as a result of executing tasks;
- *levels* which users pass depending on the points;
- *badges* that serve as rewards for completing actions;
- *ranking of users* according to their achievements.

Gamification can be viewed in two ways: (1) adopting the act of playing a video game into everyday use, (2) the act of using game elements to make non-games more enjoyable. It is applied in education, business, sports, marketing, and finance. It is currently one of the largest trends in education. Traditional education has been found to be ineffective in motivating and engaging many students. Gamification is a cutting-edge approach that produces positive results in every region of the world.

13.3 COMPONENTS OF GAMIFICATION

Gamification is a multidisciplinary technique covering various domains, including game study, human-computer interaction, and psychology. Looking at the components (or core drives) of gamification will help us understand what a gamified system actually consists of [11]:

- *Games*: Figure 13.2 shows various uses of games. Digital games involve programming computers to play games. They have become the fastest-growing section of the entertainment industry. Educators, the military, government, and healthcare providers use digital games. Games used for serious purposes or "serious games" are used by the military.

- *Gamification Elements*: These include [12]:
  (a) Awards: A particular award is given to the player on completing a behavior.
  (b) Point-based reward system: The players obtain a reward in the form of points for completing a certain behavior.

(c) Badges: These represent certain achievements of the user/player. They are common extrinsic rewards employed in gamification efforts.
(d) Levels: The users have a level that increases as they reach certain points.
(e) Quests: The tasks the player has to complete are presented as a quest.
(f) Voting: Players can vote on another player's behavior.
(g) Ranking: A ranking with the top players is presented to all players to increase competitiveness.
(h) Betting: Players/users bet on a certain event, such as an estimation, for example. The winner of the bet is rewarded.

- *Game Mechanics:* Gamification models are based on game mechanics, such as reward systems, customization, and leaderboards. The game mechanics represent the modes of interacting with games. These consist of rules, roles, and stories [12]. Figure 13.3 shows a list of game mechanics [14].

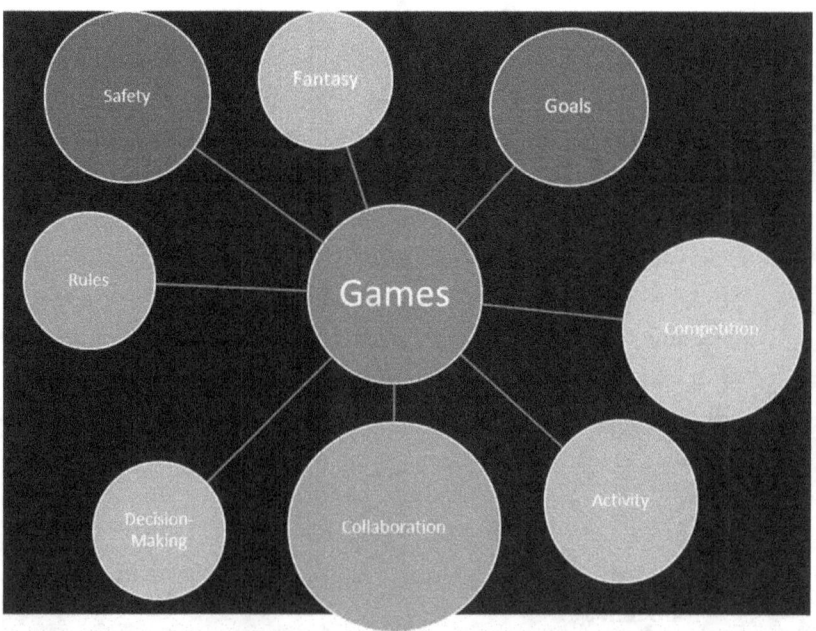

Figure 13.2 Different uses of games.

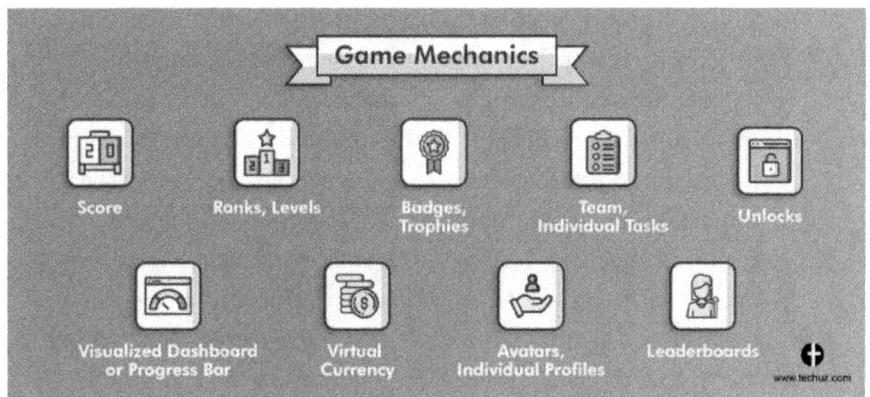

Figure 13.3 A list of game mechanics [14].

Fun is the secret ingredient that makes gamification a truly unique experience. It is a consequence of brain adaptation to pattern recognition. Like games, gamification includes goals, challenges, competition, and collaboration.

13.4 APPLICATIONS

Gamification is the application of elements of video games, game-thinking, and game mechanics to help solve everyday real-life problems. It is an umbrella term for using video game elements in non-gaming platforms with the goal of improving user experience and engagement. It can be used almost everywhere, using smartphones, tablets, and computers. It has been widely applied in different areas such as education, business, marketing, workplace, healthcare, edutainment, information studies, human-computer interaction, financial services, transportation, engineering, computer science, manufacturing, medicine, cybersecurity, and military [15]. We consider some of these applications.

- *Gamification of Learning:* Education is essentially about learning new things and enhancing capabilities. Gamification and game-based learning are used in modern learning environments to engage students. Games have some elements that make them powerful tools for human learning. Gamification is the introduction of game elements into a traditionally non-game situation. The classroom is for learning and developing innate skills. The gamification of learning is an educational approach that seeks to motivate students using video game design and game elements in learning environments. As shown in Figure 13.4, there are important elements that should be incorporated into e-Learning gamification [16]. When a classroom incorporates the use of some of these elements, that environment can be considered «gamified." Without adding extra gaming elements to the classroom, schooling already contains some elements which are analogous to games [17]. For teachers, gamification requires rethinking the classroom. Figure 13.5 shows children participating in gamification in the classroom [18].

Examples of gamification in the classroom include the following [19]:

- Giving points for meeting academic objectives
- Giving points for meeting procedural/non-academic objectives
- Creating playful barriers
- Creating competition within the classroom
- Comparing and reflecting on performance in nuanced ways personalized for each student
- Creating a range of unique rewards desirable for a range of unique students
- Using levels, checkpoints, and other methods of "progression."
- Creating challenges with more than one way to be solved and emphasize the different approaches.
- Giving learning badges instead of (or in addition to) points or grades.
- Letting students set their goals, then track their own progress.
- Create problems or challenges with more than one way to solve them.

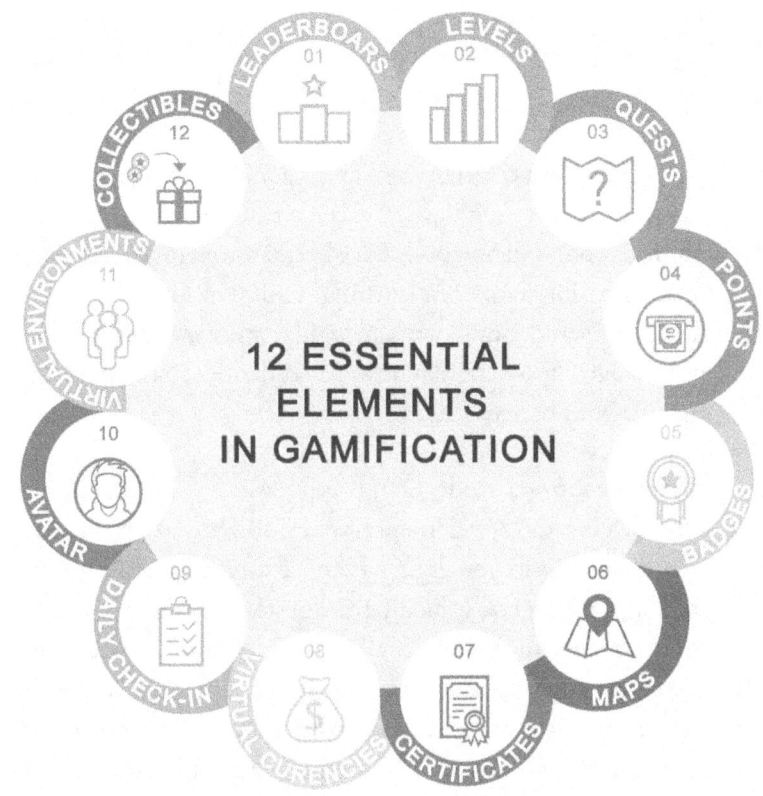

Figure 13.4 Essential elements in eLearning gamification [16].

Figure 13.5 Children participating in gamification in the classroom [19].

- *Elementary School Education:* Gamification is popular and appropriate in K–12 schools because it engages students by meeting them where they are. In K-12 education, gamification transforms the classroom environment and regular activities into a game. It requires creativity, collaboration, and play. Many children play video games regularly. Scavenger hunts, bingo, dice games, Connect Four and Scrabble, have been around for decades and can be adapted for classroom learning. Children love playing. As the Girl Scouts and Boy Scouts recognize mastery and achievement with badges, teachers may reward student accomplishments and mastery with badges [20].

- *Higher Education:* Colleges and universities use game mechanics more than K-12, elementary, middle, and high schools. Gamification is fast emerging as an effective technique to motivate and engage learners. It facilitates a better learning experience and environment, increases recall and retention, provides instant feedback, engages and entertains learners, and drives strong behavioral change. Education gamification aims not to replace regular lectures but to be a supplemental tool for students in learning concepts. Gamification simply means improving the learning that occurs in an experience. It unifies educators and engages learners through an effective, systematic approach. The entire higher education system needs to be changed and made more innovative and engaging. Gamification is useful in higher education in the following ways:

  ➢ Self-paced online learning could be more engaging.

  ➢ Gamification motivates students to use their smartphones or devices in the classroom to learn their lessons easily with more fun.

  ➢ College students are highly interested in playing games. They would be excited to complete a task and to compete with their fellow mates.

> Some of the games are based on strategizing, which helps in boosting thinking capabilities and problem-solving skills.

> In gamification, students can be grouped for a certain task. It would help students to learn and do a task in collaboration.

- *Medical Education:* It is well known that technology continues to shape the healthcare industry, providing new avenues for the delivery of patient care. Gamification techniques are increasingly been used to provide new channels for instruction and professional development among doctors, nurses, and other clinicians. They can make learning fun, memorable, and more effective. Medical students should cease seeing their education as a challenge to overcome. They should learn, seeing it as a game that can be won. Gamification in medical education is a viable alternative to some of the existing educational delivery methods. Physicians are successfully using online video games as their primary learning tool [21,22]. Over the years, medical education games, mobile applications, and virtual patient simulations for medical education have been developed. Gamification can act as a catalyst for collaborative learning, where teams of learners can work together towards a shared goal. Whether medical schools incorporate gamification in their curriculum remains to be seen. The concept of "serious games" was introduced by Abt in 1970; they are games that have an explicit and carefully thought-out educational purpose [23,24]. The main reason for using games in medicine is their ability to motivate [25].

13.5 BENEFITS

Gamification describes the process of applying typical game-like components to non-game activities to keep people motivated and participating in the task at hand. It makes us derive fun from work and everyday activities. Its objective is first to understand what drives people to play games (the feeling of accomplishment, competition, excitement, or pleasure) and apply these factors to your platform. Teachers and parents can implement gamification in various ways across countless subject disciplines.

Other benefits of gamification include the following [26]:

- Gamification makes learning visible
- Gamification increases motivation
- Gamification assists cognitive development
- Gamification can make learning a personal experience
- Gamification boosts engagement
- Gamification aids in cognitive development
- Gamification increases competition which can lead to engagement.
- Gamification involves creativity and student choice, which increases engagement.
- Gamification gives students immediate feedback and allows them to easily track their progress toward academic goals.
- Gamification provides instant feedback and reinforcement.

Some of these benefits are illustrated in Figure 13.6 [27].

13.6 CHALLENGES

There are growing concerns about ethical constraints surrounding the implementation of gamification. Teachers should be aware of the copyright protection on the elements and ensure they are not violated. If necessary, permission should be obtained from the creators of the existing game [17]. Other challenges include the following [28]:

- *Resistance:* Some educators criticize gamification for taking a less than serious approach to education. Teachers who criticize the gamification of learning may fear that the curriculum might not be covered if any time is spent on gamification.

- *Addiction:* Everyone knows that games can be addictive. It is easy to lose hours playing games. That is because the player is extremely motivated to continue playing repeatedly.

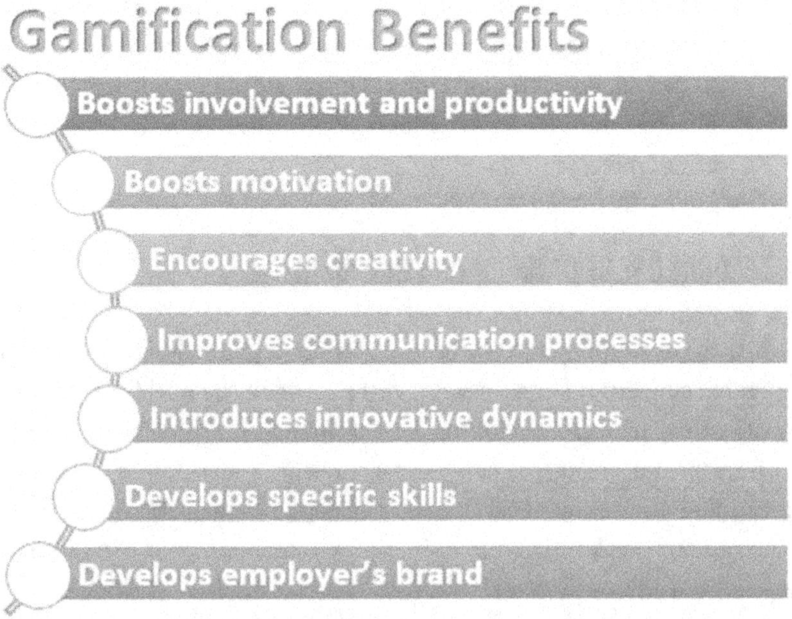

Gamification Benefits

- Boosts involvement and productivity
- Boosts motivation
- Encourages creativity
- Improves communication processes
- Introduces innovative dynamics
- Develops specific skills
- Develops employer's brand

Figure 13.6 Some of these benefits of gamification [27].

- *Overemphasizing Rewards:* Some say that giving out rewards for doing work creates the wrong type of motivation, whereby students become more focused on the treats and prizes than on the learning.

- *Ethical Issues:* Gamification can raise ethical issues, such as manipulation, coercion, exploitation, and privacy. For example, gamification can be used to influence learners' behavior, choices, and emotions without their full consent or awareness. Gamification should be designed and implemented with respect for learners' autonomy, dignity, and rights.

- *Technological Issues:* Gamification can encounter technical issues, such as accessibility, usability, and reliability. For example, gamification can be inaccessible or incompatible with the devices of the learners, teachers, or administrators, causing exclusion, inequality, or isolation.

- *Practical Issues:* Gamification can face practical issues, such as cost, time, and support. For example, gamification can be costly to design, develop, implement, and maintain, requiring financial, human, and material resources that may not be available or affordable.

13.7 GLOBAL USE OF GAMIFICATION IN EDUCATION

Gamification simply refers to the application of game design principles in non-game contexts. Gamification is everywhere in the world. In education, gamification means developing an approach for increasing learners' motivation and engagement by incorporating game design elements in educational environments. Education needs to be gamified because that is the state of the world. We consider how some nations use gamification in their educational systems.

- *United States*: Gamification of education is intended to transform traditional lessons into an enhanced learning experience. It means that educators apply game design elements to an educational setting. More and more educators are employing gamification in the classroom because it works at a time when competition for students' attention is growing. Gamification is one of the ways school districts are exploring the new education landscape. It is used in modern learning environments to engage students. Gamification is popular in K–12 schools because it engages students by meeting them where they are. Gamification can have a greater impact on learning than even its cousin, game-based learning [29]. Whether one is interested in games in education or the gamification of education, there are various examples that span everything from early childhood learning to undergraduate-level concepts. One must think critically about what makes students fun and be on the lookout for ways to make learning fun [30].

- *United Kingdom:* Gamification refers to the use of a pedagogical system that was developed within gaming design but is implemented within a non-game context. Gamification and digital games introduce fun into the learning experience and can be a powerful motivator if properly designed. Applying gamification elements to the classroom dynamic can have a multitude of benefits for the students. One of the benefits of educational technology (or EdTech) is that it can be accessed in the classroom and at home. With younger generations far more comfortable using online tools and the vast majority able to access the internet from home, schools are now in a position to flexibly incorporate these tools [31].

- *Europe:* The concept of gamification has evolved from a recent buzzword to an actual policy priority of the European Union. Gamification in the educational process might contribute to raising learners' motivation, engagement, and performance. Its main objective is to support the students' attention, promote continuity of their learning, and attract them to fulfill learning goals. The launch of the European project MAXIMUS signals the beginning of a contribution aiming to amplify the educational impact with the integration of gamification. Today's students call for new innovative educational approaches [32].

- *China:* Gamification is a process and application in which game elements apply to non-game contexts. Educational gamification is getting more attention as one efficient way to boost learning outcomes. Incorporating gamification in learning has an overall better outcome in many aspects. Teachers need to pay attention to systemization, gamification, and immersion of teaching design and ensure the attractiveness and acceptability of the teaching method. Gamification has been used to teach Chinese language to children at an early age. Chinese parents place extremely high values on their children's academic success, and some of them have a reluctant attitude are reluctant toward educational games. Gamifications have multiple benefits: make learning more engaging and enjoyable, promoting reading performance, promoting student motivation, promoting students' higher-order thinking skills, catering to different learning styles, and providing an appropriate incentive [33].

- *India:* Gamification refers to the integration of game-like elements into non-game contexts, such as education. The gamification of education has become an important aspect of education in India because it offers many benefits. It has been shown to increase motivation, engagement, and learning outcomes. It also has the potential to promote 21st-century skills, such as critical thinking, problem-solving, and creativity [34]. Gamified learning is adaptable to different learning styles and can cater to the diverse needs of students. It can be used in a variety of subjects, including mathematics, sciences, history, geography, and social sciences. In India, gamified learning has become a popular trend in recent years as more educators look for ways to make education more enjoyable for students [35].

13.8 CONCLUSION

Gamification refers to a set of activities and processes to solve problems by using the characteristics of game elements. It is an umbrella term for using video game elements in non-gaming platforms to improve user experience and engagement. It is based on the idea that "fun can obviously change behavior for the better." It works because it triggers real human emotions such as happiness, joy, excitement, and accomplishment. Gamification of education is an approach that uses game practices and elements the learning process. By increasing the student's engagement using gamification, teachers increase the likelihood that lessons will be remembered.

Gamification is still rising in popularity. While gamification is gaining ground in business, marketing, corporate management, healthcare, edutainment, information studies, human-computer interaction, financial services, transportation, and engineering, its application in education is still an emerging trend [36]. Gamification has proved to be an efficient technique to boost engagement, motivation, and competition in learning. For more information about gamification in education, one should consult the books in [37-48] and the following related journals:

- *International Journal of Emerging Technologies in Learning*
- *International Journal of Educational Technology in Higher Education*
- *European Journal of Educational Research,*
- *IEEE Transactions on Education*

REFERENCES

[1] M. N. O. Sadiku, S.M. Musa, and R. Nelatury, "Digital games," *International Journal of Research and Allied Sciences*, vol. 1, no. 10, Dec. 2016, pp. 1,2.

[2] B. Kim, "The popularity of Gamification in the mobile and social era," *Understanding Gamification*, chapter 1 or *Library Technology Report*, vol. 51, no. 2, February-March 2015, pp. 1-10.

[3] J. Dale Prince, "Gamification," *Journal of Electronic Resources in Medical Libraries*, vol.10, no. 3, 2013, pp. 162-169.

[4] M. N. O. Sadiku, U. C. Chukwu. A. Ajayi-Majebi, and S. M. Musa, "Gamification in education: An overview," *International Journal of Trend in Scientific Research and Development*, vol. 6, no. 7, November-December 2022, pp. 738-744.

[5] K. Seaborn and D. I. Fels, "Gamification in theory and action: A survey," *International Journal of Human-Computer Studies*, vol. 74, 2015, pp. 14–31.

[6] E. Hagene, "Gamification in training: 4 ways to bring games into the classroom," June 2019, https://frontcore.com/blog/gamification-in-training-4-ways-to-bring-games-into-the-classroom/

[7] C. I. Muntean, " Raising engagement in e-learning through gamification," *Proceedings of the 6th International Conference on Virtual Learning* (ICVL), 2011, pp. 323 -329.

[8] D. J. Fisher, J. Beedle, and S. E. Rouse, "Gamification: A study of business teacher educators' knowledge of, attitude toward, and experiences

with the gamification of activities in the classroom," *The Journal of Research in Business Education*, vol. 56, no. 1, January 2014, pp. 1-16.

[9] A. P. Markopoulos et al., "Gamification in engineering education and professional training," *International Journal of Mechanical Engineering Education*, vol. 43, no. 2, 2015, pp. 118–131.

[10] G. Kiryakova, N. Angelova, and L. Yordanova, "Gamification in education," https://www.sun.ac.za/english/learning-teaching/ctl/Documents/Gamification%20in%20education.pdf

[11] M. N. O. Sadiku, S. R. Nelatury, and S. M. Musa, "Gamification: A primer," *Journal of Scientific and Engineering Research*, vol. 7, no. 4, 2020, pp. 165-169.

[12] O. Pedreira et al., "Gamification in software engineering – A systematic mapping," *Information and Software Technology*, vol. 57, 2015, pp. 157–168.

[13] A. Martens and W. Mueller, "Gamification - A structured analysis," *Proceedings of IEEE 16th International Conference on Advanced Learning Technologies*, 2016, pp. 138-142.

[14] "What is gamification? A detailed guide to gamification in education & gamified learning apps," June 2019, https://www.techuz.com/blog/what-is-gamification-a-detailed-guide-to-gamification-in-education-game-based-learning/

[15] "Gamification 101: An introduction to game dynamics," https://www.bunchball.com/gamification101

[16] "Gamification in eLearning: Essential elements," August 2022, https://aristeksystems.com/blog/essential-elements-of-gamification-in-elearning/

[17] "Gamification of learning," *Wikipedia*, the free encyclopedia https://en.wikipedia.org/wiki/Gamification_of_learning

[18] "5 Benefits of gamification," January 2008, https://ssec.si.edu/stemvisions-blog/5-benefits-gamification

[19] "What are the best examples of gamification in the classroom?" https://www.teachthought.com/the-future-of-learning/examples-gamification/

[20] M. Haiken, " 5 Ways to gamify your classroom," February 2021, https://www.iste.org/explore/In-the-classroom/5-ways-to-gamify-your-classroom

[21] C. I. Muntean, "Raising engagement in e-learning through gamification," *Proceedings of the 6th International Conference on Virtual Learning* (ICVL), 2011, pp. 323 -329.

[22] D. J. Fisher, J. Beedle, and S. E. Rouse, "Gamification: A study of business teacher educators' knowledge of, attitude toward, and experiences with the gamification of activities in the classroom," *The Journal of Research in Business Education*, vol. 56, no. 1, January 2014, pp. 1-16.

[23] S. Singhal, J. Hough, and D. Cripps, "Twelve tips for incorporating gamification into medical education," https://www.mededpublish.org/manuscripts/2678

[24] S. V. Gentry et al., "Serious Gaming and Gamification interventions for health professional education," *Journal of Medical Internet Research*, vol. 21, no. 3,· March 2019.

[25] R. A. C. Marques., "Using gamification for reducing infections in hospitals," *Master's Thesis*, (unspecified university) April 2016.

[26] "Effective gamified learning setup for students," Unknown Source.

[27] "Gamification in HR management," https://www.assert.pro/gejmifikacija-u-hr-menadzmentu/

[28] "What are the challenges and risks of gamification in education?" June 2023, https://www.linkedin.com/advice/1/what-challenges-risks-gamification-education?src=go-pa&trk=sem-ga_campid.19968655396_asid.146701155774_crid.654766664810_kw._d.c_tid.dsa-2081079936479_n.g_mt._geo.9012004&mcid=7052054652627943424&cid=&gclid=EAIaIQobChMIsurN4tq5_wIVoodaBR3QbwehEAAYASAAEgLklvD_BwE&gclsrc=aw.ds

[29] R. Torchia, "What is gamification, and why is it trending in K–12 schools?" August 2022, https://edtechmagazine.com/k12/article/2022/08/what-gamification-and-why-it-trending-k-12-schools-perfcon

[30] R. Blankman, "Gamification in education: The fun of learning," January 2022, https://www.hmhco.com/blog/what-is-gamification-in-education

[31] E. Slater, " Is gamification the key to pupil engagement?" May 2023, https://www.theaccessgroup.com/en-gb/blog/edu-is-gamification-the-key-to-pupil-engagement/

[32] D. Plova and M. Vejacka, "Implementation of gamification principles into higher education," *European Journal of Educational Research*, vol. 11, no. 2, 2022, 763 -779.

[33] J. Zhu, "A study on China's tesol pre-service teachers' knowledge and attitudes on gamification," *Advances in Social Science, Education and Humanities Research*, vol. 664, 2022.

[34] "From boredom to engagement: The role of gamification in Indian education," March 2023, https://scoonews.com/news/from-boredom-to-engagement-the-role-of-gamification-in-indian-education/#:~:text=In%20conclusion%2C%20the%20gamification%20of,accessible%20and%20inclusive%2C%20and%20promoting

[35] F. Khan, "Gamification in education: A revolutionary approach to learning," April 2023, https://www.financialexpress.com/education-2/gamification-in-education-a-revolutionary-approach-to-learning/3053843/

[36] D. Dicheva et al.,. "Gamification in education: A systematic mapping study," *Educational Technology & Society*, vol. 18, no. 3, 2015, pp. 75–88.

[37] S. Kim et al., *Gamification in Learning and Education: Enjoy Learning Like Gaming*. Springer, 2018.

[38] Information Resources Management Association, *Gamification in Education: Breakthroughs in Research and Practice*. IGI Global, 2018.

[39] Information Resources Management Association, *Research Anthology on Developments in Gamification and Game-Based Learning.*. IGI Global, 2021.

[40] T. Reiners and L. C. Wood, *Gamification in Education and Business*. Springer, 2014.

[41] K. M. Kapp, *The Gamification of Learning and Instruction: Game-based Methods and Strategies for Training and Education*. Wiley, 2012.

[42] A. C. Moreira, O. Bernardes, and V. Amorim (eds.), *Handbook of Research on the Influence and Effectiveness of Gamification in Education*. IGI Global, 2022.

[43] W. Oliveira and I. I. Bittencourt, *Tailored Gamification to Educational Technologies*. Springer, 2019.

[44] V. Geroimenko (ed.), *Augmented Reality Games II: The Gamification of Education, Medicine and Art*. Springer, 2019.

[45] I. Harismayanti, I. N. A. J. Putra, and M.H. Santosa, *Gamification in English Teaching and Learning*. Nilacakra, 2020.

[46] K. M. Kapp, L. Blair, and R. Mesch, *The Gamification of Learning and Instruction Fieldbook: Ideas Into Practice*. Wiley, 2014.

[47] J. Cassie, *Level Up Your Classroom: The Quest to Gamify Your Lessons and Engage Your Students*. ASCD, 2016.

[48] T. Reiners and L. C. Wood (eds.), *Gamification in Education and Business*. Springer, 2015.

CHAPTER 14

SOCIAL MEDIA IN EDUCATION

"The best teachers I've ever had have used technology to enhance the learning process, including Facebook pages and events for upcoming projects."
—Katie Benmar

14.1 INTRODUCTION

The Internet is now an indispensable part of our life, impacting every area, from electronic commerce to online education. Its beauty is that it connects people. The rapid development of information technology has led to the birth of social media, which may be regarded as Internet-based channels that allow users to interact in real-time or asynchronously [1]. Social media (SM) are essentially online tools that provide users with the ability to collaborate and communicate with each other without any limitations by time or space.

Social media (also called Web 2.0) refers to Internet-based and mobile-based tools that allow individuals to share and consume content through varied modalities such as text, image, and video [2]. The world has become a global village, and the use of technology has made it a smaller world through social media.

Traditional social media include written press, TV, and radio. Modern social media, also known as social networking, include Facebook, Twitter, Instagram, Pinterest, and YouTube. Social media websites are online environments where users can contribute, retrieve, and explore content primarily generated by other users. Social media technology has become a medium through which educators can instruct, and students can learn.

Children were born in the age of digital technologies, which have become part of their daily lives. For this reason, they are called digital natives. They are the young generation of students (K through college) who are "native speakers" of the digital language of computers, videos, video games, and social media [3]. The 21st century has become a digital world that has produced digital natives. Social media such as Facebook, Twitter, Myspace, Google+, LinkedIn, and Instagram are used daily by millions of people worldwide, especially young people. Youngsters use social media mostly for socialization, entertainment, and exchanging ideas. Although teachers see the need to explore the educational use of these media, many teachers seem to struggle with the tension between possible pedagogical use and the tempting distraction of the relatively new technology [4].

This chapter provides the use of social media networks for education and how they are being applied in various areas of education. It begins by explaining the basics of social media. It presents some popular social media. It provides some applications of social media in education. It highlights the benefits and challenges of social media in education. It covers how social media is used globally. The last section concludes with comments.

14.2 SOCIAL MEDIA BASICS

Social media (or social networking) is a universal phenomenon. Social media basically refers to any technology that facilitates the dissemination and sharing of information over the Internet. The key purpose of using social media tools is to engage others electronically, facilitate professional communication, improve student comprehension, enhance student networking, and enable collaboration with other students around the globe. Social media applications include Facebook, Twitter, LinkedIn, and Google+, and are popular among our students. Some social media tools are powerful drivers of change for teaching and learning practices [5].

Social media (SM) is consumer-generated media that covers a variety of new sources of online information created and used by consumers to share with others. It employs mobile and web-based technologies to create, share, discuss, and modify consumer-generated content.

These are some common features of social media [6,7]:

1. *Accessibility*: They are easily accessible with little or no cost.
2. *Connectedness*: They facilitate the development of online social networks by connecting people and bringing the world together.
3. *Communications*: They foster communication between individuals or organizations.
4. *Reach*: They offer unlimited reach to all content available to anyone, anywhere.
5. *News media*: They allow political news and information, true or not, to spread quickly.
6. *Collaboration*: They are computer-mediated technologies that facilitate the creation and sharing of information and ideas.

Social media takes on many forms. The six basic forms are [8]: (1) social networks such as Facebook and Twitter, (2) blogs - websites that allow users to subscribe, update, and leave comments, (3) wikis – collaborative websites such as Wikipedia which used to edit content, (4) podcasts – audio or video files that are published on the Internet, (5) content communities which share particular kinds of content, and (6) microblogging - allows instant publishing of content via Twitter. Blogs are probably the most commonly employed social media tool. Other forms include Internet forums, photographs or pictures, videos, and social bookmarking. These and other activities on social media are illustrated in Figure 14.1 [9].

14.3 POPULAR SOCIAL MEDIA

Social media is consumer-generated media that covers a variety of new sources of online information created and used by consumers with the intent of sharing information with others. It employs mobile and web-based technologies to create, share, discuss, and modify consumer-generated

SOCIAL MEDIA IN EDUCATION

content. Consumers are most likely to leverage their power in social media to be more demanding of marketers [10]. The four most popular social media platforms are described here.

- *Facebook:* This is the most popular social media in the US and the rest of the world. It was launched on February 2004 by Mark Zuckerberg. Facebook can sensitize individuals (consumers) about many products and services. A company can use Facebook to communicate its core values to a wide range of customers.

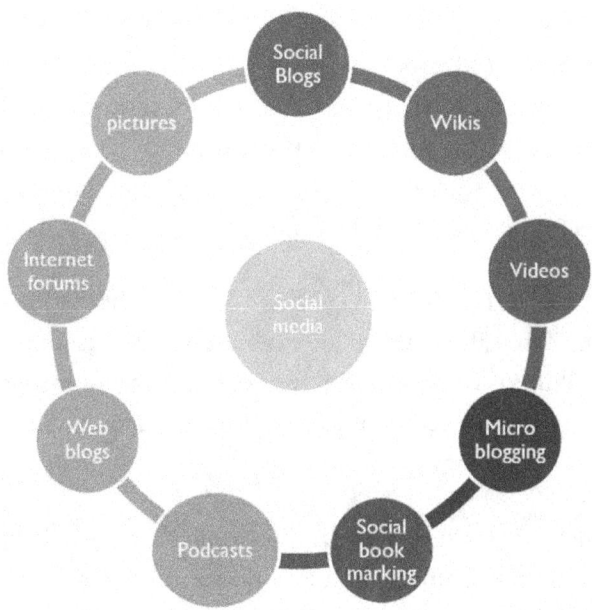

Figure 14.1 Activities on social media [9].

Facebook consists of six primary components: personal profiles, status updates, networks (geographic regions, schools, companies), groups, applications, and fan pages.

- *Twitter:* Twitter was launched on July 2006 to provide a microblogging service. It allows individuals and companies to post short messages, share content, and converse with other Twitter users. Many Twitter posts (or "tweets") focus on the minutiae of everyday life.

- *LinkedIn*: This is a networking website for the business community. It allows people to create professional profiles, post resumes, and communicate with other professionals. LinkedIn is where companies see the largest audiences.

- *YouTube*: YouTube has established itself as social media. It was launched in May 2005. It allows individuals to watch and share videos. YouTube may serve as home to aspiring filmmakers who might not have industry connections. YouTube can be both a blessing and a curse for some companies.

- *MySpace*: This social networking site bases its existence on advertisers who are paying for page views. It is an online community that allows you to meet your friends and share photos, journals, and interests. It has a lot that users can do. There are MySpace sites in the United Kingdom, Ireland, and Australia.

- *Instagram:* This is an image-based social media platform with more than 700 million active monthly users. The design is centered on a mobile visual experience. Instagram allows a simple and creative way to capture, edit, and share photos, videos, and messages with friends and family.

Other social media include WhatsApp, Reddit, Pinterest, Flickr, Snapchat, WeChat, and Vine Camera. Some of these social media are shown in Figure 14.2 [11].

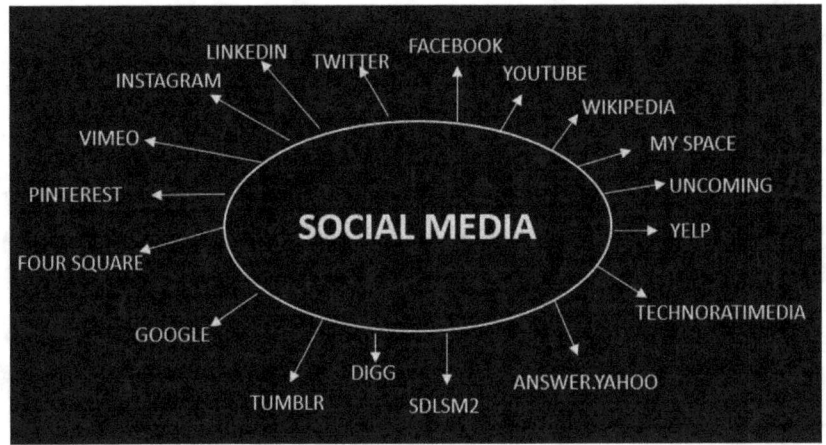

Figure 14.2 Some social media [11].

14.4 APPLICATIONS

Social media is an umbrella term that describes social networking sites where users create personal profiles and share content with others. It has penetrated many fields of educational practices and processes. Figure 14.3 illustrates several uses of social media in education [12], while Figure 14.4 shows how social media is used for teaching and learning [13]. Here we present the best practice applications of social media in various aspects of education.

- *Elementary Education:* Education is the process of learning and knowing. Learning is a process of acquiring knowledge. Technology now provides customization of the learning process to the needs of each student. This feature allows learners to actively create their learning process rather than passively consume content. Thus, learners become co-producers of knowledge. Students' perceptions of social media serve as an effective pedagogical tool. Social media is not currently being utilized fully in K-12 education. We should stop worrying about what could go wrong and realize that there is a huge opportunity here to extend the learning experience for children. Strong importance is placed on social interaction in K-12 physical and health education [14]. Figure 14.5 shows a typical use of social media in education [15].

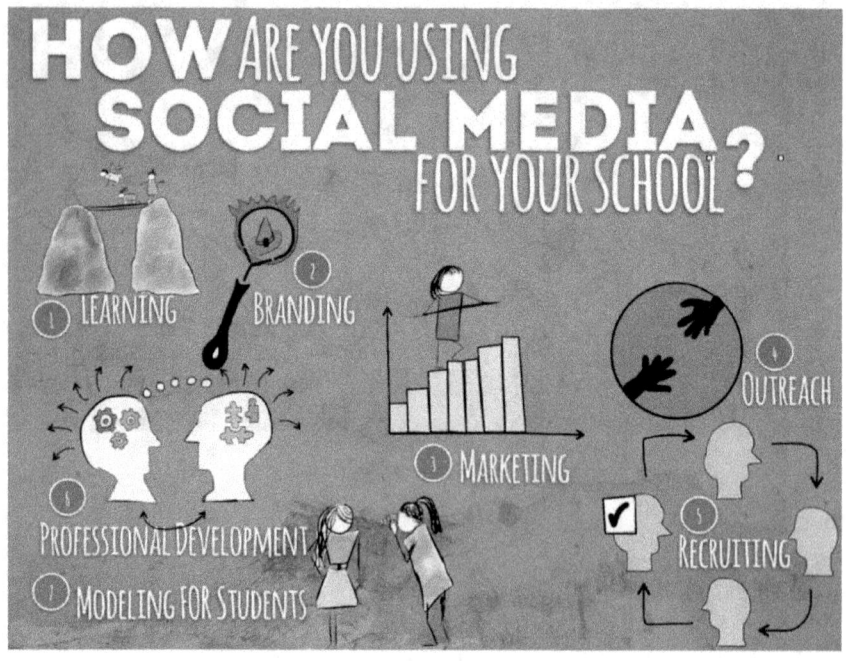

Figure 14.3 Several uses of social media in education [12].

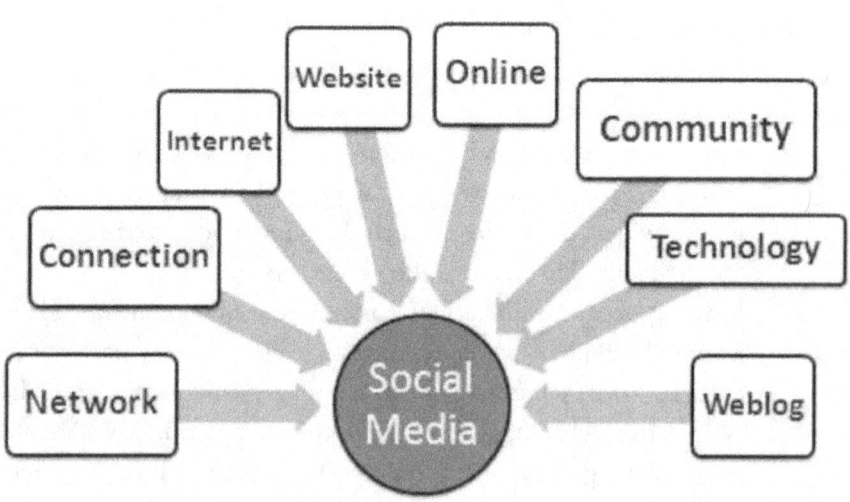

Figure 14.4 How social media is used for teaching and learning [13].

Figure 14.5 Social media in education [15].

- *Higher Education*: Higher education is usually slow and reluctant to adopt new technology, and social media is no different. Higher education institutions are now using social media to reach potential students, keep contact with current students and alumni, and enhance interaction in the classroom. The main benefit of using social networks in education is that they can enhance communication and interaction among students, and between faculty members and students. Social media can also be used to engage students, prevent boredom, and promote interactions between students and teachers. Teachers can use social media to show students videos and articles related to their classes. Figure 14.6 illustrates how Singapore uses social media in higher education [16].

Figure 14.6 How Singapore is using social media in higher education [16].

- *Business Education*: The use of social media in the business community has become almost ubiquitous. Several companies have started to fully integrate social media into their business strategies. Business educators can utilize social media as a tool in the delivery and assessment of their courses. Many business educators integrate Web 2.0 interactive tools into the business school curriculum. Some have reported success in the adaptation of blogs and YouTube in-class assignments. The advantages of such integration and adaptation include low financial expenditure, flexibility, immediacy, collaboration, exchangeability, didactic innovation, and creativity [17].

- *Medical Education:* Social media sites and applications have found their way into the toolboxes of physicians, physicians-in-training, and medical educators worldwide. Social media platforms, particularly Twitter and blogs, have been used to promote clinical concepts, disseminate evidence-based medicine, and circulate conference material to residents. YouTube is another social media platform being used to promote scholarship in graduate medical education [18].

- *Nursing Education:* Nurse educators have started to explore strategies for applying social media to nursing curricula. Social media can assist nursing faculty to help students gain a greater understanding of communication, professionalism, healthcare policy, and ethics. Blogging, Twitter, Facebook, Instagram, and LinkedIn are common places to begin social media integration into nursing programs [19].

- *Social Work Education:* This is designed to educate students and socializing practitioners in the profession. Due to the ethical issues involved in the profession, social work educators must hold students accountable for their behavior or any appearance of impropriety. Social work educators and students should be aware of how their online profile impacts their professional presence [20].

- *Music Education*: Integration of social media in music education classes can help facilitate learning experiences. Social media can assist educators to create interactive learning experiences in the music classroom. Music educators can use social networks to create online learning communities [21].

Other areas of applications of SM in education include adult education, distance education, open education, sex education, quality education, teacher education, nutrition education, management education, physical education, teacher education, homeschooling or tutoring, community education, tourism education, journalism education, religious education, dental education, and leadership education.

14.5 BENEFITS

One can confidently claim that social media and education go hand in hand in modern society. The ubiquitous nature of social media is undeniable. Social media in the classroom may be good or bad depending on how it is used. Social media can powerfully enhance the way students learn. Students in higher education rely on social media as one of the key resources for information and communication. They use social media mainly for convenience, leisure, and social connection. Social media increases teacher-student and student-student interaction and improves performance. Social media is an effective teaching and learning tool in education in developing nations. Some universities use social media to brand themselves.

It can also improve the academic performance of students in the following ways [22]:

1. Social media is an educational tool for students to get their education
2. Improve communication among students and teachers
3. Regular face-to-face communication is easier, faster, and more convenient
4. Encourage partnership and collaboration on student projects and assignments
5. Easy access to plenty of information online
6. Social media help parents stay involved in their child's learning
7. Improve literacy, communication, and reading skills
8. Provide distance learning opportunities for students who live in remote areas
9. Stay in touch with their friends
10. Prepare students for the future and for lifelong learning

14.6 CHALLENGES

Just as social media has its advantages, it has its disadvantages. Educators often face challenges in adapting to new technologies. The use of social media by physicians and physicians-in-training has given rise to concerns about patient privacy and online professionalism. Students can post inappropriate content like pornography on social media. This misuse is one of the major reasons some parents and educators strongly discourage using social media in schools; it is difficult for teachers to keep an eye on how students use social media.

Other challenges or disadvantages include the following [23]

1. It can be distracting
2. It limits face-to-face communication
3. Social media makes it easier for cyberbullying
4. Social media use poses a real risk to student privacy
5. Lack of head-on communication
6. Lack of control for inappropriate content
7. Relying on social media for all contact
8. Social media can be a time suck
9. Exposing the "haves" and "have nots."

Despite these challenges, social media use is growing rapidly.

14.7 GLOBAL USE OF SOCIAL MEDIA IN EDUCATION

Social media is people interacting and communicating with one another to share information through a web-based application. The advancement of social media is drastically impacting the whole world around us. Social media and technology are integral parts of our daily life. We all love social media, and it is difficult to resist the temptation of social media. There are many social media tools for education that can be taken advantage of for students of any age, from elementary all the way through college. Social media is changing the way the education system works in numerous ways. Social media has various uses in the classroom. We consider how some nations/continents use social media in their educational systems.

- *United States*: Social media influences how we live, how we work, and how we learn. It is now a big part of our daily lives, and there is no point in keeping it away from the education process. It provides a smoother, more direct communication tool between students, teachers, and parents. It allows for more e-learning opportunities and promotes self-directed learning, which prepares students to search for answers and make decisions independently. Professors may use any of the following social media platforms as learning tools [24]:

- Blogs with comment functionality to share and discuss information
- Twitter can be utilized as access to professionals in each field and the conversations they are having
- Skype to engage more deeply with the material and each other
- Pinterest for sharing clever ideas, inspiration, and valuable resources among students
- Google Docs, Wikis, and other collaborative document tools to store and refine data
- Project Management Apps to foster and streamline collaboration
- LinkedIn and other social networks to build a connection
- YouTube to create both course and student presentations

- *United Kingdom:* Using the Internet appropriately with children and young people can be a useful and rewarding resource for teachers and school staff. Social media is a great way to exchange information, ideas, and knowledge with friends, family, and like-minded individuals. But it can also mean big distractions and social pressures. Social media platforms seem to be acquiring a role in how institutions manage higher education. Perhaps more worryingly, social media often reproduces and intensifies various inequalities. The safe use of social media needs to be addressed for the safety of students, the safety of staff, and the reputation of schools. Higher education social media policies need to catch up with reality. The main incentive academics offer for using social media is the idea that one's research might go viral [25].

- *Europe:* Learning strategies that make use of social media can contribute to education and training in Europe. Pursuing higher education is one of the biggest investment decisions we make. It can be difficult for students to get a feel for an institution before they enroll, but social media offers insight into the personality behind the institution. Universities and colleges are using social media in the wake of remote learning and school closures. They use it to attract the best people in the world, whether they are potential students, staff, researchers, or faculty. They also use it to keep in touch with alumni, partners, and donors [26].

- *China:* Besides social, entertainment, and marketing purposes, social media has been used in academia. Academic uses include teaching, learning, and scientific research. Popular Chinese social media platforms such as QQ and WeChat are mainly used among Chinese due to language problems and the Chinese government's active censorship of Facebook, YouTube, and Twitter. WeChat, the most popular social media platform in China, was reported to have 963 million monthly active users. Social media platforms such as Facebook, Twitter, and LinkedIn are used to enhance teaching and facilitate learning in higher education [27].

- *India:* The impact that social media on India is highly significant due to cheaper smartphones, faster networks, reach to rural India, digital payments, WhatsApp, E-commerce, startups, and funding for technology. Students spend a significant amount of time on social media, and institutions cannot ignore this opportunity to engage students on social media and develop effective digital pedagogies using these platforms. Although some schools, colleges, and universities have included social media in their curriculum, the subject is not utilized to its full potential. It is imperative to understand how to use social and digital media carefully to avoid threatening children and adults [28]. Students from all over India and the world have joined together via social media apps to share information on social media platforms.

- *Africa:* Social media is regarded as a communication and interacting platform that could be used to enhance our connectivity, research, and learning. It is also seen as a learning tool that could be used to enhance student engagement and improve learning and performance. The current proliferation of social media has revolutionized our way of communicating and learning. However, if unchecked, excessive use of social media on non-academic activities can affect student academic performance and, consequently, student drop out. Social media is also seen as a distractor in students' concentration ability [29].

14.8 CONCLUSION

We live in an era of social media and social networks. Social media essentially consists of on-line communications channels dedicated to networks primarily for interaction, content-sharing, and collaboration. They have become an indispensable part of our modern lives providing new communication environments. The use of social media in education is swiftly growing and has become a global phenomenon. Today social media has become a platform where students in higher education can connect with their instructors and fellow students.

Education on social media is needed now more than ever. Social media is here to stay as a game changer, and we cannot ignore it in our lives. More information about the use of social media in education can be found in the books in [30-41] and the following related journals:

- *International Journal of Social Media*
- *Interactive Learning Environments*
- *Journal of Educational Technology Systems*

REFERENCES

[1] S. Zhu et al., "Understanding social media competence in higher education: Development and validation of an instrument," *Journal of Educational Computing Research*, vol. 57, no. 8, 2020, pp. 1935–1955.

[2] M. N. O. Sadiku, M. Tembely, and S.M. Musa, "Social media for beginners," *International Journal of Advanced Research in Computer Science and Software Engineering*, vol. 8, no. 3, March 2018, pp. 24-26.

[3] M. N. O. Sadiku, A. E. Shadare, and S. M. Musa, "Digital natives," *International Journal of Advanced Research in Computer Science and Software Engineering*, vol. 7, no. 7, July 2017, pp. 125-126.

[4] A. V. D. Beemt, M. Thurlings, and M. Willems, "Towards an understanding of social media use in the classroom: A literature review," *Technology, Pedagogy and Education,* vol. 29, no. 1, 2020, pp. 35-55.

[5] M. N. O. Sadiku, S. S. Adekunte, and S. M. Musa, "Social Media in Education," *International Journal of Trend in Research and Development,* vol. 4, no. 5, July-August 2020.

[6] "Social media," *Wikipedia,* the free encyclopedia https://en.wikipedia.org/wiki/Social_media

[7] V. Taprial and P. Kanwar, "Understanding social media," http://bookboon.com/en/understanding-social-media-ebook

[8] A. Mayfield, *What is Social Media?* An e-book iCrossing. http://www.icrossing.com/uk/sites/default/files_uk/insight_pdf_files/What%20is%20Social%20Media_iCrossing_ebook.pdf

[9] S. Bowie, "Social work and the role of social media best practices," http://www.csus.edu/faculty/b/bowies/docs/what%20is%20social%20media%20use%20this.pdf

[10] C. Kohli, R. Surib, and A. Kapoor, "Will social media kill branding?" *Business Horizons,* 2015, vol. 58, pp. 35-44.

[11] "Social media business concept isolated," https://www.dreamstime.com/social-media-business-concept-isolated-background-image195810090

[12] "The ability of social media in education and learning," May 2018, http://www.aesopmonkeyrescue.org/the-ability-of-social-media-in-education-and-learning/

[13] "Social media for teaching and learning," https://www.researchgate.net/figure/Social-Media-for-Teaching-and-Learning-category-of-online-and-create-content-share_fig1_326119163

[14] M. J. Vollum, "The potential for social media use in K-12 physical and health education," *Computers in Human Behavior*, vol. 35, June 2014, pp. 560-564.

[15] L. Chesser, "25 Awesome social media tools for education," November 2013, https://www.opencolleges.edu.au/informed/features/social-media-tools-for-education/

[16] "How Singapore is using social media in higher education," April 2016, https://www.dailybits.com/singapore-using-social-media-higher-education/

[17] C. Piotrowski, "Pedagogical applications of social media in business education: Student and faculty perspectives," *Journal of Educational Technology Systems*, vol. 43, no. 3, 2015, pp. 257–265.

[18] M. Sterling et al., "The use of social media in graduate medical education: A systematic review," *Acad Med.*, vol. 92, no. 7, July 2017, pp. 1043–1056.

[19] T. Schmitt, S. Sims-Giddens, and R. Booth, "Social media use in nursing education" *OJIN: The Online Journal of Issues in Nursing*, vol. 17, no. 3, September 2012.

[20] R. Duncan-Daston, M. Hunter-Sloan, and E. Fullmer, "Considering the ethical implications of social media in social work education," *Ethics and Information Technology*, vol. 15, 2013, pp. 35–43.

[21] D. J. Albert, "Social media in music education extending learning to where students 'live,'" *Music Educators Journal*, December 2015, pp. 31-38.

[22] M. Willbold, "Social media in education: Can they improve the learning?" April 2019, https://elearningindustry.com/social-media-in-education-improve-learning

[23] "Pros and cons of social media in education," https://www.ozassignments.com/pros-and-cons-of-social-media-in-education/

[24] "Using social media for learning," December 2021, https://www.uagc.edu/blog/using-social-media-as-a-learning-tool

[25] "Social media is reshaping British universities' value systems in a scramble for likes and shares," November 2021, https://phys.org/news/2021-11-social-media-reshaping-british-universities.html

[26] L. Davey, "How higher education social media has evolved in Europe," October 2021, https://sproutsocial.com/insights/evolution-higher-education-social-media-europe-en_gb/

[27] H. Qiao and P. C. Shih, "Use of social media for academic purposes in China," https://www.researchgate.net/publication/323547833_Use_of_Social_Media_for_Academic_Purposes_in_China [20] T. Issa, P. Isaias, and P. Kommer (eds.), *Social Networking and Education: Global Perspectives*. Springer, 2015.

[28] S. Babu, "Why should social media be included in the higher education in India?" https://www.thehighereducationreview.com/magazine/why-should-social-media-be-included-in-the-higher-education-in-india-EZME632764077.html

[29] R. Wario, "Investigating use and impact of social media on student academic performance: Case of a university in South Africa," 2022, https://www.researchgate.net/publication/362317251_INVESTIGATING_USE_AND_IMPACT_OF_SOCIAL_MEDIA_ON_STUDENT_ACADEMIC_PERFORMANCE_CASE_OF_A_UNIVERSITY_IN_SOUTH_AFRICA/link/62e2d84c3c0ea878876434eb/download

[30] J. Glazzard and C. Mitchell, *Social Media and Mental Health in Schools (Positive Mental Health)*. Critical Publishing, 2018.

[31] M. Patrut and B. Patrut (eds.), *Social Media in Higher Education; Teaching in Web 2.0*. Information Science Reference, 2013.

[32] H. S. Noor Al-Deen and J. A. Hendricks (eds.), *Social Media: Usage and Impact*. New York: Lexington Books, 2012.

[33] V. J. Callan and M. A. Johnston, *Social Media and Student Outcomes: Teacher, Student and Employer Views*. Adelaide, Australia: NCVER, 2017.

[34] T. Rudolph and J. Frankel, *YouTube in Music Education*. New York: Hal Leonard, 2009.

[35] Information Resources Management Association (USA), *Social Media in Education: Breakthroughs in Research and Practice*. IGI Global, 2018.

[36] C. Greenhow, C. Agur, and J. Sonnevend, *Education and Social Media: Toward a Digital Future*. MIT Press, 2016.

[37] C. Rowell, *Social Media in Higher Education: Case Studies, Reflections and Analysis*. Open Book Publishers, 2019.

[38] C. D. Zinskie, and M. M. Griffin (eds.), *Social Media: Influences on Education*. Information Age Publishing Inc., 2021.

[39] C. Cheal, *Transformation in Teaching: Social Media Strategies in Higher Education*. Informing Science Press, 2012.

[40] L. A. Wankel and C. Wankel, *Higher Education Administration with Social Media: Including Applications in Student Affairs, Enrollment Management, Alumni Relations, and Career Centers*. Emerald Group Publishing Limited, 2011.

[41] C. Wankel (ed.), *Cutting-edge Social Media Approaches to Business Education: Teaching with LinkedIn, Facebook, Twitter, Second Life, and Blogs (Research in Management Education and Development)*. Information Age Publishing, 2010.

CHAPTER 15

FUTURE OF EDUCATION

"Education is the foundation of equality and the path out of poverty to a promising future. It is the best investment in our present and future. And the most rewarding one."
—The European External Action Service (EEAS)

15.1 INTRODUCTION

Quality education is one of the pillars of the United Nations 2030 Agenda for Sustainable Development, which aims to ensure inclusive and equitable quality education and promote lifelong learning opportunities for all. Education is key to the future quality of human life and the sustainability of the world. Education can make all the difference in people's lives. It has a catalytic effect on the well-being of individuals and the future of our planet [1]. Education encompasses elementary, middle, and high schools, colleges, universities, apprenticeships, adult education, special education, etc. Education helps individuals escape poverty and increases the quality of life. Education matters for economic growth and power. As Malcolm X said, "Education is the passport to the future, for tomorrow belongs to those who prepare for it today." As technology advances and become more complex, the quality of education becomes more important than ever.

Our world is changing fast, and the days of a "job for life" are gone. Although the education industry is booming due to a growing global population, the traditional model of education has remained largely unchanged since the 19th century. Although the pencil has been replaced by an iPad and the chalkboard by dry-erase or SMART board, it is still the same old story. In today's classroom, students sit in rows reverently listening to a guru at the front; half are bored, while half are lost. If learning is a chore and boring, then the most important driver of human learning, inspiration, or passion, is disengaged.

The role of education has never been more critical. There are many forces influencing the future of education. Globalization, internationalization, interconnectivity, personalization, customization, and digitalization are transforming every aspect of our society, including education. To meet global expectations, education systems should prepare for the inflow of students from various backgrounds, socio-economic classes, and cultures. Students must develop global citizenship skills and be aware of the wider world. Internationalization enables institutions to have multiple sister campuses around the world. Institutions can have a global presence by just having their courses online. Interconnectivity changes education since human connections and interactions are at the heart of education. Students prefer a user-friendly, personal, and customizable way of learning. Digitalization has come to stay in education, and we can no longer ignore it. It will completely transform education. These forces provide us with several new opportunities for human advancement [2].

The pandemic exposed a need to rethink how systems leaders design schools, instruction and who they put at the center of that design. Without a doubt, education today is not what it was five years ago, and the future of education will look significantly different than it did a decade ago.

This chapter addresses how higher education institutions and K-12 schools can best prepare students for the future. It predicts the future of education by examining the future of technology, the future of learning, the future of teaching, and the future of online education. It discusses the challenges education will face in the future. It includes the global future of education. The last section concludes with comments.

15.2 FUTURE OF TECHNOLOGY

Technology transforms how we live, work, play, think, buy, sell, and worship. It has become the key to success for different sectors. New technologies that are being introduced today are eventually filling the spaces. Technological advances in education are helping to make teaching a career with an excellent future. Due to technology, education has become accessible in various villages, towns, and cities. Technology-related skills are increasingly in demand. Understanding how technologies work, what they do, and their potential for benefiting society is critical to a child's future. Figure 15.1 depicts future technologies poised to play an integral role in the future of education [3]. Some of these technologies are explained briefly as follows [4]:

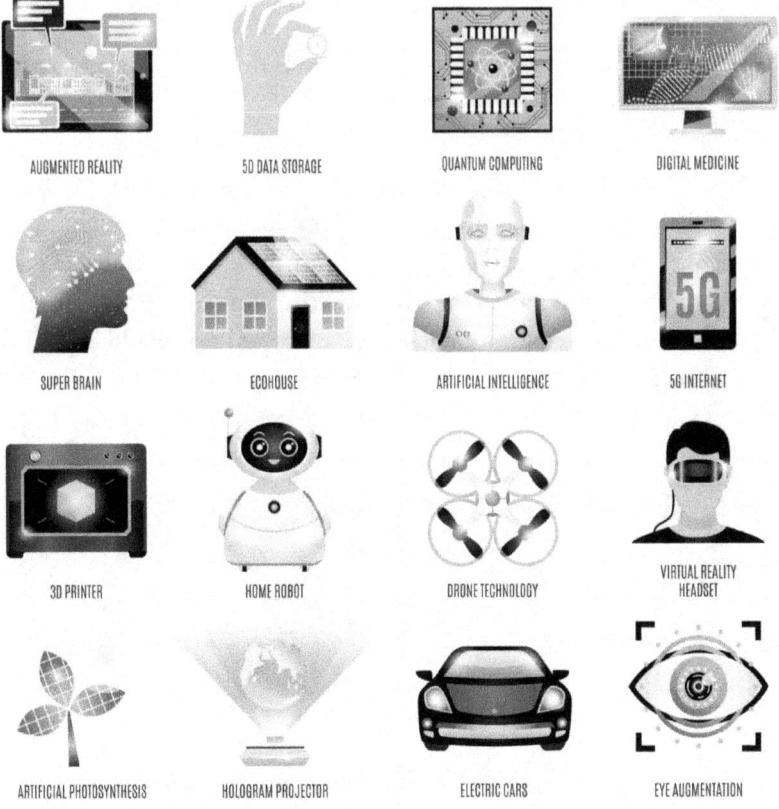

Figure 15.1 Future technologies [3].

- *Artificial intelligence (AI) and machine learning (ML)*: These are now transforming classroom experiences in schools and colleges worldwide. AI (or machine intelligence) can contribute to a 24/7 learning environment for students that achieves a deep level of personalization of how they learn.

- *Cloud computing:* It will grow with increased Internet access, leading to an explosion in the amount of data that a classroom generates and has access to. The birth of cloud-based computing and virtual learning platforms enables decentralized learning.

- *Digital Textbooks:* Students need not carry textbooks around but a tablet or a gadget with digitalized versions of textbooks stored in them. Open textbooks are digitalized textbooks in print, e-book, or audio format.

- *3D printing*: Students learn faster and understand a subject better using 3D printing.

- *Virtual reality (VR) and augmented reality (AR)*: These are growing like crazy and are popping up in education. Encouraging their use has helped the learners have complete and unrestricted access to minute details. Imagine wearing an AR headset that can superimpose educational lessons on top of real-world experiences, as typically shown in Figure 15.2 [5].

Figure 15.2 Wearing an AR headset [5].

- *Social media (or social networking):* This refers to any technology that facilitates the dissemination and sharing of information over the Internet. The key purpose of using social media tools is to engage students through electronic means, facilitate professional communication, improve student comprehension, enhance student networking, and enable collaboration with other students around the globe. Popular social media include Twitter, Facebook, Instagram, SlideShare, and YouTube.

- *Robots*: They have the potential to revolutionize education. They can improve the quality and effectiveness of learning and teaching. A robot may be used as a teaching assistant as shown in Figure 15.3 [6].

Figure 15.3 A robot is used as a teaching assistant [6].

These technologies are changing how we work and live in almost every area of life. They have transformed education. Although technology should be used in service rather than dictating, our future major challenge relates to how students use technology. Technology is not a silver bullet solution. Technology will transform education by giving teachers and students a variety of new tools to work with. For example, tools for 3D models and visualizations already exist; we just have to make them work at scale in the classroom. A science class may cover 3D printing and how it can be used to replicate prosthetic limbs. 3D printers allow students to work with mini-models to test out engineering design principles. Games can augment learning and stimulate critical thinking. Learners are naturally gravitating toward video. Education is being transformed in both formal and informal learning contexts by digital technologies.

15.3 FUTURE OF LEARNING

The traditional art of learning has witnessed a huge change with the introduction of technology. Today's learners are digital natives who are heavy users of mobile devices. They are accustomed to getting information in a user-friendly, personal, and customizable way. The formal classroom will be replaced by learning areas that allow small groups to collaborate face-to-face or virtually on learning projects, as illustrated in Figure 15.4 [7]. The future of learning depends on finding the right match between technology and teaching. Education apps are also crucial to the future of learning.

Figure 15.4 The formal classroom is replaced by learning areas that allow small groups to collaborate face-to-face [7].

The future of education is all about strengthening and incorporating student-centric learning. This feature is achieved through the following learning schemes.

- *E-Learning:* Technology has revolutionized everything. eLearning is a modern form of education that enables learning with the help of electronic technologies. It requires just a computer and the Internet. It may also be termed distance education, distance learning, online learning, Internet learning, etc., but all these refer to the same thing. eLearning has transformed the landscape of education due to its convenience for students and teachers. eLearning is here to stay. Organizations also are adapting to eLearning courses to train their employees. e-Learning is the future of education because it provides continuous learning, social learning, on-demand learning, gamified learning, and personalized learning path. It has mitigated various problems associated with learning [8].

- *mLearning*: Mobile learning is the future of education because it is flexible; it allows students to learn anywhere at any time. Brick-and-mortar classrooms do not allow mobility. Students juggle multiple jobs today, and employees are becoming more comfortable with deskless and remote settings. As shown in Figure 15.5, most digital natives have smartphones and tablets [9]. Learners prefer navigating mobile learning apps and platforms to access their training materials.

Figure 15.5 Most digital natives have smart phones and tablets [9].

- *Project-Based Learning:* This is a teaching method designed to allow students to develop knowledge and skills through engaging projects. It involves active learning and a deeper engagement, better preparing students to be creative and innovative in a project-based world. Creating immersive school areas promote creativity and collaboration in an immersive learning environment. Students can immerse themselves in whatever subject they are learning with augmented reality (AR). Project-based learning helps learners understand how the ideas we teach work instead of just memorizing and repeating facts [10]. As careers adapt to the future freelance economy, today's students will adapt to project-based learning.

- *Industry-Based Learning:* This is a learning approach to education where subjects are taught in the context of industrial applications and experiences in a commercial environment. This approach may include field trips to industries, interviews with industry experts, completing internships, etc. [10].

- *Personalized Learning:* Technology allows us to create education that is tailored to the individual, universal in nature, and decentralized in structure. Since not everyone learns the same way, personalized learning adjusts to each student's pace and style of learning. It may eventually help us to ensure that every student finds their path to success. Students are given the opportunity to make independent choices, to think, and to face challenges. Students will learn with study tools that adapt to their capabilities. Students who experience difficulties with a subject will get the opportunity to practice more until they reach the required level. For students with disabilities, new technologies mean empowerment, putting them on a more equal footing with their classmates.

15.4 FUTURE OF TEACHING

The traditional role of an educator is to be a facilitator or a guide rather than a classroom manager. With the rise of technology, the role of educators has undergone a permanent evolution. As technology evolves, educators are supposed to be updated about changes and introduce them to students. As education changes to suit the future's needs, the role of an educator must adapt and grow. Educators need to equip today's young generation with the skills to thrive in tomorrow's world. Future teachers will have to face the reality that students prefer to learn in a flexible, personalized format in a technology-focused classroom. They must adapt to changes and change what they teach to meet the needs of 21st-century learners. They must be prepared to be data collectors, analysts, planners, collaborators, curriculum experts, synthesizers, problem-solvers, and researchers. An educator now embodies a multitude of new roles: learning manager, subject matter expert, instructional designer, technology architect, multimedia developer, e-learning developer, support specialist, learning facilitator, etc. [11]. Educators will be increasingly challenged to find new ways to engage learners. Good educators derive both extrinsic and intrinsic rewards from teaching.

Educational systems and education worldwide must adapt and embrace digitization. The digital educator (or online educator) is one who knows how to use digital tools to help them simplify their work, improve classroom interaction, and make assessments. Digital solutions can allow the educator to serve the students better and unlock their full potential. Teachers use digital technologies to augment, not replace, traditional face-to face-teaching. They should be helped to figure out how to use the right technologies at the right time to do the right job for students. Then they will be able effectively prepare students for the future. Technology can be used to provide dynamic tools for monitoring student achievement. For example, integrating short videos into a lesson plan makes it easier to engage students. So, teachers will need to prepare kids to work collaboratively with machines. Figure 15.6 shows a typical classroom of the future [12].

Future educators should have the following priorities [11]:

- Embrace a growth mindset
- Be able to adapt fast to emerging technologies and teaching strategies
- Thrive in collaborative and dynamic environments
- Be student-centric, not system-centric

- Be a mentor who guides students through practical skills
- Be a coach who inspires students to reach their full potential
- Be able to design and carry out meaningful and deeply engaging learning experiences

Figure 15.6 A typical classroom of the future [12].

15.5 FUTURE OF ONLINE EDUCATION

The education industry was taken by surprise by its forced transition to digital education, also known as online education, distance education, or remote education. Remote education is already extensive, with millions signing up for online courses. The popularity of online courses has increased over the past decade, and the global online learning market is rapidly growing. Online education has expanded drastically over the last year due to school closures from COVID-19. By 2050, most students worldwide may not need to physically go to school in order to get education. From the convenience of their home, they will join students from around the globe and engage in various virtual activities. Online degree programs can provide an added layer of personal perspective for how students and teachers can leverage technology in education. Distance education already plays a crucial role in providing access to education for millions of people in the developing world. It offers extensive resources ranging from videos and tutorials to seminars, webinars, online libraries, educational websites, and more.

The appeal of online education continues to increase due to its comfort and accessibility. Its flexibility enables students to obtain the education they need in an affordable and convenient manner. Online education is more cost-effective than brick-and-mortar schools. Other advantages of online education include the following [13]:

- Online learning offers convenience and flexibility
- High-quality student-tutor interactions
- Studying online is affordable for many people
- All age groups benefit from online learning
- More students can be enrolled
- There's a vast amount of online learning resources
- Web-based learning will grow in popularity

In Western countries, launching online course provider platforms such as EdX, Coursera, and MOOC has brought the concept of distance learning closer to learners worldwide. MOOC is an open online course that allows anyone to register without time limitations, geographic restrictions, or prerequisites. The proliferation of Massive Open Online Courses (MOOCs) and other forms of e-learning will replace traditional distance education. With thousands of enrolled students, MOOCs will radically change the way education is taking place. MOOCs will change the landscape and make this a global market [14]. It is needless to say that not everything can be taught online.

At the heart of lifelong learning is the notion that students deserve a personalized experience that can weave into their daily life and help them achieve their long-term goals. Online education has a major problem; there is no physical activity.

15.6 CHALLENGES

Education is controversial because it is either a unifying social force or a divisive one. Parents quarrel about the quality of education for their children, society is divided about what to teach children, and the government is concerned about the increasing cost of education. Rising costs are no longer easy for governments and students to pay for them. Who should provide laptops for students? The government or parents? Internet access is not a major concern if a parent is still struggling to pay rent. We live in a competitive world where kids experience a lot of pressure to perform. When they fall short, they feel deflated. The lack of high-speed Internet services in remote areas is a challenge.

Technology is challenging traditional teaching and learning techniques. Educators need to think critically about how to deploy technology strategically. Although educators want the best for their students, the behaviors and knowledge required for students to succeed are rapidly changing. Can our future education system produce leaders who are able to cope with the complexities of tomorrow? [15].

These challenges look daunting, but many education systems are now well on their way toward finding innovative responses to them.

15.7 GLOBAL FUTURE OF EDUCATION

Although educators and leaders create, design, and imagine the future, technology is changing how students learn, and teachers teach. The future of education must keep up to date with the dynamic nature of the 21st century. It is expedient to take stock of the past to look forward, imagine and plan for a better future. Today, we look at education and how social, economic, and technological changes will revolutionize how children, youth, and adults go to school. Since our world is changing fast, the future of education lies in harnessing technology to make us learn quicker, memorize effectively, and teach better. Many countries chose to change the way students learn after COVID-19. Instead of traditional education, many students and instructors join virtual spaces with online meeting platforms such as Zoom, Google Meets, Microsoft Teams, etc. Education policy has for too long been restricted by short-term thinking. We now consider the future of education in some nations/continents.

- *United States:* After two years of virtual learning, many students are still playing catch up. For example, today's budget situation in California is nothing short of disastrous. Teachers in elementary/middle and high schools are overwhelmed and overworked. Good teachers are leaving because they are not well paid. This issue gives concern and worry about the future of public education in California. The community, parents, and students are increasingly pessimistic and question the value of public education. Inequities are getting worse [16]. Lawmakers and schools need to replace the traditional business model in a way that can subsidize costs and save students and parent loan debt. Education can equip learners with a sense of purpose and the competencies they need to shape their own lives and contribute to the lives of others. Figure 15.7 shows some activists protesting that education is not for sale [17]. Today's students are digital natives working in a global marketplace. The US must ensure that our students are equipped with the knowledge and skills that will ensure success in a global age.

Figure 15.7 Some activists protesting that education is not for sale [17].

- *United Kingdom:* Our world is changing fast. The education sector must adapt and change what we teach. In the past 40 years, the pace of technological change has been rapid. Assessing competence and skills like critical thinking, problem-solving, and collaboration are high on the agenda for educators, employers, and policymakers looking to reimagine an education system fit for the future. There is an opportunity to reinvent old systems and use technology to shape a new and improved education system for the future. The pandemic has forced education providers to implement digital technologies to help them engage with their audience and function. Education providers are challenged in that they have complex audience profiles with very different needs. Parents and students will demand online experiences from providers at all levels, while organizations will need to prepare themselves for a digital-first future [18].

- *Europe:* One of Europe's greatest achievements was to build bridges across the continent by creating an area of free movement for workers and citizens. In 2017, the European Commission set out its vision for how we can create a European Education Area by 2025. The Commission believes that it is in the shared interest of all member states to harness the full potential of education and culture as drivers for job creation, economic growth, and social fairness. The primary responsibility for education and culture policies lies with the member states at national, regional, and local levels. The EU joined a global call to safeguard equitable financing for education. It has chosen to put education at the heart of the post-pandemic recovery. The future of education will be dictated by the future of Europe [19].

- *China:* Over the past twenty years, China has almost eliminated illiteracy among its 1.3 billion citizens. China has a bold and ambitious long-term vision for investing in education to raise its people out of poverty and prepare them for the global economy. The current education system in China is divided into two parallel systems of general education and vocational education. According to the 2035 Plan, China's broad education goals are [20]:

1. Establishing a modern education system
2. Achieving universal attendance in quality preschool education
3. Providing high-quality and balanced compulsory education (years 1 – 9)
4. Achieving maximum attendance in senior high school (years 10 - 12)
5. Significantly improving vocational education.
6. Building a more competitive higher education system
7. Providing adequate education for disabled children/youth, and
8. Establishing a new education management system with participation from the whole society (i.e., not solely relying on government support).

To achieve these goals, the Chinese education sector needs to move beyond knowledge acquisition to promote the ability to think independently and apply knowledge in new situations. China needs to make drastic and fundamental reforms to prepare its students for success in a knowledge-intensive, high-tech, and globalized economy [21].

- *India:* Indian education system is a product of colonization. For over 100 years, the nation followed the system until the pandemic hit, and the system was forced to transition to laptops. EdTech has played a substantial role in transforming the way knowledge is accessed. India's policymakers need to bridge the digital divide among students. This action will enable them to use online tools to make learning accessible to vulnerable and marginalized communities. Currently, demand for quality education far outstrips supply. Digital learning platforms can help India overcome the supply-demand imbalance. Workplaces today expect students to come equipped with the skills they need to succeed, so schools need to shift their focus from qualification to skill acquisition [22].

15.8 CONCLUSION

Education is essential to any modern society and can influence its future. Today's education trends are shaping tomorrow's workforce, which requiring youths to be competent in a broad range of transferable skills such as problem-solving, critical thinking, creativity, and communication. Technology can be a powerful tool for transforming learning and teaching. The practice of a teacher standing in front of a room full of students is increasingly becoming a thing of the past. Introducing of e-books, digital textbooks, online learning, and electronic/mobile devices is rapidly changing the education sector.

The evolution of education brings with it future trends in education, which should be closely linked to education for sustainable development. Although the future is uncertain and hard to predict, we must be ready for it. There are often multiple versions of the future; some are assumptions, others are hopes and fears. In the future, education will become more intelligent, safer and more secure, more relevant, and intertwined with future jobs. The future of education will be much more flexible, modular, and online. More information about the future of education can be found in the books in [23-40] and the following related journal: *Frontiers in Education*.

REFERENCES

[1] N. C. Burbules, G. Fan, and P. Repp, "Five trends of education and technology in a sustainable future," *Geography and Sustainability*, vol. 1, no. 2, June 2020, pp. 93-97.

[2] M. N. O. Sadiku, G. A. Adegoye, A. Ajayi-Majebi, and S. M. Musa, "The future of education," *International Journal of Trend in Scientific Research and Development*, vol. 6, no. 7, November-December 2022, pp. 165-171.

[3] "Future technology set Pro Vector," https://www.vecteezy.com/vector-art/1392036-future-technology-set

[4] E. Polyák and Z. Vajda, "The future of education," October 2017, Unknown Source.

[5] "Future education technology: How digital trends are shaping teaching," https://online.maryville.edu/blog/future-ed-tech/

[6] D. Karambelkar, "The classroom of the future," March 2020, https://gulfnews.com/uae/education/the-classroom-of-the-future-1.1583329158534

[7] "The future of learning and teaching: Big changes ahead for education," https://www.rmit.edu.au/study-with-us/education/discover-education/the-future-of-learning-and-teaching-big-changes-ahead-for-education

[8] D. Brain, "The future of elearning: Why online learning is the future of education," December 2020, Unknown Source.

[9] J. Avelino, "The top 10 reasons why mobile learning is the future of education," September 2022, https://www.edapp.com/blog/mobile-education/

[10] "What does the future of education look like?" https://www.tomorrowsworldtoday.com/2022/08/08/what-does-the-future-of-education-look-like/

[11] "7 skills future teachers should have according to Edtech founders," https://therecursive.com/7-skills-future-teachers-should-have-according-to-edtech-founders/

[12] E. Dunwill, "4 Changes that will shape the classroom of the future: Making education fully technological," March 2016, https://elearningindustry.com/4-changes-will-shape-classroom-of-the-future-making-education-fully-technological

[13] C. Goldberg, "Seven reasons why online courses are the future of education," December 2019, https://blogs.onlineeducation.touro.edu/seven-reasons-why-online-courses-are-the-future-of-education/

[14] M. N. O. Sadiku, *Emerging Internet-Based Technologies.* Boca Raton, FL: CRC Press, 2019, pp. 109-123.

[15] A. Sheng, "Is education fit for the future?" May 2022, https://www.thestatesman.com/opinion/education-fit-future-1503069423.html

[16] "Teachers reflect on the future of education, find silver linings and offer recommendations," https://edsource.org/2022/leading-teachers-reflect-on-the-future-of-education-find-silver-linings-and-offer-recommendations/672650

[17] "Future education," https://unsplash.com/s/photos/future-education

[18] "How technology will shape the future of education," https://www.boxuk.com/insight/how-technology-will-shape-the-future-of-education/

[19] "Future of Europe: Towards a European education area by 2025," November 2017, https://ec.europa.eu/commission/presscorner/detail/en/IP_17_4521

[20] "China's education modernisation plan towards 2035," April 2020, https://internationaleducation.gov.au/international-network/china/PolicyUpdates-China/Pages/China's-education-modernisation-plan-towards-2035-.aspx

[21] "How China is preparing its youth for the future," https://asiasociety.org/how-china-preparing-its-youth-future

[22] "Future of education in India," https://bweducation.businessworld.in/article/Future-Of-Education-In-India/02-03-2023-467521/#:~:text=Equity%20and%20inclusion%20in%20education,the%20digital%20divide%20among%20students.

[23] K. Egan, *The Future of Education: Reimagining Our Schools From the Ground Up*. Yale University Press, 2008.

[24] R. Pring et al. *Education for All: The Future of Education and Training For 14-19 Year-Olds*. Routledge, 2012.

[25] G. Wells and G. E. Claxton (eds.), *Learning For Life in the 21st Century: Sociocultural Perspectives On the Future of Education*. Blackwell Publishing, 2002.

[26] J. W. Cook, *Sustainability, Human Well-Being, and the Future of Education*. Springer Nature, 2019.

[27] W. G. Howell (ed.), *Besieged: School Boards and the Future of Education Politics*. Brookings Institution Press, 2005.

[28] E. Morin, *Seven Complex Lessons in Education for the Future*. UNESCO, 2002.

[29] B. H. Banathy, *Systems Design of Education: A Journey to Create the Future*. Educational Technology, 1991.

[30] A. Toffler, *Learning for Tomorrow: The Role of the Future in Education*. Random House, 1974.

[31] L. J. Rubin, *The Future of Education: Perspectives on Tomorrow's Schooling*. Allyn and Bacon, 2007.

[32] A. Jones, C. Buntting, and P. J. Williams (eds.), *The Future of Technology Education*. Springer, 2014.

[33] I. Jukes and R. L. Schaaf, *A Brief History of the Future of Education: Learning in the Age of Disruption*. Corwin, 2019.

[34] Bauer Media Group (ed.), *Time Special Edition the Future of Education*. Bauer Media SIPS, 2021.

[35] T. Hatch, J. Corson, and S. G. van den Berg, *The Education We Need for a Future We Can't Predict*. SAGE Publications, 2021.

[36] OECD, *Back to the Future of Education: Four OECD Scenarios for Schooling*. OECD, 2020.

[37] N. Yelland, *Shift to the Future: Rethinking Learning with New Technologies in Education*. Routledge, 2007.

[38] J. Kim and E. J. Maloney, *Learning Innovation and the Future of Higher Education*. Johns Hopkins University Press, 2020.

[39] D. Clawson and M. Page, *The Future of Higher Education*. Taylor & Francis, 2012.

[40] C. O. Taiwo, *The Nigerian Education System, Past, Present and Future*. Thomas Nelson (Nigeria) Limited, 1980.

INDEX

3D printing, 6,208-225,310
    Applications of, 211
    Benefits of, 218
    Challenges of, 220
    Global use of, 221
    In education, 208
Accessibility, 87, 192, 258, 290
Addiction, 278
Additive manufacturing,
    see 3D printing
Administration, 39
Africa, 301
AI literacy, 49
Architecture education, 217
Artificial intelligence, 5, 26, 28, 310
Artificial intelligence in education
    (AIED), 26
    Applications of, 37
    Benefits of, 48
    Challenges of, 47
    Future of, 50
    Global adoption of, 42
    Possibilities in, 33
Assessments, 35
Augmented reality, 248-264
    Applications, 253
    Benefits of, 258
    Challenges of, 260

    Concept of, 250
    Global use of, 261
    In education, 248
Automation, 47

Battery life, 261
Big data, 8, 116-128
    Applications of, 120
    Benefits of, 121
    Challenges, 124
    Characteristics of, 116
    Global use of, 125
    In education, 116
Big leap, 90
Burkina Faso, 17
Business education, 296

Canada, 44
Change, 14, 145
Chatbots, 41
Chemistry, 255
China, 17, 43, 71, 92, 110, 127, 147,
    167, 199, 223, 241, 263, 281,
    301, 321
Cloud computing, 8, 79-93, 310
    Benefits, 87
    Challenges, 90
    Characteristics, 81

    Concept of, 80
    Deployment models of, 82
    Global use of, 91
    In education, 79
Coding, 66
Collaboration, 88, 259
Communication, 35
Competition, 67
Competitiveness, 47
Computer networks, 155
Computing resources, 79, 80
Convenience, 181, 192
Cost, 14, 49, 69, 87, 181, 193
Cost efficiency, 259
Cost reduction, 46

Data, 116
Data security, 90
Digital age, 178
Digital books, 164, 310
Digital divide, 14, 171
Digital economy, 181
Digital education, 155-172
    Benefits of, 167
    Challenges of, 170
    Global use of, 165
Digital natives, 10-12, 160
Digital technologies, 155, 156, 172
Digital textbooks, 162
Discrimination, 193
Disruptive Technologies, 14
Distance education, 236

Education, 1, 16, 19, 26, 52, 59, 79, 98, 111, 117, 132, 149, 155, 178, 208, 248, 302, 307, 322
    Emergence of, 140
    Generations of, 134

    Goal of, 1
    Quality of, 106, 190
Education 4.0, 40, 132-149
    Benefits of, 143
    Challenges of, 145
    Global adoption of, 146
Education industry, 248
Educational robots, 61
E-learning, 84, 103, 313
Elementary education, 254, 276, 293
Elementary schools, 36, 64, 212, 234, 276
Emerging technologies, 1-5, 10, 15
    Characteristics of, 3
Engineering education, 216
Equality, 46
Equity, 13
E-textbooks, 85
Ethical dilemma, 49
Europe, 17, 43, 71, 108, 127, 166, 198, 222, 241, 262, 281, 300, 321

Fear of displacement, 69
Five Vs, 117
Flexibility, 88
Future educators, 316
Future of education, 142, 307-322
    Challenges of, 318
    Global use of, 319
Future of learning, 313
Future of online education, 317
Future of teaching, 315
Future of technology, 309

Game-based learning, 9
Games, 268, 271

Gamification, 268-282
    Applications of, 273
    Benefits of, 277
    Challenges of, 278
    Components of, 271
    Global uses of, 280
    In education, 268
Gamification elements, 271
Gender imbalances, 69

Healthcare, 161
Healthcare education, 255,
    see also medical education
High school, 37
Higher education, 37, 64, 85, 214, 254, 276, 295
Human beings, 230

Inclusivity, 47
India, 17, 44, 72, 92, 109, 128, 147, 166, 200, 223, 242, 263, 282, 301, 322
Industry 4.0, 139
Intelligent tutoring systems (ITS), 35
Interactivity, 258
Internet, 155, 288
Internet of things (IoT), 7

Job safety, 14

Kenya, 111

Lack of communication, 171
Lack of expertise, 125
Lack of regulation, 261
Language education, 106

Leadership, 162
Learning, 42, 84, 157
Lifelong learning, 180

Malaysia, 18, 148
Mandela, Nelson, 26
Marketing education, 40
Massive Open Online Courses (MOOCs), 85, 116, 148, 187, 318
Mathematics education, 216
Medical education, 40, 215, 235, 277, 296
Military training, 256
Mlearning, 314
Monitoring, 121
Music education, 297

New Media Consortium (NMC), 15
Nursing education, 297

Online courses, 179, 183
Online education, 4, 159, 178-201
    Benefits of, 192
    Global use of, 196
Online laboratory, 185
Online learning, 183, 184
Online teaching, 181

Pakistan, 110
Personalization, 35
Personalized education, 39, 66
Personalized learning, 46
Philippines, 148
Popular social media, 290-293
Privacy, 47, 124

Reliability, 90
Remote learning, 105
Resistance, 278
Robotics, 5, 59-73
    Applications of, 63
    Benefits of, 68
    Challenges of, 69
    In education, 59
Robots, 32, 60, 311
    Appearance of, 70
    Global use of, 70

Safety, 70
Scalability, 88
Security, 88, 124
Smart learning, 104
Social media, 288-302, 311
    Applications of, 293
    Basics of, 289
    Benefits of, 297
    Global use of, 299
    In education, 288
Social networking,
    see Social media
Social trust, 171
Social work education, 297
Soft computing, 98-112
    Applications of, 102
    Benefits of, 106
    Challenges of, 107
    Constituents of, 101
    In education 98, 108
    Overview of, 99

South Africa, 17, 45
Space education, 256
Special education, 66, 236
Stability, 88
STEM education, 64, 214
Student evaluation, 105

Teacher training, 69
Teaching, 41, 84, 157
Technologies, 1-3, 172, 268
Traditional education, 1, 134
Traditional social media, 288
Trust, 48

United Kingdom, 16, 44, 71, 91, 109, 127, 147, 165, 198, 222, 240, 262, 280, 299, 321
United States, 16, 42, 71, 91, 108, 126, 146, 165, 197, 221, 240, 262, 280, 299, 320

Virtual reality, 8, 35, 230-243, 249, 310
    Applications of, 234
    Benefits of, 237
    Challenges of, 238
    Concept of, 231
    Global use of, 240
    In education, 230

www.ingramcontent.com/pod-product-compliance
Lightning Source LLC
LaVergne TN
LVHW012246070526
838201LV00090B/133